Teaching Multiwriting

Teaching Multiwriting: Researching and Composing with Multiple Genres, Media, Disciplines, and Cultures

Robert L. Davis and Mark F. Shadle

Southern Illinois University Press
Carbondale

"Cross Roads Blues" ("Crossroads")
Words and music by Robert Johnson
Copyright © (1978), 1990, 1991 Lehsem II, LLC and Claud L. Johnson
Administered by Music & Media International, Inc.
International copyright secured. All rights reserved.

Portions of the lyric from "Blues Power" by Albert King
Copyright © 1968 Albert King Music (BMI) administered by Parker Music (BMI).
Copyright renewed.
Courtesy of Concord Music Group, Inc.
All rights reserved. Used by permission.

"Key to the Highway" by William Lee Conley Broozy, Charles Seger
© 1941, renewed 1971, 1999 by Duchess Music Corporation
All rights administered by Songs of Universal, Inc. / BMI
Used by permission. All rights reserved.

Library of Congress Cataloging-in-Publication Data
Davis, Robert L., [date]
Teaching multiwriting : researching and composing with multiple genres,
media, disciplines, and cultures / Robert L. Davis and Mark F. Shadle.
    p. cm.
Includes bibliographical references (p.) and index.
ISBN-13: 978-0-8093-2754-6 (pbk. : alk. paper)
ISBN-10: 0-8093-2754-6 (pbk. : alk. paper)
    1. English language—Rhetoric—Study and teaching. 2. Interdisciplinary
approach in education. 3. Creative writing (Higher education). I. Shadle,
Mark F., [date]. II. Title.
PE1404.D3855 2007
808'.042071—DC22   2006025535

We believe that learning is powerful because it is always, by definition, autobiographical, so we dedicate this book to our families, friends, fellow teachers, and the thousands of students who have already taught us so much by employing this approach. We salute you!

Finally, we dedicate this book about evolving notions of pedagogy to our children, emblems of the future:

Rob's: Cole, Claire, and Katie

Mark's: Celeste, Astrid, and Spenser

CONTENTS

ILLUSTRATIONS

Following page 131
Tide pool on the Washington Coast
"Messages in a Bottle," a multiwriting project by Patricia Hansen
Close-up view of bottled messages in the "Messages in a Bottle"
  project
Eagle Creek, in the Wallowa Mountains of Oregon
"Stanley, I Presume?," a multiwriting project by Jim Benton
Wind-eroded, inhabited caves in Goreme, Turkey
"Shotgun: History as a Scattered (De/Re-)Construction," a
  multiwriting project by Cydney Topping
Lotus pond in rural China
"Tic Tok: Autobiography as Time Travel," a multiwriting project by
  Patricia Hansen
Rope coiled on the deck of a schooner in Maine
"The Woven Thread of Time," a multiwriting project by Connie Berry
Giant Buddha in the Bamiyan Valley in Afghanistan
"Viva La Muerte!," a multiwriting project by Neva Sanders
View of "Viva La Muerte!" with the coffin open
"Hen Party Bronze Bell, a Collaborative Remembrance" by EOU
  students
Front and back views of a *lukasa*, or memory board, of the Luba
  people of central Africa

ACKNOWLEDGMENTS

First we want to thank the legion of students who have endured the freedoms and risks of multiwriting and succeeded so well in teaching us the many things we could never have imagined learning, from esoteric Zen pilgrimages in Japan or matter-of-fact worm ranching in Oregon to cooking gumbo or building a shotgun house in the Mississippi Delta.

We both had the luxury of attending small, interesting colleges as undergraduates and Big Ten universities for graduate school. Through this combination, we came to value the collaboration of interdisciplinary learning communities in intimate classrooms, as well as the kind of research made possible by large libraries. Rob's dissertation on American writer Thomas Pynchon and Mark's on African American writer Ishmael Reed focused upon simultaneously understanding complex meaning and making room for mystery—qualities that prepared us for multiwriting.

While we have both extended and resisted their work, our mentors—some of whom have passed on—have shaped and inspired us. Accordingly, Rob would like to thank philosopher Bernard Murchland and teacher of literature Randall Waldron at Ohio Wesleyan University and rhetorician Lewis Ulman and dialectician Mac Davis at Ohio State University. Mark would like to thank philosopher J. Glenn Gray, political scientists Fred Sonderman and Timothy Fuller, and literature teacher Joe Gordon at Colorado College, and literary critic Sherman Paul, International Writing Program Director Peter Nazareth, Afro-Americanists Darwin Turner and Fred Woodard, folklorist Harry Oster, and intellectual historian Stow Persons at the University of Iowa.

Our colleagues in English–Writing at Eastern Oregon University have been regularly supportive, and we would especially like to thank Donald Wolff for his ideas and for joining the blues pilgrimages during many conferences. We also want to thank Eastern's Writing Lab Director, Susan Whitelock, for continuing to train excellent tutors in multiwriting, and Emeritus Professor George Venn, who has pointed the way to multiwriting in his diverse work in literature, history, and political action.

We're grateful to all the Oregon Writing Project teachers who have embraced multiwriting, including our frequent collaborator John Scanlan from Pendleton High School, as well as those faculty—on our campus and others—who have incorporated this approach in teaching across the disciplines, including EOU Spanish Professor Jill Gibian, whose student projects continue to amaze. Special thanks to our friends and colleagues—Doug Kaigler in Art and Michael O'Connor in Multimedia—who joined Rob to create the multiwork film, *The Hen Party*, about some hard-riding, hard-thinking horsewomen in the Wallowa Mountains. We are also grateful to the administrators of Eastern Oregon University who supported our research and writing of this book with research stipends from the Faculty Scholars Program. Mark would also like to thank the National Endowment for the Humanities, who selected him for a Summer Seminar with La Vonne Ruoff at the University of Illinois at Chicago on Written American Indian Literature, and a Summer Institute with Joe Miller at the University of Virginia in Charlottesville, Virginia. Both experiences expanded his notion of multicultural literature and history.

While we have mentioned many of them in our book, we are indebted to those scholars in rhetoric, composition, and other English Studies who have not been afraid to explore new ground, including—among many others—Winston Weathers, Kenneth Burke, James Berlin, James Moffett, Peter Elbow, Tom Romano, Geoffrey Sirc, Derek Owens, Bruce Ballenger, Cheryl Johnson, Jeff Carroll, Gregory Ulmer, and Michael Jarrett, as well as writers and thinkers outside the field who have encouraged our work, including Susan Griffin, David Antin, and George Mehaffey.

While Mark—as a blues and jazz guitarist and radio DJ who has worked in the music industry here and abroad—has spent a lifetime tracking down blues and jazz musicians, we are living proof that writing and rhetoric conferences are an opportunity to revel in this music, whether it's Buddy Guy's Legends in Chicago or Tobacco Road in Miami. We especially want to thank Sterling Warner and Martha L. Henning for making the Young Rhetoricians Conference coincide with the Monterey Blues Festival. We salute all those blues and jazz musicians who have struggled through this music of celebration, critique, and redemption that continues to entertain and move us.

We feel lucky to have found a careful, thoughtful, and encouraging editor in Karl Kageff, editor in chief for Southern Illinois University Press. Many of the photographs that appear in this book were taken by Kerry Loewen, who kindly gave us permission to publish them.

We thank our families—parents, siblings, children, and extended family—who have supported us and introduced us to reading, writing, music, and the affection that makes work worthwhile. Rob also thanks his mate, Kimberly, for love, guidance, and inspiration, and plenty of fun during the years of working on this book.

INTRODUCTION: EXPANDING THE SOUND

Crossroad Blues

I went to the crossroads, fell down on my knees
I went to the crossroads, fell down on my knees
Asked the Lord above, have mercy now, save poor Bob if
 you please

Standin' at the crossroads, tried to flag a ride
Whee-hee, I tried to flag a ride
Didn't nobody seem to know me, everybody pass me by

Standin' at the crossroads, risin' sun goin' down
Standin' at the crossroads baby, the risin' sun goin' down
I believe to my soul now, po' Bob is sinkin' down

You can run, you can run, tell my friend Willie Brown
You can run, you can run, tell my friend Willie Brown
That I got the crossroad blues this mornin',
Lord, baby I'm sinkin' down

I went to the crossroad, mama, I looked east and west
I went to the crossroad, babe, I looked east and west
Lord, I didn't have no sweet woman, ooh well, babe, in
 my distress

—Robert Johnson

As the population of college students in America and throughout the
world grows, and scarce resources, epidemic disease, and global warming
make our choices all the more important, it may be wise to ground even
a study of writing by considering "strategic" questions such as, What
is college for? What should it help people do? What do, or should, our
students teach us about the world?

Instead of acting out Robert Johnson's allusions to "running and
hiding," this book engages these questions. We have noticed that some

large composition programs—under assault from a dangerous world and a corporate business model of education—live as desperate bureaucracies trying to make writing safe in the Age of Malpractice. Graduate students teaching in such programs, like new teachers in K–12 classrooms, are often warned away from certain ways of teaching, rather than educated in alternative methods. Our working theory—that college is, or should be, a place for posing and exploring compelling questions—resists this inertia and attempts to join together those teachers and students who believe that utopian thinking is often the fastest and most practical route to the real world.

To begin this brand of practical utopianism, we would like to pose it this way: if you're a composition teacher, or are willing to see yourself as one, imagine two extremes. In one, your desk contains a neat, high stack of traditional "term papers" or research essays. All of them are written in the same form; it may be a formula you believe can help students but is one you know too well. None of these papers will be written as well as you could write it. Or imagine your office is full of writing projects that mix different genres, disciplines, media, and cultures. For example, there is a project by our student Katie Edwards on the subject of traditional logging; it stands six feet tall, its trunk made of paper boxes, each holding a different aspect of the writer's approach to the subject. One holds letters written home from logging camp by her grandfather that are accompanied by black-and-white photographs of men felling old-growth trees with whipsaws; another contains poems by Gary Snyder and Wendell Berry; a third presents an essay on the history of logging and logging companies in the American West.

This comes in at the end of the term, along with that of another student, "the Dream Trip" project on CD in PowerPoint, which is connected to a Web site that mixes maps ranging from pictographs to bird's-eye views and even satellite surveys of a remote part of China. Other projects come in as posters, ready to present at conferences in the social and natural sciences, or include audiovisuals for use in presentations at an undergraduate research symposium. Even projects that seem tame on the surface, like Shirley Crabtree's project on fleas, which came in a plain folder, contain a wealth of genres and media, and an interdisciplinary approach that fuses facts with imagination and allows writers and readers to make connections. In Crabtree's project, fleas become the ultimate survivors as she recounts the history of our failed attempts to terminate their kind and uses them metaphorically to view the many survivors of human violence against other humans, as well as other species. Natasha and Sonya, the flea characters Crabtree creates in a narrative of resistant history, become subjects of wonder and the stars of a flea circus that celebrates the triumphant persistence against extermination of the demonized and diminutive creatures of the world.

Each term, we and other teachers around the country, using a variety of related strategies—which we have termed *multiwriting*—receive a strange but inspiring harvest of such projects, from students who are often more ready for this work than are their teachers. Other instructors, we know, are still collecting that stack of mono-vocal papers. Though each has pros and cons, which of these two scenarios would make you eager to engage and evaluate student work? Which would make you run for cover, cleaning the entire house before grading? Which projects would you return to over time, as you would a key work by a theorist you admire, or a great novel? Which is more likely to show you writing styles and approaches to thinking you would quickly admit that you would not have been able to come up with on your own? And which better prepares students to compose flexibly in a world that will present them with discursive occasions, genres, and technologies that cannot be foreseen but will break upon them in an instant, like a rogue wave upon a surfer?

In the pages to come, we theorize and describe an open method of composing—where different genres, media, disciplines, and cultures may be useful or essential, depending on rhetorical situations—that we believe encourages students to grow as writers and thinkers, while taking more conscious control of their own creations. This method requires an equally open pedagogy through which students may find and follow questions they care about. Such questions, engaged with growing fascination, help students enrich and improve their work and rejuvenate teachers who guide students into mysteries and are often led by student research and discourse into places that they have not been before. Finally, such questions have the power to remake the academic experience, drawing students into disciplines, but beyond discipline-specific thinking, as they find out what they need to answer their questions, or broaden or deepen them.

We have come to this approach in part because it enacts "lifelong" learning in the purest way we know by putting questions at the center of student experience and giving students choices about how to research, write, and present their discourses in complicated relations to their subjects, purposes, audiences, and occasions. Unlike some of those advocating the teaching of academic discourse, we do not think that being the best of academicians is the end point for students or the most useful manner of being. Instead, we hope our students will be intellectuals pursuing pressing questions and fertile mysteries, who can engage, and change, the rhetorical and actual situations of their lives.

This approach is related to vernacular traditions in fields that include art, architecture, music, and politics, as it asks students to find, use,

and at times re-create or recombine the communicative forms available
to them. While these may include the familiar forms of academic discourse—such as the essay, the case study, various types of analysis and
narratives—students are encouraged to place these in a broad context
as ways of inscribing for themselves and others the trails of ongoing,
generative inquiries. We have sought to distill this manner of thinking
in the form that is pictured in the Image Gallery at the center of this
book—a *lukasa*, or memory board, from the Luba peoples of Africa. For
the Luba, the *lukasa* not only records the history of a culture by encoding the genealogy of rulers through its selection and placement of beads
but also provides an invitation to narrative and retelling history to suit
changing situations. Initiates into the Mbudye, a secret organization of
the Luba that holds a priestly power, are taught to read memory boards,
which serve to legitimize regal authority. However, this art of reading
is flexible and can be used to diminish or dethrone the undeserving. It
serves as a check on the power of chiefs while symbolizing the continuing
importance of memory. Similarly, our students find suitable forms for
their subjects, purposes, audiences, and occasions by ranging within and
beyond the genres favored by academic culture and the media of written
discourse. While their projects may use essays, dialogues, short stories,
or fables, they may also include or center upon PowerPoint presentations,
masks, intricate boxes, performances, museum displays, or community
service projects.

While we and others have used variations of this approach in courses
from the freshman to senior levels, and among honors students and
basic writers, we are especially pleased to report that some of the more
intriguing projects we have received have come from students who are
"black sheep"; they often seem full of potential but sometimes have
trouble finding their voices or gaining persuasive power with their peers.
We think, for instance, of Frank Kaminski Jr., whose mind races across
borders and whose projects on the old TV show *The Dukes of Hazzard*
and the culture of construction workers readily mixed high, pop, and folk
cultures, as well as earnest analysis and off-the-wall humor. The presentation of his projects—performance art that featured stunts, such as a car
jump using a small replica of General Lee—attracted a cult following at
the University and helped to make him the most beloved of eccentrics.
Frank went on to graduate school, then to the publishing industry in
New York City and Seattle. Dennis Rochac and Bryan Suereth were good
friends in college who created unusual projects on The Electronic Church
of Elvis and jazz experimentalist Sun Ra, respectively. They have gone
on to transform the culture of Portland, Oregon, one as a member of an
avant-garde comedy troupe, the other as the owner of an influential art

gallery and the codeveloper of an alternative installation space showcasing the work of many artists at once. We want our teaching to cooperate with the transformational potential we see in all our students and often speak of this approach as a way of lighting students up, turning them on, getting them started, then turning them loose and sustaining them.

The crossroads from which this book reports is similar to the public space in the seldom-sung "anarchist" verse of Woody Guthrie's "This Land Is Your Land," where the narrator views a no trespassing sign and notes that the other side of the sign does not say anything: that side, he believes, was made for all of us. To move to the blank but free side, we may first consider the list below, which might be labeled "unusual features, likely to draw comment" but also might be seen as crossroads of different kinds that converge here.

Alternative Tradition

Alternative composition is a term that has been used to describe our work, and we have used it ourselves, even in the titles of articles. We believe in providing an alternative approach to those we learned as young teachers and have seen continued as common practice in composition studies. However, this alternative approach does not constitute a parallel universe. We believe that we are traditionalists, in a particular sense of that word. In this book, we will examine three interrelated discursive traditions, still used in teaching discourse today: research writing, persuasive writing, and essayistic writing. We follow this with an analogy and symbolic companion: a discursive mini-history of blues music. In writing about each tradition, we seek to enact pilgrim's progress journeys toward a freer space, where a different kind of composing is possible, while the founding spirit of the tradition is reclaimed. In each case, the spirit is one of open inquiry and multiple means of expression and communication, which become available as we follow our questions through different perspectives and bodies of information, and into rhetorical situations. In this way, the compositional practices we describe are discursive analogy for the life of a mind that roves, but maintains its commitments to the world. We have sought to describe and illustrate this deep tradition of free inquiry and expression in the traditional figure of the crossroads.

Chapter 1 describes the crossroads scene for the blues player/composer and the composition teacher. Our discipline, following the work of writers still often thought of as pursuing "alternative" routes, has arrived at a meeting place of the personal and the professional, where service to the academy is gradually being trumped by a common desire to create a reflective art of discourse that ranges across disciplines and into all quarters of life. We begin to situate our work within this emerging "crossroads discipline," as Derek Owens has called it, by showing how it unites theory and practice, autobiography and academics, through the discourse of open questions.

Chapters 2, 3, and 4 show the question-centered dimensions of research writing, persuasive writing, and the essay. Chapter 2, on research writing, historicizes the research paper, which Richard Larson has famously called a nonform of writing, as a diminished, purely academic form of the modernist search for objective truth. We argue for supplanting this outdated assignment with research projects that use multiple forms to explore questions that cannot be fully answered. In a fashion that is both postmodern and ancient, such projects seek to open the minds of their authors and readers to new understandings and serve as points of entry to the mysteries of the world.

Chapter 3, on persuasive writing, continues advocating this ideal of openness in a world of others. The persuasion it describes involves opening others to our words through conversation, where even the deepest values can be discussed without fear of reprisal, and where mutual change is desirable. This chapter shifts rhetoric from an act of verbal combat to what William Covino has called an art of wondering, one that recaptures the inventive timbre of the ancient world for these uncertain times.

The essay, the subject of Chapter 4, arose from the French *essai* or "attempt" in the writings of Michel De Montaigne. The Montaignian essay differs from what Paul Heilker and Bruce Ballenger, among others, have seen as a thesis-and-support form, which shuts its writer off from continued learning and gives its audience a sealed discourse that is difficult to enter or engage. Instead, Montaigne imagined a form that would show the mind's reflections upon an increasingly complex experience in which truths were hard to know. We compare the essay to another Renaissance form, the Cabinet of Wonder, whereby Westerners recorded and sought to order a richly expanding, and threatening, "new" world that was both wondrous and disorienting.

The Blues as Analogy and Attitude

Chapter 5 moves beyond the normal boundaries of composition studies and into a province of another crossroads discipline of discourse: the musical forms and practices of the blues. This music is a method for essaying the world, moving an audience, and traveling restlessly to research and write our questions. Blues music is often seen as a stilted form, hardly open to innovation, but this is far from true. One of the qualities of the blues is its ability to stretch, taking diverse musical traditions and most of life into its restless core. The "birth of the blues" is a vexed issue, but in a radically simplified form, it entailed American musicians translating slave chants, spirituals. and perhaps the African music of their deep pasts into a new form that bears only a partial resemblance to any precursor. The supposed simplicity of blues structures ("It is just three chords!") distills this complex integration and sophistication, as blues tunes tend to refine life to a repeated refrain while hinting at the complicated experience that leads us there.

Blues also has propelled the musical present and future. Most popular American music—including jazz, rock, rap, hip-hop, and even country—is based upon blues rhythms and structures. It is a commonplace to talk about how musicians have transformed the blues into other forms. Less often acknowledged, however, is the view common among musicians that they are still playing the blues; for instance, Miles Davis's *Kind of Blue* is a kind of blues, and Public Enemy's *Fear of a Black Planet* is a restatement of the themes blues singers found years before.

The blues interests us as a parallel example to the compositional practices we admire because it is both traditional and innovative. It expands to take in more and more of reality, while also maintaining a recognizable experience that people call blues. Other musical parallels may also be made. For instance, one may compare the mixing of discourses that our students do to the musical alchemy of the dance party DJs. Even in that parallel, however, the mixers do not escape tradition, as they try to find the dance potential in music and set it against a bass-heavy groove, which is in itself a spirited restatement of the blues. We also prefer the blues as a parallel because it voices a collaborative philosophy of perseverance that finds music in experience. What better companion for a life of inquiry, writing, thinking, acting, and living could there be? We would like to echo and join the blues attitude of reflection, confession, dialogue, questioning, and hard-earned understanding, in reverence to life that remains tragicomic and mysterious, even when familiar.

The Call for Additional Expansions

Another point that may be raised against the presence of the blues in this text is whether to have a musical analogy at all. Why not simply stick to the subjects more familiar to an audience of composition teachers and scholars? We have reached outside the normal (and perhaps somewhat arbitrary) bounds of the discipline to the less familiar world of the blues because we want to expand the scope of composition and rhetoric, and we hope that upon reading this text your desire to do so will also be stoked. Other traditions of discourse, thought, music, and action can also be reopened to innovation by regathering their animating spirit, and we welcome that. In the end, all traditions of inquiry and writing lead us back to one: the inquisitive consciousness by which humans ask about the world, the cosmos, themselves, and each other. In our abstractions, it is easy to lose this essential intellectual act; but the more we reclaim it, the more inclined we are to see what's around us.

So now it is imperative to move from acknowledging our common humanity in third person to our invitation in second person: As you invent your own parallels, you may want to try a quick heuristic we have developed and used for years. What is it that gives you "the power"? We refer to the kind of power Albert King sings about in his classic "talkie," "Blues Power." King says first that everyone knows about the blues: babies cry for milk, young women want to go out, but their Mamas want them at home. Some of us have not seen our loved ones for a long time or known love at all. But this shared experience brings the audience together and empowers King to bring it (on) home. Now he is not having the blues but "doin' the blues," playing them and singing them and preaching to the crowd that loves him for it:

> The blues!
> An' when you're doin' the blues
> They so strong, that's the reason they're named
> They call 'em blues power, yeah

This is not the power to control people's lives, or political or economic power. Instead, we mean the power to keep on living, like a glow that stays with you even when you move from the source. After hearing Willie Kent and the Gents in Chicago, with two guitarists freely trading rhythm and lead, and also *comping* (that is, playing small portions of each other's parts to make a sound that is thick and complex), we believe the legacy of the sound may be just what you need to write a portfolio for a tenure review by interconnecting your scholarship, service, and teaching. When you do this, you have "blues power." Or do you, instead or additionally, have Nature power? African literature power? Progressive politics power? Good coffee power? Teaching composition power? What unites the passions of your personal and academic life, or provides the rhythm and keeps you going? What traditions of inquiry and living are at your core as insistences or intentions? In his essay "On Conversation," Michel de Montaigne writes, "The excitement of the chase is properly our quarry; we are not to be pardoned if we carry it on badly or foolishly. To fail to seize upon the prey is another matter" (190). Blues power is the spur that excites and keeps us headed toward a greater good. Our main hope for this book is that it provides a little boost of such power, for those who enjoy or are challenged by it.

The expanded sound we were going for also shows in the myriad of references we purposely try to use. Although we focus in this book on composition studies, this discipline, rightly conceived, is broad, and we need to use much of what we know or find interesting to properly study the act of writing as it links to inquiry, in a complex world of multiple meanings, media, and forms. In earlier works, as well as this one, we have often linked sources from composition studies to those from a variety of other disciplines in the hope of making a network of meaning, or crossroads, that will give readers new directions they may want to pursue. Some readers enjoy this approach; others do not. At times we have been called show-offs and know-it-alls, but we would rather believe that we are avid readers who would like to bring the various inquiries and curiosities of our lives into a pattern of meaning for others to use. We hope that readers will add references by making connections as they read, creating a crossroads of their own. We love to hear our own stories in those of others, and vice versa.

Similarly, some publishers have told us that our writing is too personal or interesting. That's because we believe all learning is autobiographical and passionate and are trying to write in ways that carry an ongoing fascination for our students and ourselves, rather than produce the traditional textbook or work of composition theory. That's why we address our words to you and your students and sometimes insist on using second person. We hope you will join us as we move toward "open source" composition that incorporates further sharing of ideas.

Theory and Practice

Our work is poised between theory and pedagogy because we see this as the natural condition of the reflective scholar/teacher. All teaching operates out of theory, whether stated or not, and theories imply pedagogy or action. We have tried to strike a balance between the theory-heavy approach to "resistant writing" of Derek Owens and the more practice-oriented work of other precursors, including Tom Romano and Bruce Ballenger. While we hope that teachers reading this book will be able to gather, modify, and use some of the writing prompts we provide, we know that these will be more meaningful if we reach the same readers on a theoretical plane where purposes become clear. Conversely, while some readers are drawn to theory, our insistence upon practice may help these readers consider how to put theories into practice, even when the theories and practices differ from those we suggest.

At the end of each chapter, we include a series of pedagogic materials that grow from its themes. These are addressed directly to students, so are ready for use as they are, although modification and recombination is encouraged. These materials are meant to be "heuristics" in the ancient sense—devices for discovery or bringing forth—which teachers and students may use or change as strategies for invention. However, they also relate to the term as used in professional fields, especially computer science, where heuristics are protocols for solving problems or establishing interfaces between unlike artifacts. These heuristics show how the messages of the main text of the book can lead to pedagogic action that expands classroom practices and enacts education as its original root, a way of "leading forth" in the world.[1] These materials lead from informal musings—like parts of conversations on back porches or front stoops—to exercises for writing or thinking inquisitively, as well as prompts for more formal or expansive projects.

These materials also include a list of additional readings, which may help you move into the chapter's subject in a different manner or provide the backbone of a reading list for a course or a series of research projects. Finally, because this is a visual culture in which people are increasingly prepared to think first with images, and through films, we have added a parallel list of films that echo or enhance the chapter's themes. Perhaps some of these will provide points of entry into, or different ways of perceiving or understanding, the discursive traditions your students are studying, writing within, or applying to their projects.

Image Gallery

Theory and practice are also linked in the student projects described in this book. In the now commonplace cultural notion, popularized in the book by Malcolm Gladwell, "the tipping point" is reached when a variety of forces and sources are brought into focus by a triggering event, action, image, or idea. In our practice of teaching, writing, and presenting, the "tipping point" for bringing the reluctant over to "the multi" has been student examples. When presenting at conferences or on campuses, we often hand around a group of current student examples as we begin. During the talk, the power of the projects is clear as, for instance, an audience member stuck or struck by/on Aubree Tipton's visually stunning project on the Grand Canyon shouts out, "Who took these pictures?" Here we have tried to recreate this effect in written words by talking about many projects in a gallery of project images to show you some of the forms.

While the photos can't fully unpack these complex collections of multiple genres across various disciplines, media, and cultures, they may offer an inkling of these amazing research projects and the way they emerge from a natural world into those we make together.

Go far enough out through a telescope or in through a microscope and the world is empty. But here inside the realm of the naked eye, we are constantly awash in a sea of recognizable and evolving forms. This includes those containers for our thinking that we describe as different styles of argument, or writing forms, like the essay. Even "place" can be seen as something we "make," by noticing, categorizing, and building upon it. If nature is an endless series of connected forms, it means that all thinking stemming from nature is connected. While students produce very specific and detailed research, most multiwriting doesn't lose sight of the larger picture—that's the gift of using samplings from (if not models of) nature.

The first image, of a tide pool on the Oregon coast, reminds us that we often delight in observing a small part of the world that has become somewhat isolated. The ocean is too enormous to apprehend, but the tide pool it leaves behind is a comfortably limited place full of the brilliant colors of marine organisms. It is the kind of place that incubated Patricia Hansen's project, Messages in a Bottle. Inspired by the traceries of starfish, we imagine a bottle floating in shallow water, a message inside from history. Patricia's bottles contained not only actual messages sent in the bottles of the past but also imaginary ones and those she might want to send. This fantasy of a message sent out into the whim of the ocean is one visited in the short stories of O. Henry or movies like *Message in a Bottle*.

Our picture of Eagle Creek is not only an inviting scene for us or someone outside our area but also a reminder of the evolving difficulties of trying to understand (as well as attempting to "manage") fish and game in model watershed projects that often involve students. The urge to the headwaters of any stream is an instinct toward history and beyond it, to mythology. Jim Benton—whose project is housed in a nineteenth-century doctor's bag—follows his ancestors' name, Stanley, toward the headwaters of the genealogical Nile. It turns out that the impulse to participate in such a journey and fame involved the renaming of the family, with mythology replacing history.

This mythology also continues to work its magic on our notions of shelter. Like the Anasazi and Mogollon peoples of the American Southwest, or the Toloy and Tellem and Dogon peoples of Mali, the religious and political refugees of the ancient Mediterranean carved caves into homes in the wind-eroded rock cones in the image of Goreme in Turkey. Like the chthonic gods that erupted from the earth in ancient Greece, our ancestors learned the safety of living in the earth and rock as cave and cliff dwellers. The image of Cydney Topping's framed composite of two types of "shotgun house" from the deep South—part of her project on Southern architecture—shows not only the vulnerability of any free-standing home but also its vulnerability to both hurricanes and the shotgun that can fire through the open front door at anyone leaving through the one in the back. Our architecture is at once a meditation upon beauty and comfort, and both terms have been assaulted by modernist practice. In the wake of hurricanes Katrina and Rita, how do the residents of the Mississippi Delta and New Orleans want their homes to look and work? These are the questions that look for answers in the genres of Cydney's project, stored in appropriate parts of the house.

Time and space may remain the two great obstacles and pillars of philosophy. In India and China, especially in Buddhist meditation, the quiet natural beauty of the lotus pond is a place for escaping the un-lived future and the nagging past and journeying deeply into the present moment, as it changes. You may want to take a moment to disappear there in the image Mark took in China on a trip that visited various Tai Chi Chuan schools. Then look at the image of Patricia Hansen's Time Machine Project, which also indulges meditation on the future through science fiction's reoccurring question: "what if?" If you were making a time capsule, what would it look like? What would it collect? How much does the future depend upon the past? These are the kinds of questions that are included in, or implied by, this multiwork.

Property must have once been a burden, for it had to be worn or hauled. The photos of rope coiled on the deck of a schooner in Maine remind us of the long history of weaving not only the rope that would pull a cart or horse but also the clothing and paper made of fibers carefully entwined. Connie Berry's elaborate multiproject on weaving follows not only the variety and beauty of woven materials but also their many uses. Its enormous book of woven samples and mini-artifacts all fit snugly into an enormous woven box. This grid is not only the warp and woof or wool but also the tapestry of literature and the geography of the four directions that are omnipresent in our culture.

In his new award-winning film *The Giant Buddhas*, Director Christian Frei recounts the fascinating history of the world's largest statue of Buddha in the Bamiyan Valley in Afghanistan. The image Mark shot in the early 1970s already portrayed a face that had been chiseled off by Islamic invaders. But recently the Taliban blew up the statue. How can a representation of the past invite such animosity? The image of Neva Sanders's project, Viva La Muerte!, examines this paradox of how the Mexican Days of the Dead honor the living. The coffin unfolds into a startlingly beautiful collage of color, with a path leading toward the gaudy complexity of the Mexican version of Catholicism. Statues become the animation of the living. An array of genres are tucked into the pockets of the coffin, as if they belonged to the "deceased."

The next image of the bronze bell created by sculptor Doug Kaigler and his students to honor the horsewomen of the Hen Party, who roamed the Wallowa Mountains, is a microcosm and synecdoche of the way nature invites culture into its abode. Like the dinner bell that might be kept in the shotgun house, or the dinging of bottles full of messages against rocks of a tide pool, or those bells full of incense swung during Days of the Dead, this bell's rope beckons us, like the rope coiled upon the deck of the schooner, to grasp and use it. The earth's metal, transformed into art and placed for commemorative use, becomes the trailhead into the Wallowa Mountains. But these projects all stand as, and before, the further journeys of their creators and classmates. Most multiwriters continue to work on their topics/projects long after the grades are in. The last image, of the lukasa of the Luba people of central Africa (mentioned earlier), is a sophisticated and dynamic artifact; in the hands of its practitioners, it is the wood and beads of the natural world remembering migration routes, secret clan information, and the sacred layout of the chief's abode—often in the shape of a thumb piano, which implies the music waiting to be performed again, with new improvisations.

None of these, however, quite equal the project we once toured from the inside at Baker City, Oregon, where a high school student showed his classmates how he had restored his vintage Oldsmobile Cutlass in a project that was presented inside, outside, and around the car. Texts and images were everywhere, with the glove box holding the student's most private thoughts about the car in, and as, his life. His mock insurance policy is a genre that adults worried about deductibles, accidents, floods, and fires may also want to try.

In discussions of the use of student examples in the profession these days, we find two contradictory strands: the idea that "using students" in this way in unethical, and the argument that it is ONLY student examples that are fresh and interesting, especially when compared to the other sources we usually site. We have tried to mediate these positions while taking an alternative approach: we value students as colleagues and composers and have tried here to place them on equal footing with the published authors we cite. Many of our former students have become teachers, gone to graduate school, or are doing other interesting work in the world. Their progress suggests what most of us secretly know: these roles of "teacher" and "student" are reversible, mutable and, in some ways, temporary. So, while we have "used" our students to help us write this book, we hope that they are "using" us in similar ways, with their students and in their lives.

Terminology of the Crossroads

We call our compositional practice *multiwriting*. It is a coined term and as such stands out. However, we have chosen it with some care and are using it in a single way: multiwriting is a practice of composing in which multiple genres, media, disciplines, and cultures are potentially open to use. It differs from an allied term in vogue today—*multi-genre writing*—in that it stresses not the formula of composing in a number of different genres but a more flexible stance, where authors may use any means to compose effectively, reflecting in engaging ways. Writers using this approach link practice to theory by taking into account all they know or are finding out about their subject, purposes, audiences, occasions, as well as the selves they continue to generate. They enact a copious spirit of expansion and pleasure in discourse, which our former student Neva Sanders captured in giving advice to English majors about what they need to do to succeed in learning: "More multi, more multi, more multi!" One of our reservations about our term, however, is that it suggests that student discourses of this kind are *only* expansions, organized, if at all, through difference. The teacher's nightmare in such a case is to be handed a stack of writings that each scratch the surface of a different feature or aspect of a subject, without making the connections necessary to begin to find unity or show a depth of thought.

However, the deeper insights of this method make finding and enacting a rough unity, or web of meaning, a desired goal. The better projects we receive create complex thematic and stylistic links that allow for a focus to remain clear even as it expands across a discursive field. We also require, at times, univocal discourses, where students familiar with this flexible approach consolidate rhetorical power in a single genre of writing, suggestive image, or way of knowing. Experience in the multi can also help students writing in more limited academic situations. In an interview, student Chris Wolfe, now a language arts teacher, told us that the strongest evidence that this approach had worked came when he was asked to write in a univocal way: "I never just sit down and write a paper anymore," he said. "I am always constructing a voice and looking for the right style."

The use of the term *multiwriting* may also be puzzling, since many of the projects we describe here have visual, aural, cinematic, textural, architectural, or design components. We have chosen in this text to use *writing*, however, to suggest that our view of the kind of work these students produce remains tied to the traditions of composition, rhetoric, and discourse studies. We want students to come to see, by working with each other and preparing to show their work to different audiences, how ancient rhetorical concerns of accomplishing purposes, moving audiences, inhabiting occasions, or working with *kairos* remain powerful ways to organize, form, or sharpen their work. However, especially as colleagues have spread this approach to other disciplines in the fine arts, the term *multiwork* has also been used to describe projects in multiple or mixed media that follow, or help to discover, the vision of their creator(s). Predecessors of this work are myriad and include the collage tradition in art, talk performance in theatre, and many types of music and song. While we have chosen the blues as an example of such work that combines lyrics and music to encode a series of related attitudes, stances, and ways of living, we also consider other parallel ways of working across boundaries to enact a commitment to the world and living inquisitively within it—ranging from traditions of vernacular architecture that make use of materials at hand to clowning to ease political crises. We would like readers to consider this an open text, to which other examples of multiwork—as well as evolving terminologies—should be added.

We also use the term *crossroads discourse*, suggested by a reviewer, to whom we are grateful, as useful for describing a broader set of discursive practices that emerge at the crossroads of disciplines, cultures, political practices, values, ethnicities, histories, and ways of being. In times like ours, when so much is uncertain, many discourses arise in the seams and open spaces, where new forms for thinking, acting, and being in the world may emerge. While Mary Louise Pratt has studied the arts of living in contact zones, where cultures meet and grapple, often in asymmetric power relations (33–40), other thinkers join multicultural writers Gloria Anzaldúa (especially in *Borderlands/La Frontera*) and Gerald Vizenor (beginning in *The Heirs of Columbus*) in envisioning and practicing a future belonging to the *mestíza* or *cross-blood*, respectively. While we see multiwriting as another way to practice the discourse of the crossroads, we do not want to conflate the terms. The crossroads is a symbolic setting where new cultural forms can emerge; multiwriting is a pedagogy, a set of classroom practices and the student discourses that emerge from them. Ideas migrate with people, just as writer Sherman Alexie, after viewing the classic little film *Crossroads*, wrote a novel in response; in *Reservation Blues*, blues guitarist Robert Johnson gives his magical guitar away to young Native American musicians on a "reservation" that has become a "delta."

Another term of importance to us is *invention*, which, as Sharon Crowley and Debra Hawhee, among others, have seen, was also the centerpiece of ancient rhetorical education (xiv). This book may be seen as a guide to rhetorical invention that spreads, potentially, from autobiography, to the academy, and into the rest of life. Many things are being "invented," or discovered, in this practice: discourses, cultural perspectives and understandings, bodies of knowledge, methods for finding out more, and versions or emanations on one's self. In this broad agenda, the book focuses upon the act of "getting started" in its many manifestations, which is central not only to the writing process but also to the continued development of the mind. As Meredith Sue Willis suggests in *Deep Revision*, revising is an inventive act dependent upon an open stance that fosters the new thinking needed to reenvision discourse. We believe this inventive openness is also needed in composing lives, especially today, when the world is held prisoner by authoritarian extremists who, even as they fight one another, are perhaps more understandable as linked by their common vision of exclusive holiness.

We would like this text to participate in the revolution of multiplicity, which we believe is growing in the world, largely unheralded. As Thomas Pynchon saw in *Gravity's Rainbow*, the "counterforce" to a singular war threatening to swallow the world is the multiplicity of life and experiences, and an attitude of joy, dialogue, and communion that allows us to participate in it. We have learned from the idea of "nomadology" developed in De Leuze and Guatari's *A Thousand Plateaus: Capitalism and Schizophrenia*. However, instead of focusing upon nomads as unconscious incubators of war, and seeing the tension between any culture's need to nest and wander or disperse to the point of schizophrenia, we are interested in the way nomads act as potential healers, as well as traders, translators, mediators, and emissaries. This inventive nomadology can happen by traveling the world or staying at home; the lone monk in James Cowan's *The Mapmaker* makes a *mappe mundi* of the whole world without leaving his cell, by transcribing the accounts of travelers who visit him.

An Implicit Politics of Imagination

Although seldom overtly political, this book is designed to give the world a small, but firm, push into open territory, where old conflicts can be put aside and new alliances formed. We argue against the politics of stratification and objectification and look instead toward the rising and suggestive ambiguity of the world, which shrill declarations of certainty anxiously try to cover. As the American Indian artist Harry Fonseca, a Niseran Maidu, says of his "stone poems" series, which update petroglyphs using textured acrylic paint and canvass: "[It] is a chance to confront myself in a new world. It is a world where the blacks and whites are slowly, very slowly, turning into grays—grays with all their shades of uncertainty, growth, and wonder." Fonseca's subtle grays contain a world of color. Discourse in the "gray" world is similarly nuanced, complex, and mixed. Never pure in voice or logic, it is heteroglossic, multi-vocal, and open-ended.[2]

Part of the pleasure of living in this world of many grays—the time after the master narratives foreseen by postmodern thinkers such as Jean Francois Lyotard—is traversing the boundaries of self, by reimagining identity or regenerating autobiography. This is traditionally part of the work not only of writing but also of reading, as Azar Nafisi, author of *Reading* Lolita *in Tehran: A Memoir in Books*, has shown. In "The Republic of the Imagination," an essay in the *Washington Post Book World*, she writes,

> Curiosity is essential. No amount of moral preaching or political correctness can replace what the imagination gives us when it places us in other people's experience, opening our eyes to vistas and views we never knew existed. It is this process of dehabitualization, of discovering the magic in what another person might consider mundane, that presents the world anew, washed and clear, evoking the ecstasy that only a great work of imagination can provide. (10)

Practicing writing as inquiry can lead to a similar imaginative and empathetic border crossing, preparing students to live in a world that will often surprise them. We would most like to counter in others and ourselves the tendency to retreat from the unknown toward the shelter of what was thought to be true. It is not even enough to say that one has a tolerance for ambiguity or sensitivity to the different experience of others. Instead, the continual presence of difference should lead us into a sustained fascination and learning that deepens our appreciation of the world, even as we come to better know its troubles.

Realizing this grand purpose will require unlearning old habits and forms of discourse and action, as well as learning new ones. We propose some transformative steps here. For instance, the research paper as an attempt to contain and control knowledge becomes the multiwriting research project, which invites both writer and reader to trace an open question across genres, media, disciplines, and culture. Similarly, persuasive writing moves from the state-and-defend form of argumentation to the "loose talk" of informed conversation that deepens our questions about the world and appreciation for our interlocutors. The essay drops its academic stance of presenting knowledge to become, again, the collection of items of wonder by which we first know the world. The blues is then seen not as a forlorn tradition but as a living art of endurance, resistance, and philosophic reflection, which oppression, violence, or bad luck cannot crush. We have sought to redouble this message through the crossroads form, where the texts our students have composed join with many other sources to move discourse from its old certainties and scales to a sound we are learning to hear, make and, appreciate.

"Open Source" Composition

As Socrates saw, one of the limits of the written word is that it repeats itself, saying the same things again over time. These days, however, the fluidity of discourse is ever upon us, as, for instance, Internet bloggers supplant the mainstream media as investigators and the source of the rapid spread of information, and disinformation, and strangers almost instantly come together in social action through "flashmobs" and "meet-ups" announced online. As texts go out of print increasingly quickly, even the permanence of print, outside of library collections, is called into question. The best methods for sustaining a discussion, sharing results, or collectively pursuing questions, outside of a small set of real-time friends, may also be online, in discussion forums and chat rooms, or in the collective programming projects, such as Linux or Apache (as well as a burgeoning number of smaller projects) of the Open Source movement.

In *The Success of Open Source*, Stephen Weber describes the movement not only as a group of related theories and practices for making software but also as a social organization offering an altered understanding of property rights. In our culture, property rights traditionally cohere around the right to exclude. When you "own" something, others cannot use, access, or reproduce it without approval or payment. Michel Foucault points to the danger of such individualism—and may project the way multinational corporations now sometimes appropriate constitutional rights reserved for individuals—when he notes, in *Madness and Civilization*, the moment during the French Revolution when debtors were thrown into prison alongside murderers. This meant crimes against property were seen as equal to crimes against people; conversely, we might say that property was seen to be an extension of the individual who owned it. This is very different from an African king saying, "I am the elephant." A "oneness" among people, plants, and animals is distinct from, and nearly opposite to, the abstractions of property (that move inside language as metonymy).

However, open source works far differently, by configuring concepts of property around the right to distribute. This open source is not always "freeware," available without monetary charge, but its code is publicly available and can be replicated for any purpose. In higher education, the open source principle is seen in "open courseware projects" in which universities distribute course materials—including syllabi, lecture notes, and assignments—freely on the Web.[3] Sharing scientific knowledge was part of the founding of the Internet. Many are also familiar with current knowledge-building projects such as the *Wikipedia* "free content" online encyclopedia, which volunteers write and edit. This project is mind-blowingly ambitious, as its goal is the communication to every person on Earth the sum of all things known. At the time of this writing, *Wikipedia*'s content had spread through 187 languages. This is a giant step away from the "last scholarly edition" of the *Encyclopedia Britannica* in 1911, when each entry was written by the alleged world expert in each subject. From the centralized authority of the medieval king and expert—and the master-apprentice pedagogy that followed from it—in a world built upon slavery, we are coming full circle toward a decentralized, more democratic collaboration.

We would like to help bring a similar spirit, with more modest goals, to the field of composition by working with others to create an "open source" project that will continue to expand and reach new parts of this and other fields, as different people add to it and enhance it over time. This book, therefore, is supported by the *Horn of Mystery*, a Web site for composition, to which all may add. The *Horn of Mystery* site is itself the "system" we may improve, through the addition not only of programming code but also of content such as student projects, sample assignments, scholarly texts, and contributions to discussion boards. This site is useful for teachers but also aimed at students worldwide interested in experiencing new perspectives and materials about inquiry and writing. So, if you like this book, or would like to talk back to it, please check out or check in at www.mysteryhorn.org.

Pooling our knowledge is a constant project against the drought that shrinks that pool into puddle. And the crossroads, like rivers, change locations through time, one oasis giving way to another. Somehow we must learn to live with mystery and find, as Terri Tempest Williams tries to in *Refuge*, a sanctuary *within* change. In American culture, mortality is often masked with a restless adolescence that encourages the kind of tinkering that lives inside of change without reflecting upon it. But mortality reminds us that we must discover our uniqueness before we die; paradoxically, this uniqueness must encompass the way we negotiate the crossroads and navigate back to our common humanity. Our ability to discover this flexibility begins with childhood. Stories made familiar through repetition may not be comforting. Grimm's fairytales are, alas, "grim." The "long ago and far away" is no protection for the cautionary tale. Whether because we lack experience or a developed cerebellum, as children we confuse the actual and imaginary. This is why we, or some child we knew, had an "imaginary friend," or why Max's bedposts turn into trees and the carpet into grass in Maurice Sendak's *Where the Wild Things Are*. Edith Cobb, in *The Ecology of the Imagination of Childhood*, reminds us that ecology can provide the overview necessary to appreciate the kind of reflection that allows us to develop the habit, as learners, of using steady reflection as the dead reckoning that helps us follow and map our passions and intentions. So how can we recover the imagination and sense of the whole needed to live in an imperfect world driven by a necessary mystery beyond our apprehension? All teachers and students must answer this question. In the next chapter we begin to map, simultaneously, into and out of this mystery as pedagogy.

1 A CROSSROADS IN SPACE AND TIME

It is no wonder that bluesman Robert Johnson wanted to run from the crossroads, and perhaps he should have, given his short and violent life. But the gifts he left are extraordinary. To older musicians, including the great Son House, Robert was a pesky kid at the juke joint, wanting to play when he could not. Then, after disappearing from the scene for a time, he could. And he played as no one had before, a blues that continued to haunt his listeners. Where had he learned it? The story is archetypal and manifested many times in the history of the blues: The singer goes to the lonely delta crossroads late at night, in an apocalyptic wind or disturbing stillness, and is greeted by the Devil, in rags or fancy threads, who can make him a player for the price of his soul. There is a voodoo version as well, where it is Papa Legba in all his ambiguity—as teacher, guide and trickster, devil and angel—who points the initiate toward a unique musical birthmark. He tunes the hopeful, desperate wanna-be's guitar so that it plays divine music, never before heard, that extends the blues along a route now opened.

But the legacy of divine intervention is hard work. The opportunity and duty remain with the player, who has to make this music, working out the implications and potentialities of Legba's idiosyncratic tuning. It is further left to the musician to help the world recognize this as music by providing the bridge that's needed and waiting for others to catch up to where she is or by forging ahead, knowing that some listeners can't resist following. Legba—often modest and humble, eating rice from a cup, then smoking a corncob pipe—is not likely to take the credit or push the player to perform. He gives her the knowledge that there is a special way for her, which she can take or leave, as she makes her lonely way back into the world and on to the next leg of her journey.

The classroom practices and student projects we review and describe and have called multiwriting reside at a similar crossroads, where routes for invention and composition converge. Our teaching is directed toward work that is multiple in genre, media, discipline, and culture. Writers creating such discourses find their routes of inquiry and the shape, structure, style, and slant of their works within complicated rhetorical and actual relations of content, purpose, message, audience, and occasion. While one project is a dialogic argument on gay marriage that persuades by examining the lives of selected couples, another finds its unity through the form of a snowman and becomes a folkloric and psychological study of children's play. While PowerPoint is the right solution for a project that leads to a presentation for the student government on the need for a university community center, a presentation on the connections between dyes and weaponry in chemistry, politics, literature, and World War II history for a student research symposium takes form as a series of posters forming a museum display.

Within a single course with a common purpose, the range of forms, contents, and styles may be extraordinary. As we write this, a term is ending and Rob has collected work from a 300-level writing theory course using a cultural studies approach. They include Kathleen Cathey's interview-based research project on the experience of students upon leaving an alternative elementary school and entering mainstream public education; Naomi Hatfield's study of a Desraize woman from Tajikistan now living in the United States, who is perpetually amazed at American excess; and Christine Winde's project on the culture of body piercing, which includes a mini multicultural history of piercing, monologues from people who have recently been pierced in unusual places, and ethnographic observations from a local piercing parlor. Perhaps most compelling of all is Ryan Browne's project, *Through the Eyes of a Soldier: Cultural Iraq*, which is based upon a series of interviews with a good friend who had recently returned from the fighting. Browne begins with an objective description of his project as interview-based research but then takes us deep into the war zone using the first person of his friend's haunting descriptions of a desolated landscape, sudden violence, and other interactions the young soldier sees as more hopeful, such as football (soccer) games played at camp, in which Americans were schooled by skillful Iraqi youths.

The projects come from a multifaceted, sustained curriculum that spans projects, courses, and disciplines, through which students learn to follow their questions and communicate these to others through projects that take form from their contents, audiences, and occasions and allow for both personal and collaborative development. For instance, the students in Mark's first-year Exploratory Writing course working on "dreamtrip" projects on international destinations have often been inspired to study abroad and have come back to encourage other students as part of the university's internationalization initiative. This term, Cydney Topping's dreamtrip to Italy begins to inhabit her love of *Il Postino*, the film about the exile of Chilean poet Pablo Neruda in Italy. She writes letters that both apply and hire her to be a mailwoman in Italy. She creates poems that parallel some of Neruda's and includes various maps and mini-research essays on the politics and cooking of various parts of the country, as well as film clips from the movie to introduce her own genres built upon the experience of the senses. She performs the trip as a PowerPoint presentation. Matthew Arrington plans a trip to Japan, where he can continue his strong interest in martial arts. His dream-trip multiwriting project includes a variety of genres that introduce, explain, and apply the connected aesthetic of relaxation, art appreciation, politics, and combat of Japan. His performance, in full Samurai regalia he has made, includes demonstrations of traditions of combat with wooden weapons he has created for the occasion.

Students in the Cornerstone Program in Experiential Learning, which Rob directs, have similarly worked together to turn individual community service projects into collaborative programs, such as a multidisciplinary study of hunger and food security, which has included food drives, nutritional studies, consensus-building dialogues with local agencies, and a community garden. Next year, students and faculty are planning a statewide symposium on hunger, food security, and community food systems at the university and are working together to build a university consensus center that will sponsor the event. This center will also work across agencies and the private and public sectors on other issues, including air and water quality and sustainable economic development. The necessity of knowing and using a variety of languages and discourses is evident in this pubic work with partners from diverse backgrounds and viewpoints.

During fall term, Mark's students in two large first-year expository writing classes investigated the rhetoric of citizenship and the 2004 presidential elections, then worked in small collaborative groups on community service projects. These projects ranged from helping at the local animal shelter to raking leaves for seniors to helping with the shelter for victims of domestic violence or environmental groups with the restoration of local streams. Many of these students met most of their Cornerstone requirements in community service. Their collaborative projects used whatever genres they deemed important for reporting back to the larger class as agents for change. One group made a flashy promotional brochure for the animal shelter, while another made a scrapbook of photos and texts showing the work of the local Court Appointed Special Advocates group (CASA), which advocates for the interests of youth in court cases. Another group of physical education majors reapplied their academic learning by creating a curriculum and handbook for exercises and sports for elementary school teachers, as well as teaching elementary students some new games.

This book accompanies this expansive sense of engaged learning in the world, as it conceives a widened range of discourse arrayed across multiple genres, media, disciplines, cultures, and forms. In its flexibility and potential variety, multiwriting can be a close match and pedagogic support to the many kinds of active learning students now follow in college and beyond: business case studies or business plan writing; political or journalistic blogs; natural or cultural studies approaches to engaging topics, including recently published works on love, blood, the pencil, and the number zero; or the partnership building implicit within community service learning or public work. We further believe it helps students to increasingly become aspiring experts in the art of discourse, who not only know some of its multitude of forms but also can freely apply those that are appropriate, using ancient rhetorical considerations such as purpose, audience, message, and occasion.

While college writing is never fully without givens or preconditions, the approaches this book begins to describe rely upon choices made as students study the tools and stances within discursive traditions and apply these to their own situations. Ours is a question-based method that enacts texts as journeys that can transform both writers and readers. We like to think of each course as its own crossroads of ambiguity and potential, also enriched by the multiple discourses students carry with them on their routes. The challenge of teaching is to help individuals and groups find that unique tuning leading to a different music that changes all they know.

We especially want to report the following outcomes, achieved during more than a decade of teaching this way:

This approach gets students excited about learning. It gives them an element of control that they may lack in courses using more conventional approaches or understandings of discourse. However, most are surprisingly prepared for this control, as it either fits lives that have involved multiple choices or because it provides choices that have been lacking. Students who seem detached from other approaches often take to this one as if they have been waiting for it. While students can be overwhelmed by the free choices of multiple subjects and forms, a cagey teacher can bring them along more slowly by relying upon discursive traditions, such as the discourses of cultural studies or civic engagement in the courses described above, or the traditions we describe in chapters to come.

We have found that this way of teaching is particularly helpful in getting students excited about and helping them to access difficult kinds of academic learning, such as theory. It works, we believe, in part because it links the public and academic with the private and personal. While all learning is autobiographic, this method also helps students to see how autobiography can be transformed through theory, and how telling a life story is often a matter of embodying experience in forms. In a chapter in *Research Writing Revisited: A Sourcebook For Teachers*, edited by Wendy Bishop and Pavel Zemliansky, we discuss this at more length, showing how one of our students captured both her life history and the theory she was beginning to engage and apply in the familiar de/re-constructive form of the piñata.

It leads to additional learning and "student retention." Administrators fear disaffected (or poverty-stricken) students will leave college never to return, and as faculty and representatives of higher education to the world, we should also, as our work involves spreading a gospel of enlightenment and empowerment through information and intelligence. The approaches we describe here—including the pedagogic exercises and reading lists provided in each chapter—favor getting started or finding a route to open the world. Like the ancients, we put emphasis on the act of invention as key even to the "revision" and "editing" included in a writing process designed to produce finished texts. See, for instance, Meredith Sue Willis's *Deep Revision: A Guide For Students, Teachers, and Other Writers*, which reenvisions the five "latter stages" of the writing processes as reconception and invention.

For our students, the deadline draft of a course project is often a means to further learning that suggests the next project to come. Although strategies such as careful degree planning and cohort foundation are essential, another way to retain students is to get them "hooked" on the power of their own questions and the value of their academic work in ways that can extend beyond individual courses or academic programs. This internalization of inquiry may turn the drudgeries of their service jobs—taken during "down times" for college to earn money for the next round, or to begin to pay off daunting student loans—into opportunities for learning, through cultural observation, problem-solving, or the revolutionary consciousness that asks why college students and most others work on behalf of corporate interests.

It makes them hungry for discourse. They become both ravenous eaters and connoisseurs of written and spoken words. One of our precursors, further discussed below in this chapter, is Winston Weathers, who has served as exemplar and sensei to the current wave of scholars envisioning alternative practices for composition. In *An Alternate Style: Options in Composition*, Weathers includes a "jotting"—part manifesto, part request—found among the papers of Professor X, which may have been written by X or by a student. The author looks toward a practice of composition that will include not only conventional academic discourse but also the grand variety of discourses of the world. She does not want to be saved from the five-hundred-word theme but to experience it as part of a larger whole:

> I'm asking simply to be exposed to, and informed about, the full range of compositional possibilities. That I be introduced to all the tools, right now, and not be asked to wait for years and years until I have mastered right-handed affairs before I learn anything about left-handed affairs. That, rather, I be introduced to all the grammars, vehicles, tools, and compositional possibilities *now* so that even as I "learn to write" I will have before me as many resources as possible. I'm asking: that all the "ways" of writing be spread out before me and that my education be devoted to learning how to use them. (2)

This smorgasbord of discourse is reminiscent of the "information overload" that can cripple any of us in postmodern times, but it also leads to the craving that keeps people searching, say, for alternative sources of news beyond corporate "mainstream" infotainment. While developing critical judgment is one cue for intellectual life in these times, another is the sense of nomadic inquiry that sustains and drives us as we search the Web, read the print, and talk to others in search of the finest source or most appropriate or provocative discourse for any occasion.

It de-mystifies academic prose. As Australian aborigines know, sometimes we can get to where we are going only by walking hard in the opposition direction of the presumed destination. Knowing a plethora of discursive alternatives is excellent preparation for writing conventionally in academic settings. No longer are students prostrate before the academic essay with proper citations as it crashes seemingly from nowhere upon their heads. Gradually, through the overplanned improvisation of finding the free spaces within traditions, students come to see that all discourses have histories, with conventions that developed over time. Each discourse they write increasingly involves constructing a voice, inhabiting a form, and breathing life into a dry set of rules. Because they can see the boundaries, students may also be better able to write beyond the form, exceed the conventions as well as fulfill them, and give the new twist that many faculty wait for as they wade through the stack.

It asks students to be self-directed. Compositionists often define their goal as helping students gain admission into discourse communities, like those within specific disciplines or professional fields. But don't we secretly want more for them? Is admission into the status quo even minimally enough when the human world needs badly to change? Intriguing thinkers often work beyond the boundaries of a singular community and write to a greater pool of interested people who also swim through discourses, bodies of knowledge, and cultural perspectives like the philosophical sperm in John Barth's "The Nightsea Journey," in *Lost in the Funhouse*. It is this global intellectual "community"—ever in the midst of being formed through dialogue, argument, and acts of resistance to pat answers—which we want our students to join.

This sense of reflective, sometimes contentious, always persistent, wondering is at the core of the blues music we love and that often inspires our teaching. While such blues is often deeply autobiographic and connects aspects of the world to emanations of the self, it also rejoins us with others as the audience is soaked by the lazy rain or mighty storm of a blues guitar or joins with a singer in the repeatable but differently nuanced chorus of "Everyday I have the blues." Such blues is lifelong learning sustained by the processes of inquiry and communication. It is an art of creative endurance that allows us to take in, reflect upon, argue with, survive, and transform experience.

We want students to similarly take reflection and inquiry to the heart of their experiences, and we find them most often eager to do so. Our belief, borne out over the years, is that despite the massive energy in the culture suggesting that the use of college is to get a better job, people would like it to be about something more. Ellen Condliffe Lagemann, dean of the School of Education at Harvard, is among those reconnecting the career training of professional education with the ideal of vocation or calling in the world. Her speech at the 2004 National Meeting of the American Association of Colleges and Universities described this sense of vocation as the binding force connecting liberal arts to professional education and integrating aspects of academic and life experience. We suggest, however, that this call of vocation is one aspect of a broader sense of learning, which, while sometimes concentrated in a sense of mission, may also be dispersed through the multiple, often complex, or contradictory situations of life that call for reexamining the world and regenerating the self. Our teaching is an attempt to prompt such creative learning, as well as to help students strive toward a "calling" or sense of interconnected inquiry that begins to unite experience.

For teachers, we offer a set of outcomes that parallels the list above: heightened excitement in teaching; an approach to theory and pedagogy that sets academic discourse as a portion of the discourses of the world; a potential reawakening of the teacher's appetite for student work; and a new way to view teaching as a jump start for the life of the mind. We also offer a more hidebound discussion that may be liberating as well. Our intent is to show how an altered practice of composition can grow from a reinterpretation of discursive traditions. The initiative to span multiple genres, media, disciplines, or cultures comes in part from loosening energies held in check by conventional readings of traditions. We join many other teachers and scholars in questioning and moving past these limits to experience traditions of persuasion, inquiry, and essayistic writing as—in the lyrics of legendary Texas blues guitarist Stevie Ray Vaughn—a "Texas Flood" of discourse for use in multiple contexts.

We offer a crossroads in place and time, where an avant-garde present links to a past filled with potential. This landscape is like the one anthropologist Keith Basso describes in his study of the history-bearing place names of the Western Apache, in *Wisdom Sits in Places*. For Basso, learning to see the marks of the past in familiar places or artifacts leads to an awareness deepened by the dimension of time. As we become more cognizant of the past, we are increasingly "present" in and absorbed by the world. He describes the process by which this consciousness of time begins to take hold by beginning with the familiar and workaday world:

> Many of these places are also encountered in the country of the present as material objects and areas, naturally formed or built, whose myriad local arrangements make up the landscapes of everyday life. But here, *now*, in the ongoing world of current concerns and projects, they are not apprehended as reminders of the past. Instead, when accorded attention at all, places are perceived in terms of their outward aspects—as being, on their manifest surfaces, the familiar places they are—and unless something happens to dislodge these perceptions they are left, as it were, to their own enduring devices. But then something does happen. Perhaps one spots a freshly fallen tree, or a bit of flaking paint, or a house where none has stood before—any disturbance, large or small, that inscribes the passage of time—and a place presents itself as bearing on prior events. And at that precise moment, when ordinary perceptions begin to loosen their hold, a border has been crossed and the country starts to change. Awareness has shifted its footing, and the character of the place, now transfigured by thoughts of an earlier day, swiftly takes on a new and foreign look (4).

By adding the dimension of time to this work, we hope to create a foreign appearance that leads to a new familiarity born of a different recognition. For those who enjoy or are on the verge of alternative practices in composition, we provide a double sense of tradition. We reinscribe theories and practices of alternative composition as a fledgling nomadic tradition in the field, through which an expanding collection of thinkers has gradually turned the margins of the profession into a center for different kinds of writing and new conceptions of discourse. In this sense, the crossroads is a caravansary—a sanctuary on risky routes through the world. But it is not the kind of caravansary Mark photographed as a young traveler in the Afghani desert, where the walls were crumbling and a power pole had no wires attached. It is more the kind that comes to the moveable feast of an oasis, like Oahu, where Hawaii—like it or not—is the nexus of more fiber optic cable running in every direction than anywhere on earth.

Our alternative reading of discursive traditions shows how they evoke and enact the arts of the crossroads in its multiple forms as an oasis—a place that, over and over again, provides inspiration beyond protection. For those whose interests and practices remain more tied to conventional practices, we suggest that there is more room to operate within the traditions with which we are more familiar than may be immediately seen. For the committed avant-gardist, we hope to strengthen the argument, for use with colleagues or students, that even traditions thought of as familiar invite leading-edge work. We also would like to build consensus between all by suggesting how a broad landscape of inquiry and writing with many possibilities may provide a common ground that we all may traverse. Here the crossroads is a diverse community, where trading groups from cultures moving in all directions also, at least temporarily, settle and remix their differences. Just as the gumbo and blues/jazz music of New Orleans continues to mix Creole and world traditions, we envision multiwriting not as a static language but as a temporary, evolving tongue of nomadic traders, like the Chinook Jargon of the Pacific Northwest, which has over twenty different words for *voice*.

From the charged landscape of the crossroads, this book works through a series of retunings. This metaphor of tuning is not just our salute to, or appropriation of, the blues, but a bow to the way it has been developed by interdisciplinary thinkers like David Antin, especially in *Tuning*, his collection of talk performances. Prosody—as poets like Antin, Allen Ginsberg, and Jerome Rothenburg have shown in their work and collections of literature from around the world—is the history of the music behind poetry and words.

So, in Chapter 2, research writing is reclaimed from the staid practice of the nonmusical term paper and recast as the tracing of inquiry opening to show students an increasingly mysterious and beckoning world that holds the key to their survival. Chapter 3 reveals persuasive writing as a way to move both writer and audience into a deeper understanding of issues, rather than a retrenchment of positions. Chapter 4 recasts the essay as a crossroads (and cabinet) of wonder, where different kinds of writing and ways of thinking may be collected and provisionally ordered by an emerging question or theme. In Chapter 5, the blues is explored as an open expression and communication of living, able to take in and eventually syncretically affirm each round of experience.

Again, we are reminded of a figure in the gallery, the *lukasa*, which serves not only as the ultimate record of the culture that provides a central narrative that other mnemonic forms including statues and stools extend but also as an invitation to narrative that allows the culture to enter into changing situations with a sense of both tradition and preparation. Initiation into the Mbudye, a secret organization of Luba that makes and interprets the *lukasa*, is a training in rhetorical flexibility and a kairotic sense of community. The work of the Mbudye holds the culture together and helps both to direct and buffer it from changes. It formalizes the combination of official and subterranean narratives that keeps the culture from becoming stultified or too diffuse.

Perhaps because of its complexity, life at the crossroads throws us back upon the simplest terms as we reflect on where we have been and decide how to proceed and make parallel choices about recording our experience and helping others to follow where we are headed. Geoffrey Sirc, one of the writers in composition studies we rely upon, supplants abstract considerations of purpose and audience with the heuristic that matters most, "that the person who reads this—and it is one specific person, saturated in a lived desire—will that person be changed?" (11). In the crossroads, we write, read, think, and ask in order for the changes to continue, as we know that they must in a world that does not wait.

The particular arts of the crossroads that we record and invite others to follow are the pedagogic acts and student-written texts of multiwriting. These discourses are example of those Derek Owens foresees in "Composition as the Voicing of Multiple Fictions," where the focus is on assemblage across a broad discursive field and the craft of composing in multiple dimensions:

> Feasibly, taken in its broadest sense, composition studies is a crossroads discipline, a catalytic zone where a motley assemblage of discourse communities and arenas for intellectual exploration converge, metamorphose, and regenerate. At the same time, we cannot study multiple disciplines without being brought back somehow to the art of composing: musically, syntactically, lexically, orally, dialogically, socially, politically, poetically. (160)

Multiwriting may also be defined as a series of choices, where all manner of utterances are open to us, but perhaps only a few are the most appropriate, or moving. Often, students become interested in the marriage of content and form and compose a research project in unusual containers: a meteorological and cultural study of Oregon coastal weather comes in an umbrella, and an oral history of local women in the armed services during World War II is presented as a gift that comments upon the learning of these women as the life of the writers who now pass it on. While PowerPoint is useful for presentations, students learn through the study of forms that blogs may be best for keeping an issue alive and building community over distance. At times a single form may dominate the project, as in Tim Lucas's research on surveillance, which came as an intimidating, classified exposé. Other students find a broad theme where one project leads to another. For example, Michelle Skow studied Japanese-American poetry in literary criticism, cultural cuisine through ethnography, and the internment of her grandparents and many others during World War II in a project that combined historical narration and fiction.

Multiwriting also has a creative relation to history. The copious nature of discourse and thought—coupled with the blooming of interactive technologies, the acceleration of cultural mixing, and history's determination toward liberalism (despite alarming current trends in this period of reaction)—cooperate with the causes of multiplicity and dialogue toward unity as the world heads toward the crossroads. Perhaps our activity as teachers and writers is meant to cooperate with this progression and help direct it in intelligent ways. Instead we often see that the opposite approach disenfranchises the students by isolating the strands. Teaching one way of writing at a time, through a false purity of definition that denies the *metis* or mixed blood quality of all discourse, may make sense in a curriculum that dedicates courses to particular ways of writing. But the most successful students are often those who cut against the grain to mix discourses in intelligent ways, despite the structure of the course, while those who struggle cannot find voices despite, or because of, being told how they should sound.

We argue instead that traditions contain many possibilities and stretch to bring in more. Blues music is a case in point. It is highly traditional—one recognizes a tune as blues almost at once—but its flexible forms expand to take in all of life—the pride, pleasure, and joy, as well as the heartache, violence, and misery. Further, blues has stretched to provide the backbeat of all later American music—jazz, rock, rap, hip-hop, punk. What is not a restatement of the blues? It is the foundation of American music, although too few still seem to realize it. Attending classes at Julliard as a young man new to New York, jazz great Miles Davis saw how limited an understanding trained white musicians and scholars had of African-American music, and the blues in particular:

> I remember one day being in a music history class and a white woman was the teacher. She was up in front of the class saying that the reason black people played the blues was because they were sad and that's

where the blues came from, their sadness. My hand went up in a flash and I stood up and said, "I'm from East St. Louis and my father is rich, he's a dentist, and I play the blues. My father didn't never pick no cotton and I didn't wake up this morning sad and start playing the blues. There's more to it than that." The way I was thinking about music was that people like Fletcher Henderson and Duke Ellington were the real geniuses at arranging music in America. This woman didn't even know who these people were, and I didn't have the time to teach her. She was supposed to be teaching me! So, instead of listening to what she and the other teachers said, I was looking up at the clock and thinking about what I would be doing later that night, wondering when Bird and Diz would be going downtown (59).

Playing with Bird (Charlie Parker), Diz (Dizzy Gillespie), and many others and following his insatiable creativity and musical curiosity wherever they led, Davis extended the blues, moving from bop to cool to an increasingly Afro-centric fusion. His way of learning his art included a wide range of study, which again set him apart:

> Another thing I found strange after living and playing in New York for a little while was that a lot of black musicians didn't know anything about music theory. Bud Powell was one of the few musicians I knew who could play, write, and read all kinds of music. A lot of the old guys thought if you went to school it would make you play like you were white. Or, if you learned something from theory, then you would lose all feeling in your playing. I couldn't believe that all them guys like Bird, Prez, Bean, all them cats wouldn't go to museums or libraries and borrow scores by all these great composers, like Stravinsky, Alban Berg, Prokofiev. I wanted to see what was going on in all of music. Knowledge is freedom and ignorance is slavery, and I just couldn't believe someone could be so close to freedom and not take advantage of it. I have never understood why black people didn't take advantage of all the shit that they can. It's like a ghetto mentality telling people that they aren't supposed to do certain things, that those things are only reserved for white people. (60–61)

We mean to cultivate a similar, boundary-crossing inquiry. Rightly practiced, discursive traditions are blues of inquisitive living that accept no ghettoes and project the rich past into the future, where it is needed. The discourses we refer to in this book may seem alternative or avant-garde, but they can also be understood as the late manifestations of ways of thinking, writing, and asking that, while connected to the rhetorical practices of the academy, also predate it. Our use of tradition heads into a deep past, where the initial human acts of questioning, the ur-inquiries, lay shrouded. But this archeology also leaves us better informed and prepared in the current scene, where ancient arts are remade. We want to help teachers refill their rhetorical backpacks for the classroom and the world while giving them a new but strangely familiar tune to hum as they go and perhaps an altered perspective on the daily blues as it unfolds. Miles Davis said that he and his band play what the day recommends. We would like readers to see that practicing composition in new ways does not mean flouting tradition, acting carelessly, or coming at discourse from outside academic conventions. Instead, we suggest that conventions can be revised or infused with a new sense of purpose by knowing some of their history and seeing that their use is often dependent upon rhetorical choices involving purposes, messages, audiences, and occasions.

When Mark began using the approach we describe here, he was so worried about the judgments of the senior faculty and dean that he had students rewrite their already gargantuan research projects as twenty-page reflective essays that both explained all their choices and showed how the project contained the great array of information that it would have held if written as a traditional term paper. The students, who saw themselves as defenders of an approach they surprised themselves by loving, obliged. Not so friendly were the audience members the first time the two of us presented together at a conference on "unusual student texts" as works of literature and theory. The bizarreness of the approach, the audacious claim that students could write complexly and that a project on tetrahedrons could be compared to Charles Olson or Jacques Derrida nearly led to a stoning with examination copies of grammar handbooks collected from the textbook publishers in the flush days when such texts were handed out for free.

While we have not kept up with that crowd, we can say that twelve years later, many of those same faculty members at our university use multiwriting themselves, including the dean, when she teaches courses. The approach has spread across the disciplines and out of our university to others nationwide and internationally and throughout high schools and secondary schools. It has met up with other related approaches for pursuing discourse differently, ranging from multi-genre writing in some high school and college classrooms to writing for the Web to writing across disciplines for first-year college seminars and learning communities. Crossroads discourse is on the rise in a world of cultures that are mixing and morphing into new combinations. We are attracted to the approaches and arts of the crossroads because they offer us a chance to participate in these new cultural formations while practicing the crafts of writing and teaching in new ways.

Despite our emphasis upon traditions, we identify with theoreticians and practitioners of alternative educational and compositional practices. Later chapters include figures who revise discursive traditions from an alternative point of view, including Richard Larson, Bruce Ballenger, and Michael Blitz and C. Mark Hurlbert for research writing; William Covino and Theodore Zeldin for persuasive writing; Paul Heilker and Susan Griffin for the essay; and Angela Y. Davis and Albert Murray for the blues. Here, however, we focus upon and construct an alternative tradition in composition constituted by selected works by Geoffrey Sirc, Derek Owens, Winston Weathers, and Tom Romano. These writers develop their visions of boundary crossing discourse by placing composition into dialogue with "alternative traditions" in music, art, and literature. While Sirc relates counterculture composition to the Happenings movement in art, Owens shows how the experience of academic writing may be broadened through reference to and practice of resistant avant-garde and ethnocentric discourses. In Weathers, the alternative style of "Grammar b" allows writers to break out of the container of conventional discourse, while Romano opens the classroom to passionate discourses and inquiries modeled upon complex and lyrical expressions like multi-genre novels. Each writer practices what Sirc terms allegorical history or criticism, which reopens the history of composition and reexamines its practices and values by relating it to another variety of discourse.

In *English Composition as a Happening*, Sirc recollects the nearly forgotten composition pedagogies of the late 1960s and the 1970s. His return to composition's past is akin to a suspension of history: he reads the weathered pages of old articles from *College Composition and Communication* as if entering a room long ago sealed, with its furnishings still in mint condition, but covered in white sheets. The spirit of the Happenings allows for such a suspension: a Happening is an experience that privileges the present. It is nonrepeatable: one has to be there to understand it. For Sirc, such an ethic of spontaneity, surprise, innovation, and invention is the countermeasure to the simulacra called academic discourse, in which composition students replicate the conventions of other disciplines, which our field, prostrate, serves. In 1968, composition could still be "writing"—an act of expression in search of authentic being in the sum total of the here and now. Back then, courses had atmosphere, as Sirc recounts through a passage from William Lutz's 1971 article, "Making Freshman English a Happening":

> The next class was held in the same room; only this time I made a few alterations in the physical arrangements. There were no neat lines of folding chairs. The students sat, stood or lay wherever they

wished. When everyone was comfortable, I closed the drapes, turned off the lights, lit a candle in the middle of the room and a few sticks of incense, and played the same music as before [Sirc inserts: Ravel's "Bolero," Strauss's "Zarathustra," some Gregorian chants, selections from the Association, the Doors, Steppenwolf, Jefferson Airplane, Clear Light, Iron Butterfly, Simon and Garfunkel, and others]. The class just listened to music in the dark with the flickering candle and the scent of incense permeating the room. Again, when the period was over, the students were asked to pick up their books and leave. Some of them did not want to. (W. Lutz 38; Sirc 1)

Retrenchment against the pedagogy of the Happening began in the same era. The counterculture met with a reaction we are still living within and which has defined us as a profession. Sirc narrates the development of composition studies:

I began to realize that something questionable happened in our field in the late sixties and early seventies: our insecurity over our status as a valid academic field led us to entrench ourselves firmly in professionalism. To establish composition as a respectable discipline, we took on all the trappings of traditional academia—canonicity, scientism, empiricism, formalism, high theory, axioms, arrogance and acceptance of the standard university department-divisions. We purged ourselves of any trace of kookiness, growing first suspicious, then disdainful, of the kind of homemade comp-class-as-Happening that people like Lutz tried to put together. (6–7)

This is especially true at the margins of composition, in writing center and writing across the disciplines programs, where faculty still struggle to receive tenure and promotion and respect. Writing centers often had to become writing "labs" to suggest the necessary respect. Mark, who directed our busy writing lab for many years, once got a cranky letter from a famous composition scholar imploring him to change the address for the lab, which was, like so many, in a library basement. A publication devoted to writing center pedagogy once returned Mark's intentionally funny article, "Secrets of the Whitehouse Writing Lab," as "too unprofessional to gain respect outside our group."[1]

By depriving ourselves of both humor and the Happening spirit, we have prevented composition from being the encompassing intellectual practice it may still become. We have practiced a "material restraint" that upholds the conventional and have formed a carefully bounded canon, when we might have resisted canonization in order to continue to discover ideas, forms, and texts that we find significant. Now, the traces of composition as a discipline have begun to vanish in our eagerness to please or become the others. Examining the practice often called writing-in-the-disciplines, Sirc retorts: "Frankly, I don't care how a biologist writes. I assume it's pretty conventional stuff, thoroughly implicated in the traditional department divisions that stultify the academy" (8). Into this bleak scene, he projects a Happening: "If the folks in biology want to get together with me and talk about how to reevaluate the form and subject of biology, I'm there" (8).

People operating out of the Happening ideal undertake the improvisation through which one makes new sense out of matters long engaged. The structures they build together would take on vernacular forms as the architecture was modified due to circumstances, available materials, local customs, or idiosyncratic tastes. Such compositions accept, resist, critique, or change the conditions of life by turning it to art:

> Happenings were all about blurring the boundaries between art and life. They understood what [John] Cage maintained, which was that "what we are doing is living, and that we are not moving toward a goal, but are, so to speak, at the goal constantly and changing with it, and that art, if it is going to be anything useful, should open our eyes to this fact." (Sirc 9; Kirby and Schechner 60)

Happenings artist Ken Dewey's "de-determination of the idea of theatre" refines the relationship between art and life: "'[T]he further out one moves, the simpler one's understanding becomes of what theatre is. I now would accept only that theatre is a situation in which people gather to articulate something of mutual concern'" (Sirc 10; Dewey 210). For Sirc, Dewey's inclusive but specific vision speaks to the heart of composition and allows us to restate who we are or can become and what we might get done. "Dewey shows a basic, unoccluded desire for communion. That, along with passion, beauty, lyricism . . . why is that not our core? Why do we not insist on it? Despite all the lip service we give to empowerment in our ideological curricula, we don't really believe in the power of composition to change the world" (10).

The spirit of the Happening, however, is that of collective change. It grows out of the work of "expressivists," including Lutz, Charles Deemer, and Ken Macrorie, who have been obscured by the rise of "academic composition." Building a bridge through time, Sirc reminds us of declarations such as Macrorie's in *Uptaught*, published in 1971: "'[T]eachers must find ways of getting students to produce (in words, pictures, sounds, diagrams, objects, or landscapes) what students and teachers honestly admire'" (Sirc 7; Macrorie 186). While it invites individual departures, the Happenings spirit sets these within a public project of transformation.

Imagine the brilliant and varied structures to be built in academe from the work of biologist, compositionists, students, and teachers, all walking the line and making the exchange between experience and discourse, living and making meaning. And think of the exotic fun of it. Sirc calls us to this pleasurable, surprising work through a metaphor drawn from the sunny side of architecture:

> I offer, then, these backward glances in the fervent hope: to capture the Happenings spirit for our own in Composition, shaking off more than a decade of conservative professionalism; to fracture our field's genres open for possibilities, risks, and material exploration, leading to a Composition in which faith and naiveté replace knowingness and expertise; to put pressure on Composition's canon, recalibrating the field according to a general economy of composition arts—a destabilized site of various competing schools, under-cut by an ongoing, productive tension between the academic and the avant-garde; to liberate thinking in our field from the strictly semantic, reopening Composition as a site where radical explorations are appreciated, where aesthetic criteria still come into play, but criteria not merely cribbed from an endless, formalist tape loop. Put simply to resume building Compositions' hacienda. (32)

In *Resisting Writings (and Boundaries of Composition)*, Derek Owens surveys a similar scene using metaphors of geography and nautical navigation. It is as if the discourses of the world are islands in the sea, "a great many islands, some in chains, some scattered in isolation." Academia resides on one archipelago, where the natives share a discourse that is not a single language so much "as an array of conflicting communicative habits" linked by a mutual tolerance and a mythical unity:

> Although numerous dialects thrive on these plots of ground—many of them wholly incompatible with one another—there seems to be a shared consensus among most of the different users; as if some implicit albeit abstract institutional rubric ideologically joins the different islands, thereby metaphorically linking them into a solid "chain." (3)

Transit among the islands is surprisingly limited to the armada of administrators, who speak a "colonizing, enforcing language system" to which everyone must submit. "In this sense the Academic Discourse Islands aren't all that different from the IBM Islands, or any other incorporated discourse conglomerate" (5).

An aerial view reveals the academic archipelago as "a splotch of closely knit freckles" with many other islands, "each of them sites of equally fascinating, equally serious tribal dialects":

If we travel not too far we find islands where various African American rhetorics govern language usage. Elsewhere bodies of land pop up marked by feminist principles of composition, which try their best to dissociate themselves from the typically masculine grammars of academic power. Some islets are noticeable by their modernist, "postmodern," and avant-garde workings. The further we look, the more we become aware of the alternative spread of writing and communication strategies alive and well outside the academy. Viewed from distance, it's an amazing constellation. (6)

The islands do not exist in isolation. Migration is common, as is mixing of discourses through electronic media, "a babble of multiple voices and conversations, operating non-stop." Students coming to the academic archipelago carry the discourses of the wider world, "which resist and mimic one another in continual flux" (6).[2]

The permanent residents of academia, however, have been hesitant to make creative use of their opportunities to aid in the building of polyvocality; instead they stick to instruction in the tried forms they find comfortable, with confined places for only sanctioned alternatives. Owens parrots such critics when he says:

The point of education is to teach discourse from an *academic* framework. Functional, formalist, institutional literacy is important, not call and response or African-American "signifying." Students write according to current-traditional formulas, not projective verse. Though we might encourage personal narratives in student journals, less attention is paid to constructing oral performative texts, say those representative of much Amerindian discourse. Making well-honed, finely polished linear arguments in response to assigned readings is valuable; experimenting with fragmentation, mixing of genre, or multiple personas isn't. In other words, learning how to make written language look, sound, and read so that professors will validate the results—not discourse that would succeed by a host of alternative, nonacademic standards. (7)

Against this landscape of isolation and exclusion, Owens reimagines composition as inquiry into the many ways that people communicate. The crossroads discipline he envisions would expose students to the varieties of discourse and provide them with a "polyfocal vocabulary of discourse." He advocates mixing theory and practice or critical judgments and creative work. Students should not only read the discourses of the world—and study the history of them, and unmask the ideologies behind them—but also try their hands at writing the resistant texts of feminism, the signification of African-Americans, and the surreal or parodic collages of the avant-garde. His book tours the discursive varieties he has begun to learn while sampling a pedagogy based upon inclusion and variety, rather than expertise in only "academic" forms.

Against the charge that failing to focus on the prescribed rhetorics of the academy leaves students ill prepared for writing in college and beyond, Owens shows that a generalist's appreciation for variety may be the best response to the times. For instance, even a lifetime of reading across cultures, languages, and genres will yield only a partial, idiosyncratic understanding of the experience we call literature. He cites Buckminster Fuller's claim that computers have supplanted humans as specialists" "[F]rom here on out we are all generalists, selecting our way through an incomprehensible flood of information, our paths governed only by taste and by chance" (193). From this generalist perspective, Owens shows how pockets of expertise or experience can be established through courses in subjects such as Traditional Academic Discourses; Writing Personal Narrative; Ethnorhetorical Investigations; Experimental, Avant-Garde and Feminist Writing; Computers in Composition; and Developmental Writing.

In offering generative critiques, which expand the field of composition while showing why the limits we have set for it are needless and defeatist, Owens and Sirc follow in the wake of authors such as Ken Macrorie and Winston Weathers, each of whom argued for an opening of composition to include alternative methods and styles. Macrorie's famed "I-Search Paper" allowed students to shift research writing from the abstract subjects of the academy to matters of personal concern. Weathers bracketed the rhetorics and conventions of academic prose as a single "grammar" while offering a series of alternative styles derived from modern literature and the new journalism, grouped under the heading of "Grammar B." While Macrorie argued for the right of college students to pursue subjects they deemed important, Weathers preceded Owens and Sirc in arguing for the empowering effects of discursive diversity.

Weathers's *An Alternative Style: Options in Composition* begins with the rebellious secret thoughts of the late Professor X or, an intervening voice tells us, perhaps it was not X but a student who wrote these indiscretions. Like Sirc, Owens, and Macrorie, Weathers's "X" returns us to a fundamental scenario, full of potential, from which the limits and abstractions we previously imposed have been removed. Writing is

[w]ords on paper/one of the ways I—the human being—communicate. There are all the other ways, of course. Talking. Gesturing. Moving my body. Costuming my flesh. Participating in events "out

there"/in observable actions. But tremendously important always/ words on paper/the string of words in the code of written language, effecting the composition—the "thing made"/the verbal artifact— that I transmit to others for them to negotiate into the miracle of understanding what it is/has been inside the otherwise inaccessible regions of my very human, mysterious brain. (1)

The range of transmissions is broad. We communicate information but also emotion, attitude, and stance. Even our style is part of what we transmit; as Weathers says:

> "Look," I often want to say. "This is anger!" "This is confusion!" "This is enigma!" "This is the way I see the universe—mixed up, ambiguous, disorderly." Or, "simplistic, barren, vacant." Or "complex, baroque, impenetrable." Even, at times, I want to say, "The message is: 'there is no message.'" (1)

Schooling, however, is the limiting of contents, styles, and forms. The every-person X replicates the system he was taught within:

> What I've been taught to construct is: the well-made box. I have been taught to put "what I have to say" into a container that is always remarkably the same, that—in spite of varying decorations—keeps to a basically conventional form: a solid bottom, four upright sides, a fine-fitting lid. Indeed, I may be free to put "what I have to say" in the plain box or in the ornate box, in the fragile box or the study box. But always the box—squarish or rectangular. (1)

Now, the X figure begins to envision a discourse, and container, beyond the box:

> And I begin to wonder if there isn't somewhere a round box or an oval box or tubular box, if there isn't some sort of container(1) that will allow me to package "what I have to say" without trimming my "content" to fit into a particular compositional mode, (2) that will actually encourage me to discover new things to say because of the very opportunity a newly shaped container gives me (even though I can never escape containers—e.g. syntax—altogether), (3) that will be more suitable perhaps to my own mental processes, and (4) that will provide me with a greater rhetorical flexibility, allowing me to package what I have to say in more ways than one and thus reach more audiences than one. (2)

As X begins to suggest, even the simplest messages may require multiple styles and stances to make their way into the world. It is this knowledge of the multiple, untaught styles that the student/scholar desires. He is not asking to be excused from the common work of college students; instead, he wants it to expand. Sensing a great beyond, he requests what James Moffett once termed the universe of discourse.

In response, Weathers, or the narrator of the rest of the book, constructs an alternative "grammar of style," termed Grammar b, with its own conventions, values, and characteristics, including "variegation, synchronicity, discontinuity, ambiguity and the like" (8).[3] It is an alternative style, not an experimental one, as it stems from a tradition dating back to at least the end of the eighteenth century residing within literary culture and found in the work of writers including Laurence Sterne, William Blake, Walt Whitman, D. H. Lawrence, F. Scott Fitzgerald, Marianne Moore, and Tillie Olsen, to name a few. This style has developed its own traits, which allow for a flexible organization within complexity and variegation. These devices include "crots," independent bits of discourse, often used for dramatic effects or abrupt leaps, that allow for unusual connections; labyrinthine sentences or fragments, suggesting the convoluted or isolated qualities of existence; the list, indicating the simultaneity of variety, where readers are left to provide the commentary, create connections, or make choices; multiple voices, lexicons, or languages, evoking complex relations among discourses; and repetition, repetends, or refrains that auspiciously scaffold plural texts. Such devices respond and grow out of human life on Earth, in its richness, complexity, multiplicity, and sense of serendipitous connection.

It is not correct, Weathers argues, to see Grammar b as ancillary to Grammar A, or as its shadow, or corrective: "The alternate style is not a style that 'comes after' the traditional style. It is not a 'subsequent' skill." Instead, each style is part of the writer's repertoire, and each should be part of the writer's education:

> Indeed, if one style is anterior to the other, Grammar b has the greater claim: it is probably the fundamental and essential style, out of which a secondary Grammar A has been developed for specialized logic/clarity of goals; but, because of the "system's" long inculcation of Grammar A and disapprobation of Grammar b (the sort of displacement that William Blake "howls" about throughout his prophetic work), we are led to the very need to "teach" Grammar B—a teaching that is perhaps, actually, a restoration. (51)

Like Weathers, Tom Romano sees literary works as models for an alternative composition that extends the discursive knowledge and skills of students. Romano also shows how varieties of language encode different ways of being and perceiving. In *Writing with Passion: Life Stories,*

Multiple Genres and *Blending Genre, Altering Style: Writing Multigenre Papers*, he describes teaching multi-genre research papers as a creative process by which interest and research is made into art.

In *Writing With Passion*, he describes the multiple ways language mediates our view of the world:

> Perception is all.
> Ways of seeing.
> Ways of knowing.
> Ways of learning.
> Sometimes I see the world through poetry: a bit of cadenced language suddenly saying itself in my head, an indelible image ever sharp, a surprising metaphor with extensions following close behind.
> Sometimes I see the world through prose: a description that holds in place an unforgettable scene, a pointed story that clarifies experience, a monolog that marshals points I wish I'd made during a disagreement.
> Sometimes I see the world through dramatic encounters: before a student arrives for conference, I play out the dialog that might occur between us; I talk with my father, he dead now three decades.
> Each genre offers me ways of seeing and understanding that others do not. I perceive the world through multiple genres. They shape my seeing. They define who I am. (109)

This multiplicity carries into the multi-genre paper, which enacts an evolving set of perceptions and voices. Inspiration for the multi-genre form came from reading *The Collected Works of Billy the Kid*, a multi-genre novel by Michael Ondaatje. The novel is factual and poetic, research-based, and highly imaginative: "The author's inquiry easily matches that of a dissertation. Out of his learning, however, Ondaatje did not write exposition. Instead, he created a complex, multilayered, multivoiced blend of genres" (111). The experience of reading it is like listening to jazz: ". . . the reader feels something satisfying and meaningful, but may not be able to articulate what it is right away" (124).

Romano reports his continued zeal over the book as he begins to consider how to turn students toward such writing:

> After reading and rereading the book, I began to wonder what if . . . what if students wrote in Ondaatje's multigenre style? The notion was so big I carried it around with me for nearly a year, talking with friends and colleagues in the Ohio Writing Project and the University of New Hampshire Summer Writing Program. Look at this book, I'd urge them. Look at the poetry and fiction, the character sketches

and songs, the pictures and scenes. Listen to all the voices. Have you ever seen anything like this? (111)

He asks not only if students would be capable of similar work but also what they would derive from it. His theory is that writing in multiple genres may provide multiple means and layers of perception and feeling, helping students to experience their subjects and writing in a deep, layered, and nuanced manner. He tries the method first in an advanced high school course, asking students to write in multiple genres about a person who interests them and constructing a series of inventions and reflections to help them turn their growing research into a creative product. He reports on the results:

> I have never read anything like these multigenre research papers before. Most of them were genuinely interesting in style and content. The visions were complex, the writing versatile. Brian's paper was one of six or seven I found astonishing. All was not glory, though. Three of the papers were disappointing, showing little depth, breadth or commitment. And rest assured, like Reverend Dimsdale, I did a requisite amount of self-flogging: What did I do wrong? What could I have done? (127)

This agenda for practice, reflection, and refinement is ongoing, as Romano continues to teach this method, spread it to others, and gather their results, as well as his own. This collective experiment, now institutionalized at many high schools and expanding to colleges, has gained momentum in part because of the interest of students in this kind of work and due to its natural links to multiple ways of being and perceiving.[4]

Our work echoes and recombines elements from Sirc, Owens, Weathers, and Romano. Through a pedagogy that is in part a series of invitations to a Happening, our students follow exercises or heuristics into an altered world of inquiry and discourse. We have adopted an approach to courses and even academic programs as Happenings, where students can build on the work of one another and pursue interrelated inquiries in ways that no one can foresee from the beginning. Like Owens, we want composition to navigate waters beyond the bays of academe, because we believe that ours is indeed a "crossroads discipline" that gives students not only tools for working in particular discursive situations but also the opportunity to form a whole, where different discourses can be brought together to address central questions. Like these writers, we know that the act of composing extends into music, art, science, politics, conversation, consensus building, mediation, friendship, and love. Our students' products are linked to the multi-genre works described by Romano but also likely to include multiple media and perspectives from different disciplines and cultures.

The crossroads discourse we join resides not solely in composition studies but also potentially in many or multiple traditions for expression, communication, inquiry, reflection, or action. So, while some of our readers may think alongside this book about how to turn literary criticism, ethnography, or technical writing toward a more open approach, others may find parallels in different disciplines, such as emergence theory in physics and biochemistry; open source computer programming; or the theories of public work, now reshaping many fields.[5] Cultural parallels may also be found: East Indian men taking the inquisitive journey called Sunyata; Aborigines finding an "alternative" reality in a dreamtime that evokes their history and destiny; or the Brazilian martial art Capoeira, which allows its students to absorb, deflect, or transform all that life sends them.[6]

Purposes and forms for writing lurk within each analogy. We imagine student projects that follow these parallel tracks: an ethnography that includes the science and culture of Capoeira, with a performance of this Brazilian martial art as the student has so far learned it; an enactment of the wandering mind in writing, music, and travel, through an internship in Africa that produces a journal or series collages, like those of Dan Eldon's in *The Journey Is the Destination*[7]; or a collaborative project on spiritual practices in diverse cultures that includes interviews with participants; readings of central texts; and observation of, or participation in, a spiritual practice, during a workshop for the campus community.

Faculty reading this book may charge themselves to support or foster such student work by expanding their own practices and visions, to include cross-disciplinary courses, teaching with experiential learning toward study abroad, working on curricular reform projects aimed at crossing disciplines or cultures, or helping students to search for a deeper sense of vocation or calling in the world. At the crossroads, the world is still coming awake and is full of potential for change.

Seeing the act of seeking as fundamental to our lives and to the work we ask of students entails reversing a libidinal economy, turning inside out the desire for acquisition and control that has driven Western history. Attempts at world conquest, all delusional, are the (bi-) polar twin of the analytic drive to separate experience into component parts in fitful attempts to gain mastery. This method is parodied beautifully as the "baby steps" therapy in the film *What about Bob?* The title character, played by Bill Murray, cannot control the smaller parts of his life but wrecks the frenzied attempts of the analyst (Richard Dreyfuss) to "make it" as a celebrity. A life of inquiry involves neither separation into the smallest units nor creating a single therapy for all problems, although both may be interesting experiments to try along the way. Instead it involves finding pleasure in continuation and happily receiving the questions that recast themselves when our overarching theories break down or we realize that a whole is needed to make sense of the parts. We live, think, and write between baby steps and master theories, where the richness, confusion, tragedy, violence, and joy of life rush at us where we are and await us where we go.

Musing: Practice in the Habit of Questions

Those who work out in the gym, train for road races on foot or bike, or prepare for backpack adventures by carrying a heavy pack as they walk the dog each day know that different kinds of training or exercise are essential for different activities. While you may run "gassers" or wind-sprints during basketball practice, learning to golf requires working on swing fundamentals on the driving range. Athletes also often cross-train to build desirable skills: for instance, professional shortstops sometimes learn ballet or jazz dancing to help them choreograph their movements on the baseball diamond, while NBA player Richard "Rip" Hamilton attributes his tirelessness on the court to his training as a marathoner.

Students and aspiring intellectuals and writers need a similar sense of training to acquire the conditioning, skills, and attitudes needed to bring the mind more fully to life. In particular, we must "train" for the awareness and curiosity needed to find, recognize, and articulate questions and for the stamina, restlessness, and sense of mystery required to follow questions wherever they may lead.

Learning to recognize the questions we live by is one of the hardest tasks for those entering the intellectual world, and one of the most habitual for those at home there. Here are exercises—from conversational musings to a more formal writing project and readings—for finding the questions within experience. We continue to try these not only with our students but also with ourselves, as we become more comfortable in the ambiguous milieu of questions.

After his wife died, blind blues musician Paul Pena went through a period of depression for six months, spending most of his time listening to HAMM radio broadcasts in a basement. One night he heard a strange new kind of music. He had no name for it but was fascinated. For over seven years, he did his best to describe what he had heard and asked others if they knew what kind of music it was or where it came from. One day a guy in a record store gave him a recording that turned out to be the music he had heard. Playing it over and over, he somehow taught himself the music, which showcased very high and low harmonics. It was Tuvan throatsinging.

Unbeknownst to Paul, the famous astrophysicist Richard Feynmann had brought up the former country of Tuva in a dinner conversation with friends, deciding he would like to go to this place. While Feynmann died before he could go, a group known as Friends of Feynmann investigated Tuva, which had been a country in the middle of the twentieth century, and was situated near Mongolia, China, and Tibet. They communicated with Tuvans still living in the area and brought one of their leaders to Pasadena to ride in the Rose Parade and give a throatsinging concert.

A friend of Paul's told him about this visit, and he flew to L.A. and introduced himself to the Tuvan leader by doing some throatsinging. It was impressive enough that he was invited for the national Tuvan throatsinging contest the next year, where he competed with many other singers. The Friends of Feynmann got Paul there and made a fascinating documentary film about it, *Genghis Blues*. Paul wins over Tuvans not only with his singing of their music but also by performing blues for them. This long, arduous, unusual journey began with both the dinner conversation of Feynmann and friends, as well as all the conversations Paul had with friends and record shop employees. From casual conversation came travel, cultural and linguistic exchange, and a work of art.

Exercise 1.1: The Discourse Diary

Although we may not have heard Tuvan throatsinging, each day we make, hear, absorb, ignore, and reflect upon many kinds of discourse. Here is a list of some of the genres of oral discourse students use or encounter in a typical morning:

> singing in the shower
> listening to funny morning radio shows
> chatting with friends or family over breakfast or coffee
> internally reviewing what they must do that day
> asking about assignments or social events as they wait for class
> laughing at amusing stories about the night before
> listening to instructors lecture
> discussing a reading or idea
> daydreaming about many things
> answering questions asked by professors or classmates
> reminding themselves what they need to do once class ends

This list, of course, can continue as the day goes on. For our purposes, let's try something a bit more focused. For a few days, keep a

Discourse Diary focused upon the purposes of speech and writing in your life, and the questions behind these purposes.

For instance, you may begin your day by making a list of things you need to accomplish during the day or the events, errands, and projects you must remember. The purpose of the list, we might say, is to aid your memory. However, perhaps the list also has a subtle persuasive effect: you have made the list long enough so that it is not overwhelming but it is ambitious. If you scratch off all the items on the list after having done them, you know that you will be able to relax with a sense of accomplishment. If you start to slack off, the list will make you feel guilty, which may lead you to get going again to see what more you can get done.

Beyond this self-information and persuasion, however, interesting questions reside. Why do you want to get so much done today? Why have you chosen these particular items? Does the list keep you from being spontaneous as new opportunities arise? Or does it keep you focused when you might have drifted away? Do you need the list? Are you in charge, or is the list?

Here are some specific instructions for your diary:

1. Pick about four examples of speech and writing you make, hear, read, or write during the course of the day. These may be conversations you take part in or overhear; arguments, debates, or discussions; readings for courses or pleasure; writing you do for yourself or others; even discourses that occur in your mind.

2. Describe each item in a few sentences.

3. Then list the purposes you see at work in each example. Did this discourse mean to entertain, inform, persuade, question, arouse, perplex, please, and/or annoy? Or do you see other purposes at work? You may find several purposes for each example.

4. The effects of the discourse must also be considered, as they may not be the same as the purposes. For instance, a friend may want to convince you that you need a new vehicle. This may instead have the effect of reinforcing your love of your old, beat-up ride. Similarly, you may set out to explain why you want to study abroad next year to your roommates and instead find yourself in a debate or philosophic discussion about the roots of terrorism or anti-American sentiment.

5. Finally, see if you can detect the questions behind the discourses. For instance, even a grocery list can have been a product of inquiry. Perhaps, for instance, you are trying to construct the perfect meal to impress someone you like, or throw a great party for your friends, or treat yourself to a favorite food. Why have you chosen the items on the list? Will this meal accomplish the purpose you have in mind? More broadly,

how does food create a reality? What other elements are needed: Music? Mood? Conversation? Luck?

Finding the questions is often the hardest part of this exercise. Many times, friends, classmates, tutors, and instructors can suggest questions that we may not have initially identified but may be at work, or may change our discursive experiences.

If this exercise works for you, you may begin to see what many writers know: discourse is complicated and often has multiple uses, purposes, and effects. It also arises from the questions that help to make our lives interesting and expand our thoughts and perceptions. As you prepare to write in college and beyond, it is useful to recognize this complexity and learn how better to work within it, even as it continues to surprise.

Exercise 1.2: The Daily Inquiry

What questions, inside or outside your academic work, occupy you today? Perhaps the question is about a course project, a job, an interest, or a relationship with a person or group. It may also be a political, social, or philosophic question: Why do humans seem to want to be at war? Why are some friendships lasting while others start hot and fade quickly? What about your favorite style of music is so compelling?

Here is an exercise to help you track the questions that arise in your own life. You may find that once your start doing this, it is hard to stop. The experience may be akin to keeping a dream journal, which, for many people, helps more dreams to come.

1. Record a question per day. It can be in the evening, as a souvenir of the day's events and thoughts, or in the morning (or the night before) as a way to set the tone for the day. You should also record answers, insights, or theories discovered or received, or your stray thoughts or stories relating to the question. For instance, is there an incident that may have caused the question to arise?

2. Observe and note your habits as a questioner. For instance, do you return to the same questions, or similar ones, or do you tend to move on? Do you focus upon one question at a time, or do you "multi-track" so that several questions of different kinds are open for you at once? Do you tend to be satisfied with answers you receive, at least for a time, or do you quickly reject most of what you hear or conceive?

3. After a week of daily inquiries, review what has occurred. Do any questions stand out as particularly intriguing or worth pursuing? Share these with classmates and talk together about how you may find out more about your questions and their possible answers.

You should find satisfaction in learning to ask and reflect upon questions, as this is an important skill for academic success and intellectual life. Many great discoveries, inventions and innovations—as well as the personal insights by which people shape their lives—come from curiosity and asking questions. For writers, questioning is essential, since writing is often an act of following questions along their trails.

Project: The Autobiography of a Question

To pursue research subjects as questions, it helps to see your life as a mystery that is open to interesting new explorations or well-known insistences. Here is a project that asks you to see yourself as a mystery and then trace a question of importance to you.

1. Find "official" documentation. Our culture generates many kinds of texts and documents about each of us. Some of these are written by us. For example, you may have already used a resume to help in a job search or filled out an application to get a credit card, to work abroad, or to join a club or organization. Others write some texts about us, like the credit card you finally received in the mail, which shows that someone wants you to spend money! The bill from your college or university implies another idea of where that money should go and who you are. The state authors your driver's license with information you provide. Your high school yearbook may include a "blurb" about you written by the staff: "a quiet, steady friend." Collect at least two examples of such texts about you.

2. Use these texts as invitations to narrative by telling a story about yourself that the official documentation may miss or mask. For instance, no one looking at your fishing license would be able to guess that you almost accidentally caught a dolphin or nearly drowned in heavy river currents. Perhaps the entry under your name in the phone book leads you to reflect on the house where you used to live and to tell a story showing why it haunts you. Write at least one story in response to each of the official documents.

3. Now look at the stories together. Is there anything that connects them—a personality trait, behavioral pattern, way of viewing the world, personal philosophy, or alter ego? What is the "hidden" you like? Does the public know or understand you? How have you been misunderstood? Have you even misunderstood yourself? Talk to classmates in a small group about these questions, as well as the connections you see and those they do.

4. If you are generating some interesting thoughts, go on to step five. If you aren't satisfied, you may want to try steps one or two again. We all

have various official documents, and many stories, so you should be able to try multiple routes. Remember, too, that this assignment is an experiment, so you may find that, in the end, no pattern emerges among your stories; or you may find one that is quite unexpected or seems wrong.

5. Now try the next step in seeing yourself as a mystery: instead of looking for conclusions in what you have written and discussed, look for interesting questions. What do you want to know more about regarding yourself and your life? What parts of you don't you understand? What aspects of your life or ways of living would seem alien to many other people? What things about you seem the most interesting to the people in your group, or to your friends? List at least three questions you have about yourself.

6. Next, reconsider the relationship between you and the world. Certainly there is more to it than a series of official documents suggests. What in the world do you feel passionate about? What about the world troubles you? What questions do you have that you would like answered? What work do you see yourself doing in the world? What have you already begun?

7. Try for one more imaginative leap: as you think about the person you are, think of the person you want to be. What experiences do you crave? What hasn't happened so far that you would enjoy? What, besides wealth, power, or even family, would signal success to you? What kind of relationship do you want with the world and the others in it? What sort of world do you want to live in? Try to think beyond the cliché of "world peace," imagining actual steps people could take toward a more equitable world. What is needed, for instance, to make this happen?

8. After a few days, look back on the results of this exercise, make adjustments, and decide on a way to present a part of your life to the class. You don't have to be too revealing. What would you like others to know? Present a part of your findings in an interesting way, such as a story you tell about an unusual experience, a postcard you send to the class from your better world, responses from a survey filled by family and friends about you, a humorous list of the minor disasters you have to wade through each day, or a motto or slogan for living that you are thinking of adopting. Be prepared to talk about the reasons for presenting what you have chosen.

9. Alternatively, you may want to work as a class on a collaborative but personal project. For instance, a class might create a personal philosophy message board to mount in a public space where others could readily add to its collection of short statements on how to live or questions designed to help people become more philosophical.

10. Now you should be better prepared to make a more formal product. In an essay of at least three pages, trace a single question as it has made its way through your life and into the world. You may think, for instance, of how your interest in the body started long ago as you played that goofy game Operation or showed your friends that you were double jointed for humorous effect. Perhaps now this interest shows up in your declared biology major or in your habitual viewing of *CSI Miami*. Conversely, a new question may have recently arisen in you, such as why people are homeless near your prosperous campus, or whether the world's economy can run on something other than fossil fuel. Write the history of the question in your life and explain why it interests you. Be sure to say what you plan to do next to continue your exploration of this question.

Readings: Experiments with Truth, Autobiography, and Social Action

Great social leaders have also been questioners, as we discover when they write or talk about themselves. For instance, reading the autobiographies of thinkers and leaders such as Martin Luther King Jr., Mohandas Gandhi, Jane Addams, and Malcolm X show how they centered their lives on the quest for truth, the right way of being, or the proper course of action. While in college, it is especially interesting to consider how these leaders educated themselves and prepared for a life of social action.

Martin Luther King Jr. did not live to complete a full autobiography, but Clayborne Carson, a historian who has edited the many papers and documents written by King or related to this life, has compiled King's own personal writings into *The Autobiography of Dr. Martin Luther King, Jr.* Here, we read King's accounts of his days as a student at Morehouse College, Crozer Theological Seminary, and Boston University. King read many of the great thinkers of history and did so with an eye toward finding the right way to live ethically in the world and combat the racial prejudice he experienced and saw around him. His study of Gandhi, prompted by hearing a sermon on Gandhi by Dr. Mordecai Johnson, showed him that the power of love, actualized in nonviolent resistance, or what Gandhi called *Satyagraha*, the love/truth force, could transform the world by showing the common spirit that bonds all people to one another.

Gandhi wrote his autobiography not to rehash his many accomplishments as a social leader but to show others his method of working to improve himself and find the correct manner of life. *Gandhi: An Autobiography* is thus subtitled *The Story of My Experiments with Truth*. These experiments include finding the proper diet, spiritual fasting, celibacy, and organizing people, as well as developing the *Satyagraha* method of nonviolent resistance in the service of democracy and equality. Gandhi believed that all these experiments were spiritual in nature and saw them as part of his search for Hindu *Moksha*, the condition of living in truth and coming to know the Divine.

Jane Addams founded Hull House, the first of many settlement houses in America that served as educational, cultural, and economic centers for immigrants and the poor. Her autobiography, *Twenty Years at Hull House*, includes the story of her education as a restless activist student at Rockford Seminary (now Rockford College) who took the "Grand Tour" of Europe common for young women from privileged backgrounds. Addams broke from the usual regime of museums and social affairs to seek out the poor in the factories and slums of the European cities. The cathedrals inspired her to conceive of a "cathedral of humanity" beautiful enough to inspire people to recognize and embrace their solidarity with others. While this education readied her for life to come, where the cathedral would be enacted in the unpretentious neighborly conditions at Hull House, an impatient nature and abundance of energy led her to concur with the Russian writer Leo Tolstoy in speaking of "the snare preparation," which entangles the young in a morass of distractions or inactivity while they long to construct a more ideal world. Young people today also experience this frustration or boredom.

For Malcolm X, the snare was more literal. After years as a street criminal, in which he abandoned the education of his youth, Malcolm X was imprisoned in Massachusetts and eventually sent to the experimental Norfolk Prison Colony. Here, he began a correspondence with the leader of the Nation of Islam, Elijah Muhammad, who taught that the true knowledge for black Americans began with the worship of Allah. Inspired by Muhammad but ashamed of his diminished capacity for carrying on an intellectual correspondence, he began an intense program of self-improvement, which included voracious reading and hard practice in writing. As he recounts in *The Autobiography of Malcolm X*, as told to author Alex Haley, he began by copying the dictionary, a page at a time, which greatly expanded his knowledge of words. He then read widely, in history, science, and religion and formed a view of the proud history of black people, which directly countered the racial violence of American culture.

Films: Personal Problems and Insistences as Social Action

At one extreme, autobiography can lead anyone toward a life of public service when the filmmakers live questions about social injustice. Dan Eldon's death as a correspondent in Somalia led his mother and sister to make a documentary film, *Dying to Tell the Story*, about reporters who believe in risking their lives in war zones, with considerable personal sacrifices and for different reasons. This kind of movie owes much to the 1966 movie *The Battle of Algiers*, which recounts the violent struggle in the late 1950s for Algerian independence from France. *Hearts and Minds* is a documentary in the same tradition about the horror of the Vietnam War that makes neither side happy politically and seeks to counter the mainstream media approach to war as both necessary and "winnable." *Fog of War* shows Robert McNamara living up to his middle name of "Strange" and examines the way the U.S. government looked at conflict in general and the Vietnam War in particular. These films prepare the ground for politically charged documentaries (or perhaps "mockumentaries") like Michael Moore's *Fahrenheit 9/11*, which focuses upon the fall of the World Trade Center, insisting upon face-to-face interviews.

Other films unravel questions about ancestry. For example, *Daughters of the Dust* looks at several generations of African-Americans in the Georgia and South Carolina Sea Islands. In a different way, *Malcolm X* explores the way Malcolm's dangerous habit of asking tough questions led him out of crime and into religion and politics. Similarly, *Gandhi* portrays the way Mohandas Gandhi refused to accept the givens of Western Civilization and lived both his questions and the resulting beliefs.

2 RESEARCH WRITING AS A KEY TO THE HIGHWAY

From "Key to the Highway"
I got the key to the highway,
Billed out and bound to go.
I'm gonna leave here running;
Walking is most too slow.

I'm going back to the border
Woman, where I'm better known.
You know you haven't done nothing,
Drove a good man away from home.

When the moon peeks over the mountains
I'll be on my way.
I'm gonna roam this old highway
Until the break of day.
        —Charles Segar and Willie Broonzy

Between conquest and vacation, the blues models the restlessness of the New World, where the only key we need is the one that unlocks the open road. Whether it is for fleeing slaves, land-hungry pioneers, bereft hobos, jubilant Beatniks, hallucinating hippies, or greedy investment bankers, the United States is the ever-shimmering crossroads where gender, race, and class constantly collide. The most important proof of being American is to, in the words of break-dancers, "bust a move." In the film *Butch Cassidy and the Sundance Kid*, Paul Newman and Robert Redford play outlaws constantly on the run from the law. When they audition for a job guarding a gold shipment, they draw their guns and fail to shoot their targets. But when the Sundance Kid is allowed to move, he rolls around on the ground firing with deadly accuracy. Whether it is the Appalachian families moving westward in his novel *The Grapes of Wrath* or John Steinbeck traveling east with his poodle in *Travels with Charley*, it's all about circulation. William Least Heat-Moon follows the blue veins of highways on the American map in his car, then back into print in *Blue Highways*.

This chapter discusses research writing as a method of intellectual movement that takes writers out of their earlier understandings and sets them on journeys the outcome or destination of which can never be entirely predicted. While some college "road trips" are larks, taken for pleasure or to find a sense of release in the midst of encroaching responsibilities, travel may also be the key to intellectual survival as we avoid the stagnation of clinging to earlier selves or confront and begin to move away from the disarray or violence of life. Further, such motion, often into and through different bodies of knowledge or ways of viewing the world, can lead writers into questions of form as they consider how to represent the story of all they have learned. Mary and Allen Roberts say of the Luba peoples of Africa, "What is most certain is that as a collective term, 'luba' has many different applications to many different realities." (211). Similarly, blues musicians find their key to the highway, or *lukasa*, in the music itself, as when a band finds an extra burst of energy and tell each other to "take it on home."

One of our methods for starting students on their own research journeys is to show them published texts that model this restless motion while coming to rest within localities of subjects, cultures, or forms. *Airstream: A History of the Land Yacht*, by Bryan Burkhart and David Hunt, recounts the authors' history of discovery as they researched Airstream trailers and the homespun trailer industry from which Airstream emerged. Spread through its pages is an archive of photographs of Airstream models; trailers being made; Airstreams in locations ranging from the Oak Creek Canyon in Sonoma, California, to under the Arch of Bost in the Dasht I Margo desert in Afghanistan; and trailers in formation, in the great Airstream caravans of the 1950s and 1960s that rolled through Africa, India, the Middle East, and Central and South America. Besides being a study of a peculiar part of consumer history, the book also explores Airstream's classic silver tube design as part of Streamlining, a broad movement in design. We learn to compare the trailer to trains and airplanes from the same era, study the clever intricacies of the many plans for Airstreams, and follow the manufacturing process. The book also focuses on the philosophy of travel, adventure, and diplomacy of Wally Byam, Airstream's colorful President, which the authors discuss in their main essayistic texts, as well as asides, such as a reproduction of the Wally Byam Creed, the "Four Freedoms" of Airstream life, Byam aphorisms, and itineraries for international caravans.

This multi-genre, multimedia text also shows how even travelers under "safe" conditions can learn through friendliness and curiosity.

While on caravan, Byam consulted with world leaders, including Haile Selassie I, Emperor of Ethiopia and Rastafarian deity, and common people everywhere. Byam said, in 1960, "Whether we like it or not, any fool can see that this earth is gradually becoming one world. Nobody knows what the form of the 'one' will be, but it is going to be one or none" (17). Burkhart and Hunt continue Byam's work of connecting the travel trailer enthusiast to the rest of us so that Airstream reminds us not only of crowded RV parks or slow rigs holding up traffic on the freeway but also, in more romantic images, of trailers camped at trout streams in the West, or circled next to a village on the African savannah. The authors define their work as "cultural diplomacy rather than cultural history" (141).

To see how thoroughly the open road has been incorporated (and tamed) into the cultural mythology of America, we can turn to the books that accompany the expensive American Girls Collection of dolls. For example, there is *Molly's Route 66 Adventure*, a multiwriting book that chronicles pigtailed Molly McIntire down the infamous Route 66 of the American West. Her scrapbook has dozens of genres, including foldout mileage charts, car decals, a micro envelope holding a Royal Oil Mystery Decoder, postcards, amusement park ride ticket stubs, photographs, a wee book of Ranger "Rithmetic" (math problems about forests), meal receipts, animal prints, and more.

As works of border crossing, these books join many we find these days that use multiple discourses to explore a subject of interest or fascination and follow this subject where it leads. We use such works in teaching as "starter texts" that quickly illustrate to students some of the possibilities for writing in motion. These we do not always link to assignments but instead typically hand around at or near the beginning of a variety of courses to invite students into a different world of research and writing. We may begin a course, then, with examples such as these that illustrate and complicate an emphasis upon form by suggesting that cultures make meaning through forms, appearances, and values, whether these choices are encoded in colors, houses, or bodies:

> *Chihuahua: Pictures from the Edge*, with photographs by Virgil Hancock and an essay by Charles Bowden. This is a bold mix of media used to capture a cultural message. Hancock's photographs shows what he calls a "discovery of the community use and power of color" (ix), while Bowden sees Chihuahua as an edge world where races and cultures mix, colors radiate unashamed, and geographic borders and the labels for people that result from them do not apply.
>
> *Dwellings: The Vernacular House Worldwide*, by Paul Oliver. Vernacular construction is a parallel to multiwriting, as it involves making

use of what is available and bending form to fit cultural situations, so this is a volume we return to often with students. Most houses throughout the world are self-built by their owners or built by a community according to designs that carry cultural values. Oliver studies such houses around the world, showing how homes carry both personal and shared meanings.

A Little House of My Own: 47 Grand Designs for 47 Tiny Houses, by Lester Walker. This is another architectural study that makes the vernacular tradition more personal. From an anonymous settler's cottage or frontier cabin to famous dwellings like Thomas Jefferson's Honeymoon Cottage or Henry Thoreau's Cabin, this work studies historic, prefabricated and paper houses. Some are permanent dwellings, while others are vacation dune shacks, picnic enclosures, or road houses. Some are even mobile. All are tiny, and most ingenious, each with a design that can be copied. This is a reference we use both at the beginning of courses and with an exercise for students to consider their growing projects as tiny houses, which require intricate and clever designs to hold their contents.

Zeropolis: The Experience of Las Vegas, by Bruce Bégout, with photographs by Julie Cook. If the vernacular house represents the most authentic or natural of human structures and architectural forms, the simulated city of Las Vegas is among the most artificial. This book shows Las Vegas as a paradigmatic postmodern city, a spectacular cipher that is the stage for the fragmented mini-dramas of a noncommunity. For our Western students, this book, like Jean Baudrillard's *America* and some revisionist histories, such as *The Legacy of Conquest: The Unbroken Past of the American West* or *Desert Passages: Encounters with the American Deserts*, by Patricia Limerick, shows how familiar landscapes can be rendered strange and how visions alter as powers of analysis grow.[1]

Shoes: A Celebration of Pumps, Sandals, Slippers and More, by Linda O'Keefe, with photographs by Andreas Bleckmann. In this book, shoes are not only a means of getting around but also the culturally symbolic and artistically shifting representations of how and what we stand upon and for. Various histories are entwined in the various categories of colorful shoes and boots represented from around the world. A similar work is *Glass, Paper, Beans*, where Leah Hager Cohen studies the cultural meanings and histories of the paper on which she reads her morning news, a thick glass coffee mug, and the coffee within it. *One Good Turn: A Natural History of the Screw and Screwdriver*, by Witold Rybczynski, shows students how familiar objects and habitual parts of life are themselves worthy and enlightening subjects for study.

Girl Culture, by Lauren Greenfield. This is a photographer's report on the conflicted and often difficult lives of adolescent women in America, who are often self-consciously torn between competing expectations to be thin, smart, strong, feminine, sexy, studious, and, above all, "themselves." Along with photographs of beauty queens, partiers, athletes, women-next-door, and taboo-violators of different kinds, the book includes monologues from the women photographed that are startling, sad, and frequently insightful. This book can be used to open an ongoing meditation on the multiple meanings of the body. We have found this a good approach to help students get interested in research, as nothing is more personally meaningful than our physical beings. The body also provides an entry into many disciplines and allows for a grounded approach to theory. Many sources can be used to continue for reflection on the body, including works that suggest ways to write with the body in connection to the mind, such as Gloria Anzaldúa's *Borderlands/La Frontera* or Susan Griffin's *The Eros of Everyday Life*. For a lead-in to a variegated study of the body, we have also used Dani Cavallaro's *The Body for Beginners*, which turns the genre of the illustrated novel or comic book to an intellectual study of corporality.

Together, these sources suggest that topics for research, wonder, and inquisitive critique are all around. Some may enrich our appreciation of the familiar; others may problematize our day-to-day lives or lead us to processes of transformation. Some subjects beckon from far away—other countries, planets, or galaxies. Michael McCrae's *The Siege of Shangri-La: The Quest for Tibet's Sacred Hidden Paradise* is an account of explorations over a long period of time that have failed to "conquer" a very beautiful and remote valley in southeastern Tibet, which is hidden by nearly impossible terrain. Time and history can add a further dimension to distance. Peter Sís's *Tibet Through the Red Box* had its genesis in childhood as Sís listened to a father who was sent to China and ended up teaching filmmaking to the Tibetans. He told his son stories of his travels and left a diary in a red box. Years later Sís opened the box and used the form of a children's book to reconnect with his father through paintings, pictures, and words.

In *The Art of Travel*, Alain De Botton relates this lure of the exotic as a chance to reconsider our happiness:

> If our lives are dominated by a search for happiness, then perhaps few activities reveal as much about the dynamics of this quest—in all its ardour and paradoxes—than our travels. They express, however inarticulately, an understanding of what life might be about, outside

of the constraints of work and of the struggle for survival. Yet rarely are they considered to present philosophical problems—that is, issues requiring thought beyond the practical. We are inundated with advice on *where* to travel to, but we hear little of *why* and *how* we should go, even though the art of travel seems naturally to sustain a number of questions neither so simple nor so trivial, and whose study might in modest ways contribute to an understanding of what the Greek philosophers beautifully termed *eudaimonia*, or "human flourishing." (9)

Others begin to show us that our happiness may involve traversing well-known ground anew. For example, Chet Raymo (who teaches physics and astronomy) in *The Path: A One-Walk Through the Universe* and Wendell Berry (who teaches writing and literature) in *Traveling at Home* both write about how daily walks over the same terrain constantly vary and provide a sense of wonder.

We also use earlier student multiwriting projects as invitations to the crossroads and as illustrations of how a good project is both personal and public. A perennial favorite of students is Linnea Simon's project, *The Way of Tea*, which connects her own use and love of tea with the ancient history of this subtly potent leaf. Her introduction, "My Obsession with Tea," details some of her own tea ceremonies, while essays later in the project talk about the ceremonial functions of tea in other cultures. She retells the Chinese myth in which Shen Nung, the Divine Cultivator, brings tea to the people, helping them to become fully human. The project also includes a tour of some of the varieties of tea—with the qualities and folklore of each described and samples given in small cellophane envelops—and provides basic instructions for reading tea leaves.

At the end of the project we return to Simon and her tea. She has chosen the right tea and cup, prepared the water, and now the tea is steeping:

> There is something calming in this, and the culmination is in enjoying the tea, relaxing, and smelling and tasting the tea. It is like finding my calm center when life has become chaotic and disorganized. I suppose this can be found in different things, but many have found it in tea, which, I think, attests to its powers of allurement and its unique energy. Perhaps it is foolishness, but, as Kakuzo wrote, "Let us dream of evanescence and linger in the beautiful foolishness of things" (Okakura 17).

Christine Dilworth's project on the Paiute Ghost Dance and Tabbie Roberts Coulter's on the prehistoric, still-living fish, the aruana, convey a similar feeling of connection as the writers guide us into history and a world of others. Dilworth's project recounts the spiritual resistance of some native tribes as they sought to shed the oppression and violence of the white man. Spread first by the Northern Paiute prophet Wovoka, the Ghost Dance sought to resurrect the past, save the culture, and raise the dead. It tapped into traditional discourses of transformation and redemption—Dilworth also examines creation myths and finds patterns of connection. However, Wovoka's explications of the dance also made use of Christian themes, and his appeals to other Indians included the claim that Jesus was on the earth to bring back the ancestors and make the world young again. This cross-cultural determination was a powerful force.

In the aruana, we have a different version of the "dead" who have never left. This species of prehistoric fish still resides in Asia and the Amazon River Basin of South America, as well as in large fish tanks in the homes of collectors, including, much to her surprise, Coulter's. A neighbor on his way to a stint in the county jail asked if she would "fish sit" until he got out.

> I obliged and set up the 30-gallon tank with this little 8-inch, pre-historic looking fish in my living room. I was instantly more relaxed each night when I would come home and stare at this rare, graceful, elegant creature and I dreaded the day when he would have to leave. Luckily, that never happened. When my neighbor got out of jail, he was hard up for some cigarettes so he sold me the tank and this magnificent fish for $20. In a matter of months I was shopping for a larger tank.

With the need for inquiry swimming before her, Coulter began finding out all she could about this intriguing creature and continues to do so. Her project featured a photographic essay and a PowerPoint presentation that showcased her expertise (and wowed her classmates in a first-year exploratory writing class), but it also revealed how much she is still just beginning to know: aruana will attempt to jump out of the tank; do not approach the fish tank wearing red or bright pink or a commotion of misplaced water will follow. Worldwide, aruana are the subject of fascination and even commodities on black markets in places where trading this barbeled, large-scaled "dragon fish" is illegal.

Although knowledge is useful, these texts and projects, whether published or unpublished, seem born from curiosity more than expertise. They involve finding out what is not known, through reading, travel, talking to others, and experiencing life. The act of writing such works involves bringing various sources and ways of knowing into a pattern, but the process begins with questions worth following and tracing. Susan Orlean recounts in the introduction to her collection of journalistic essays, *The Bullfighter Checks Her Makeup: My Encounters with Extraordinary People*, how her ambition to be a writer was mixed with curiosity and wonder about the world:

> In junior high school I took a career guidance test that suggested I would do well as either an army officer or a forest ranger but I didn't care: I wanted only to be a writer, even though I didn't know how you went about becoming one, especially the kind of writer I wanted to be. I didn't want to be a newspaper reporter, because I never have cared about knowing something first, and I didn't want to write only about things that were considered "important" and newsworthy; I wanted to write about things that intrigued me, and to write about them in a way that would surprise readers who might not have expected to find such things intriguing. (ix)

This attitude of finding fascination in both the unusual and the everyday while understanding that these two categories are often joined is one that composition teachers should want for their students. It will not only make them more intrepid writers, able to follow questions into many subjects and fields, but also help them respond to and take hold of the times. In a world of information overdose, when more knowledge is recorded than ever before, writers become guides finding routes through the matrix and makers of provisional webs of meaning for others to link to, recombine, or wander—while wondering—within.

Among new genres is the Weblog or "blog," where authors post up-to-the-minute thoughts about the news or their lives. While blogs have been installed as instant propaganda by shrill voices on the right and left, and as online diaries of triviality by Web literati without much to say, other functions will follow. They are already reporting news from afar, with consequences for both travelers and politicians. An example is *Salam Pax: The Clandestine Diary of an Ordinary Iraqi*, by (codename) Salam Pax. This secret blog gathered a significant worldwide readership and chronicled, often with humor, the violent toll of both Saddam's dictatorship and the occupation that followed it. A futurist might say that this form is the harbinger of instantly updateable writing by which statements will turn into processes and discourse will be a record of commitment to ongoing inquiry—an open text in pursuit of its own continuation. Even now, a blog in need of updating inspires guilt.

Restless writers in this complex world need openness more than certainty, persistent querying more than rigid beliefs. The composition classroom is a perfect place to help students develop into such writers, as it is here that the acts of inquiry and writing are most likely to come together as practices and subjects of study. However, making the best of this opportunity involves altering, even reversing, the restrained practices of research-based academic writing. The practice of writing conventionally should give way to a deeper study of writing, inquiry, and conventionality that shows how genres and forms are made.[2] Rather than focus upon presenting evidence to support or force conclusions, it is time to better consider how questions can be sustained in a piece of writing while evidence is gathered and examined. Instead of separating domains of writing into the personal and the academic, or the public and private, we ought to take up more fully the study of the border texts that lead us into the world and return a meaning that is both idiosyncratic and understandable, like a blues that changes during a performance or an exciting new house built with lumber others had discarded.

Years ago, Richard Larson declared the term paper "a non form of writing" but saw inquiry residing in every discourse. The problem for writers is inhabiting this inquiry, doing the research, finding things out, or discovering messages and purposes by heading into often deepening questions. "Our responsibility as instructors," Larson asserts, "should be to assure that each student reflects in each paper the appropriate research, wisely conducted, for his or her subject" (182). We are aided in the task by ignorance, which, once admitted, is an invitation to know. The job becomes teaching, and trusting, a process of research and invention to find messages, purposes and forms.

Ironically, students can gain an advantage by not knowing if we free them from the burdensome expectation of premature expertise. Cub reporters are often told that thinking they know the truth of a story is dangerous because it can prevent them from listening to their sources. As David Bartholomae showed those in our field in "Inventing the University," what we experience as improper usages or convoluted constructions in student writing should be seen as apprentice attempts to write in the voices and manners of academic discourse, or to sound as they think academic writers sound. Students doing research are similarly apt to feel they must know what experts know before they can say something meaningful. With the assignment coming due, the choices seem to be to write with temerity that betrays uncertainty or to take on a false confidence that belies it.

Similarly, in *Beyond Note Cards: Rethinking the Freshman Research Paper*, Bruce Ballenger recounts the case of "Carrie," a student writing a research paper on the social value of the television show *The Simpsons*. Carrie knows that her subject requires her to state and support an opinion while exploring other views as well. It is in the province of what she calls the "I thinks" rather than the "I knows" (63–64). Yet a peer reviewer convinces her that the research paper requires authoritative statements. Carrie removes the "I thinks" but, as Ballenger notes, does so half-heartedly, convinced, at least for the moment, that the rules of research writing demand dishonesty marked as knowledge.

It seems to us, as it does to Ballenger, that it is smarter, more productive, and more truthful to re-pose research writing as an act of finding out, aimed at holding questions open for further exploration, rather than shutting them down with falsely authoritative answers. Students have been taught to write what they know and to know before they write, but as with most old saws, the opposite side is as sharp: we should write what we don't yet know. We start with the holes in our current understanding and need to begin with an open mind, ready to welcome a question to trace, a theory to test, a hunch to follow, or an incongruity to explore. As Ballenger suggests, shifting the aim of research writing from teaching an academic style of discourse to introducing students to the a spirit of inquiry will not only make for more interesting papers but also help them to practice habits of mind valued across the disciplines. He cites the Boyer Commission Report, "Reinventing Undergraduate Education," which cites inquiry, investigation, and discovery as the heart of academic work: "What better place to introduce this 'shared mission' than in freshman composition—usually the one universally required course—and especially through the one assignment that is the most common in that course: the research paper" (Ballenger, 16).

Much of the research people do occurs because of a sudden need to find out. A medical problem, war, home disaster, prehistoric fish, crime or lawsuit, or new job—each of these may lead us to become mini-experts on a subject we never cared about before. This accidental approach parallels self-chosen "lifelong learning," which follows passions or scratches an intellectual itch. Such learning connects reason and emotion, private interest and the public good, work and pleasure. As teachers and fellow inquirers, we need to cooperate with such learning, foster it, and, when necessary, get out of its way. We are working within and against a culture that fragments knowledge, regards education as job training, and leaves little time for conversation or thought. But we have an ally in the power of questions, which have a way of finding their way through the barriers and often gather urgency when they are denied. Inquiry and writing should be ways of reflectively participating in and tracing life's serendipitous, intriguing course.

We have remained committed to multiwriting because we know it to be a way of working the changes that readily cross boundaries, turning potential obstacles into chances for connection. However, we came to it for more selfish and mundane reasons. Mark often says that it was the endless series of elk-hunting essays, a genre handy for where we live, which did him in. An avid reader of everything from architectural manuals to detective novels, he knew a rich discursive world. Why not find a way to teach this universe of forms and to help student find ways to connect the diversity?

Rob arrived from Ohio State, where he had worked with other teachers and their students to turn persuasive writing "inside out" through a questioning essay that asked students to sustain their thinking on a subject, rather then settle into a fixed opinion. Together, we envisioned a Protean or "coyote" discourse that could change in form and freely mix formal or academic ways of writing with those that are more personal, intimate, or familiar. When we took this idea to our media-maniacal students, they fused and juxtaposed the written word with film, anime, music, performance, street rhyming, video games, and computer simulations, to name a few. Quickly, this became a compositional method open to anything that worked. We found that removing a few of the givens made rhetorical choices more interesting, complicated, and real. Now what was said and the way it was said rested more squarely upon how the purpose, message, content, and form was constructed to reach and move an audience. This approach has led to student projects in many forms, which fill our offices and often the hallway outside them, too. While we cannot say that every project we receive is perfectly conceived or executed, we can say that the cumulative effect is inspiring. Students are extending themselves well beyond the province of the static elk-hunting essay.

The method began in a 200-level composition course we call Applied Discourse Theory, where students were originally asked to make multi-genre biography projects, like those described by Tom Romano in *Writing with Passion*. Influenced by the richness of discourses outside of formal schooling and stoked by Michael Ondaatje's multi-genre novel *The Collected Works of Billy the Kid*, Romano asked his students to complete similar biography projects on subjects of their choosing, with memorable results. As Romano wondered if his students could write like Ondaatje, Shadle was eager to see if his could produce like those of Romano.

So Mark and his students put "the multi" into action, immediately stretching multi-genre work to include multiple media and often disciplines and cultures. Mark received projects on singer Joan Baez, comedian Robin Williams, poet Adrienne Rich, and Nez Perce Chief Joseph. The projects included unusual forms: one on Bill Cosby came in a sweater like the comedian wore, while the performance component of the project on space shuttle astronaut Christa McAuliffe was constructed as a model of the Challenger, which the student "crashed." When the model shuttle hit the ground, it unfolded to reveal a cascade of origami forms and genres.

The project on magician Harry Houdini by Randy Kromwall included show bills and posters and used a circus poster font for headings describing some of the sensational events from Houdini's life. However, the project also contained more intimate, private pieces that probed into what motivated Houdini to take such chances. The Houdini who emerged was seduced by the edge of death and wanted both to come nearer to death and pull himself out. The analysis centered upon Houdini's famous Water Torture Cell, perhaps his most dangerous apparatus. In a piece that is part dialogue and part monologue, Houdini tells the machine, "I love you, but you terrify me."

This project, written by an aspiring magician, and the one on Chief Joseph, by a student whose family owns horses descended from the Chief's appaloosas, helped Mark to see that a good biographic project had to be autobiographic, since students were exploring individual takes on a research subject and their connection and/or disconnection to her/him. We quickly added, therefore, an autobiography project to begin the course that asked students to engage the unknowns about themselves. This inquisitive approach to the self prepares students for inquiry that stretches into the world, and it can also become this inquiry, as the process of self-questioning leads students into a world of others, where they discover and use new possibilities for self. Katie McCann's autobiography showed that inside she was a castaway, disassociated from her life and studying it from afar, as if in memory. The project was formed as a basket of blue bottles, gathered on a beach, sent by a person on a far away isle. Catherine Hefferan styled her project as an oversize (about three feet tall) fairy-tale book that tells the story of the way her life failed to live up to the Cinderella story she wanted to it to be but became more like the story once she learned to take care of herself, rather than being victimized by others or awaiting her prince. Nadine Galinsky's subtle project centered on a series of questions she continues to ask about life, while Connie Berry's contained several meditation devices, including a model labyrinth. Tracy Terrell's project, entitled *The New Unofficial Resume*, filled in the bare facts of her "official" resume, just made at the campus Career Center, with vignettes showing what her life was like during its various stages.

Rob's original contribution to the Applied Discourse Theory course was a third project, placed between the autobiography and research projects, called the multi-body. Here, students analyzed cultural forms of bodylore and expression, used these to describe a theory of the body in our culture, then generated counter-theories through the use of alternative, or hidden, examples. This project counteracted students' tendencies to get too abstract when thinking about their multi-selves while bringing them back to the world through our prime interface with it, the human body. As with multiple forms of autobiography, the multi-body project often suggested avenues for further inquiry, as multi-body projects beginning with quick weight loss schemes led to research on the functions of fat in the body and a project on images of breast cancer became a study of the performance artist Matuschka, whose bodywork has made others confront and witness cancer and mastectomy. Another project chronicled the history and uses of the bra, including its use for the recipients of mastectomy. Two projects by different students made the surprising discovery that a fourth toe that stopped growing in childhood was genetic, rather than the result of the divorce of parents in both families.

We have since moved the course's large research project into a more open space, where students can pursue a variety of topics and themes, instead of biography. Recent topic selections include E-bay and the History of Auctions, Theories of the Apocalypse, Spoons, Fireflies, A Bosnian "Transnational" in America, Yoga, Feathers, The Vietnam Wall, The Game of Monopoly, The Azores, The Urge to Destroy What We Cannot Be, Doors and Thresholds, The Chinese Cultural Revolution, The Work of a Marine Science Center, Oregon Meteorology, and New Technologies for Oil Exploration.

We and our colleagues have gradually adapted this approach within other parts of the English/Writing Program, including courses in Argumentation, Folklore, Science Writing, Introduction to Literature, Multicultural Literature, Writing Theory, Advanced Prose Writing, Imaginative Writing, Methods of Tutoring, two first-year composition courses: Expository Writing and Exploratory Writing, and senior Capstone Projects. In 2005, the program will debut an approach to developmental composition in which students craft Macrorian "I Search" projects that explore majors, careers, and vocation. Multiwriting has also spread across the disciplines, to psychology, government, modern languages, and education. It is the pedagogy of "Creative Composition," an interdisciplinary foundations course in theatre, art, and writing that is part of the university's First Year Seminar program. It has been fascinating to learn from teachers using similar approaches that respond to their situations and purposes, especially as we have come to know the work of K–12 teachers in the Oregon Writing Project.

Increasingly, we have studied how this approach relates to the current conditions and history of discourse and inquiry. We have come to realize that traditions are more open and encouraging to improvisation and invention than we imagined, as seen both in their original purposes and often their emerging forms. Often, our readings involve a project of recovery in which submerged possibilities—present in the discourse from early on, but hidden in conventional practices—are brought to the fore, developed, and used in a myriad of ways.

This chapter practices such reading toward invention by opening the academic practice of research writing to the larger history of human inquiry. Although it has been made into a static system for displaying the known, research writing should be a key to the highway of discovery and travel into generative mysteries that offer us new ways of seeing the world and ourselves. It is this transformation of research, which involves reclaiming its original purpose as a way of marking the world that we focus upon here. While part of this revision of history involves reclaiming and recasting the modernist project of creating new knowledge, we also attempt to look before the modern, toward earlier human attempts to talk back to a dangerous but fascinating world. Our attempt is not to regain a premodern mode of being but to suggest how travel into a mystery is a perennial key to the highway of human survival, which is based on the intelligent capacity for adaptation. While life is in motion, our ability to think inventively, engage new situations, find a number of homes for ourselves, and discover or create different version of self leads to fruitful citizenry in a diverse world and the multi-vocal capacity to write in altered situations. We want our students to connect to a long, splintered tradition, whereby they can appreciate the culture of ancient Egypt while rethinking postmodern America. For this, they need to re-inhabit the academy, even as they think and work beyond it, as emerging intellectuals becoming versed in their questions.

Implicit in this view is a critique of academic ways of writing and knowing, and the withered act of researching writing in particular. Elsewhere, we have reviewed the history of research writing in the academy as a diminishment, in which the modernist project of knowledge-making became an exercise in following arbitrary rules of style and format.[3] Research writing as practiced in the academy was among the innovations of the Germanic university model, which privileged discovery using rational processes. While for faculty this ideal has taken on hyper-real qualities in the drive to publish, for students it has waned to research writing as the stringing together of facts made by others into arbitrary assemblages that often lack the animating energies of inquiry, opinion, or interest to hold them together.

As Robert Connors noted in *Composition-Rhetoric*, research writing as conventionally practiced today was born as a modernist concern with ethical research, including giving credit to sources, that is part of an agenda of intellectual property rights within the law and jurisprudence of the nineteenth century. The true program of work was erecting the free-standing individual while formalizing its connection to others and clarifying the messiness of identity as constructed in a variegated world.

The dispirited presentation of the known, detached from the lived experience of the author or reader, which came to be called the term paper, ironically supports the unitary individual, bound by law, through its negation of student authorship. Since beginning students were not yet ready for discovery or to claim aspects of the world under the unimpeachable banner of their names, they must at least be kept from trespassing. The role of the teacher—perhaps a relief given the boundaryless nature of discovery—was to enforce abstract zoning rules that kept property within clear demarcations. As David R. Russell notes in *Writing in the Academic Disciplines, 1870–1990: A Curricular History*, the teacher/enforcer saw poor writing as a sign of poor thinking, which was a threat to all that academic culture had achieved:

> The "undisciplined" gropings of student prose were of course far from the research ideal held up by the disciplines. As faculty never tired of pointing out, student papers were replete with ignorance and errors of all sorts, which could never be entirely eradicated. Because faculty tended to regard poor writing as evidence of poor thinking, not as evidence of a student's incomplete assimilation into a disciplinary community, faculty sensed that the discipline's "store of knowledge," acquired at great sacrifice, was "tarnished" by poor writing. (74)

The scouring that continues to characterize composition instruction is part of a broader narrative, in which the chimera of a unified law, logic, or language, meant to reveal the nature of the world, collapses into a proliferation of difference, hyper-reality, and impotent power. While this is not the place to attempt this long history, we can examine views from the end. Looking back from the postmodern scene of panic sex, art, ideology, bodies, noise, and theory, Arthur Kroker and David Cook cannot see where the demise of the modernity began:

> It is our general thesis that the postmodern scene, in fact, begins in the fourth century with the Augustinian subversion of embodied power, and that everything since the Augustinian refusal has been nothing but a fantastic and grisly implosion of experience as Western culture itself runs under the signs of passive and suicidal nihilism. Or was it not perhaps even before this, in the Lucretian theory of the physical world that Serres called the *simulacrum*? Or was it later, in the abandonment of reason in Kant's aesthetic liberalism of the

third critique? And what of late twentieth-century experience? Ours is a *fin-de-millennium* consciousness which, existing at the end of history in the twilight time of ultramodernism (of technology) and hyper-primitivism (of public moods), uncovers a great arc of disintegration and decay against the background radiation of parody, kitsch, and burnout. (8)

History is overdetermined, and the causes and signs of its collapse are multiple and profound. Kroker and Cook's stance is reminiscent of the position of Angelus Novus in the Paul Klee painting by the same name, as described by Walter Benjamin in "Theses on the Philosophy of History." The angel stares agape at an unseen object:

This is how one pictures the angel of history. His face is turned toward the past. Where we perceive a chain of events, he sees one single catastrophe which keeps piling wreckage and hurls it in front of his feet. The angel would like to stay, awaken the dead, and make whole what has been smashed. But a storm is blowing in from Paradise; it has got caught in his wings with such a violence that the angel can no longer close them. The storm irresistibly propels him into the future to which his back is turned, while the pile of debris before him grows skyward. This storm is what we call progress. (257–58)

In history's storm, when—as Jean Francois Lyotard proclaimed in *The Postmodern Condition*—the *gran escritas* that organized history have collapsed into shards, vernacular reconstruction is the moral imperative. While research writing as an objective or determinate text vanishes in a quantum university where perspective is essential, the need to piece together a meaning of one's own becomes more urgent. The modernist project of discovery arises in a new, more intimate, but still public form. As Susan Griffin envisioned in *The Eros of Everyday Life*, when the exhaustive economy of violence, power, and hierarchies give way, we are left not with a void but with a second order of being—which she calls a "collaborative intelligence"—where the connections among people, and between our species and others, are felt and known in the body and mind. This collaborative intelligence also takes us deeper into history, where we know that our presence on earth is part of a mutual unfolding that involves other beings and forces.

Alongside the remarkably static background of our slowly evolving genes, our differences and the way we grow this adaptive intelligence travels through the arteries of our experiments and the veins of our adopted revisions. As poet Charles Olson saw, the heart is a listening organ, where we feel life flowing in the blood. Native American "magic" is the way the idea of story parallels the "red" blood cells, which collect environmental electromagnetic data when they pass through the eyes. Here we will remember that this science is paralleled in Native American literature with the story of "Coyote the Eye Juggler," where coyote loses his eyes in a gambling match and must steal the eyes of other creatures until he can get his own back; thus, he is forced to see the world through the eyes of other animals. In his novel, *The Heirs of Columbus*, Gerald Vizenor mates Columbus with a New World shaman, making us all crossbloods traveling with "stories in the blood" and thinking with our hearts as well as minds.

The crossroads of connected being, where body and mind are integrated into the world, is realized through travel, whether figurative or literal, into the mysteries that reason, tradition, or the reports of others cannot fully explain. As Charles Olson reminds us in *The Special View of History*, Herodutus's original rendering of history was as "istorin" or "to find out for yourself." Perhaps instead of propelling us further from an original disaster, as Kroker and Cook and Benjamin suggest, history has returned to this root, where we can begin to regather the stances, habits of mind, and ways of writing that allow us to inquire within an abiding sense of a suggestive unknown. With a backpack full of our insistences, we set out, over and over again, to reorient ourselves toward shifting destinations and previously unimagined routes.

In times of micro-specialization, when diasporas splinter and the somnambulant voice of scandal spins its selective memory on Fox and CNN, it is easy to lose sight of the wonder of being here in this world and the communicative impulse by which we say, "Yes, here it is." Curiosity begins with this original wondering—an openness to the oddity that we are actually alive. Emerging from the cave at Lascaux, Pablo Picasso is said to have uttered, "We have discovered nothing." The figures of animals and people on the wall cut through time as tokens of knowledge and mystery. They remind us of presence, the sheer fact of being, and they are evidence of our uncanny desire and ability to record the world and leave conscious traces of our having been here.

Similarly, in *A History of Reading*, Alberto Manguel views two Sumerian tablets from the fourth millennium B.C. on which is carved what is thought to be a count of sheep or goats. These are the earliest specimens of "writing" yet found. Manguel describes his experience viewing these tablets the year before the Gulf War in the Archaeological Museum of Baghdad. They are simple objects in a bare display, "each bearing a few discreet markings: a small indentation near the top and some sort of stick drawn animal in the center." Archaeologists believe that the notches refer to an astounding abstraction: the number 10. Our history, Manguel writes, begins with carved pieces of stone. From them, he conjures a primordial human world not distant from ours:

> There is something intensely moving in these tablets. Perhaps when we stare at these pieces of clay carried by a river which no longer exists, observing the delicate incisions portraying animals turned to dust thousands and thousands of years ago, a voice is conjured up; a thought or message tells us, "Here were ten goats," "Here were ten sheep," something spoken by a careful farmer in the days when the deserts were green. The mere act of looking at these tablets lets us prolong a memory from the beginning of our time, preserved as a thought long after the thinker has stopped thinking, and makes us participants in an act of creation that remains open for as long as the incised images are seen, deciphered or read. (27–28)

The tablets are both an early receipt or statement of accounts and a piece of quantitative research where form comes from purpose. We imagine the herder, clever and harried, using such counts etched in stone to get a momentary fix on a changing world. At first, others may have feared the herder's technology of counting. As William Covino notes in *Magic, Rhetoric, and Literacy*, the ability to read and write has long been associated with magic. The Egyptian Thoth or Theuth, the scribe of the gods, who the Greeks renamed Hermes, gave writing to mortals in his role as messenger bearing divine gifts. Theuth is warned by his master, the supreme god Thamus, that some powers should be confined to the occult realm because only the gods will use them well.

The power of communication is confirmed by the tablets, which make us see the original wonder within an act as mundane as counting. At a time seemingly without escape from a violent system for wasting resources that threatens the future of the world, evoking wonder may be seen as identifying one last sign of uncorrupted humanity to strip away—or another nostalgic aftereffect of what Kroker and Cook, following thinkers such as Nietzsche, see as a disaster that has already occurred. In our more hopeful view, however, such wonder is also a precondition for rethinking the human project on Earth and the beginning of a new freedom to choose and construct a different social scene.

In *The Eros of Everyday Life*, Susan Griffin points out many experiences that lead us to the second order of being, wrought with a spirit of energetic connection. These include the process of making or viewing art; reconnecting with a natural world through careful observation as well as experience; and developing the "outsider consciousness" that often originates through being part of a racial, sexual, religious, or political minority. Childbirth is a paradigmatic portal into the second order, since it indicates beyond a doubt that human beings are intimately part of one another. We believe that inquiry and communication, whether realized in stone tablets or a blog, can also constitute "second order" experiences if they enact a sense of connection leading to an expanded sense or understanding of the world and self. Mundane and everyday, omnipresent in the academy, and often practiced in trite ways, research writing should be a special occasion to invite entry to a new way of being through the following and tracing of questions.

This is a powerful message to bring to students and can be problematic, given the conditions of their lives and their sometimes uneasy relationships to the academy, their instructors, and each other. When we have students pre-write about the ten most unusual experiences of their lives, they frequently report that they have never written about these incidents because they didn't fit the image they or others were making of them. Students need to be safe enough to explore the amazing, or deadly, things that happen to them, as long as they are emotionally ready to express themselves. Writing is therapeutic not because it is the catharsis of confessing but because writing about topics that writers are passionate about can help transform lives.

As Michael Blitz and C. Mark Hurlbert show in *Letters for the Living: Teaching Writing in a Violent Age*, our students know violence, disarray, and death and have powerful stories to tell. They suggest that evoking and listening to these stories should be at the center of our teaching because "the teaching of writing is connected to living. Not living in the abstract, but living—and dying" (1). Blitz and Hurlbert write of the lives they have learned about from reading student texts:

> We find that our students face deaths of all kinds every day—of the body, of spirit, of hope, of desire, of the ability to care. When we address some of the struggles just to live that our students face, we also address the tensions that tear at the health of the world. It is time to ask ourselves: as teachers of composition, are we prepared for the truly powerful stories our students are ready to tell? (1)

Perhaps because we are not prepared, these narratives are often held in abeyance or covered by the busyness or quiet living that masks what is really going on. Besides their classes, students often have jobs to attend to or families with continuing needs. In such a culture, it is easy to construct college education as a race for the credits needed for the degree. Hyperinflationary costs only exacerbate this tendency, as students feel the pressure to make every credit count. In this accelerating system, where the clock is always running out on the semester, term, or block, college can be divested of personal meanings except for the relief, accolades,

or hope for income that await upon graduation. As Blitz and Hurlbert
suggest, teachers and students are often strangers stuck in abstract, if
comfortable, roles designed to keep the noise and urgency of living carefully contained.

The sadness that hangs over this efficient system for alienation comes
from the knowledge that college should contain more. We have all been
visited by the student, sometimes immature or withdrawn, who does not
seem to "get" college and disappears from our class and perhaps from
the college scene entirely. Just as worrying are the "good students," who,
like the academically successful women who populate parts of *Women's
Ways of Knowing*, have learned the rules and play the game masterfully
but seldom find in it any intrinsic meaning beyond grades or credits. A
third class of students, seldom discussed, is the quirky or eccentric black
sheep, who seem intelligent and humorous but have become cynical and
do not produce as they might. These students often come to college thinking it will be different from the regimented cliques of high school and are
disappointed by the continued use of busywork and the constant emphasis
on conventions or grades. While the idea of college as personal and cultural transformation is a figure of the popular imagination, it may also
be heard as a challenge to create the conditions by which transformation
may occur. Why cheapen the experience, given the sums people pay for
it, or give way to easy cynicism even if it is all around?

Blitz and Hurlbert remind us how to enact this transformation, first
by listening. In one of the e-mails that comprise much of *Letters for the
Living*, Blitz recounts the work of his students at the John Jay College of
Criminal Justice in response to a prompt they came up with and agreed
to write on "What's Wrong with This Picture?":

> They wrote for nearly 25 minutes and didn't want to stop. They will
> have a chance to work further on the piece over the weekend and
> have agreed that it will be a major paper of the semester. And I have
> to tell you, this worries me. It's nothing new to fret over having to
> grade my students' writing. But the things they wrote about, so far,
> make me feel particularly reluctant. One student wrote:
>
>> What's wrong with this picture? An eighteen-year-old kid
>> comes home to find his mother totally drunk, as usual. His
>> little sister has most of her clothes off with her boyfriend
>> who is older and bigger than the eighteen-year-old so what
>> can he say? The father? Well he's no place, nobody knows
>> where he is or if he is dead. The eighteen-year-old finds a
>> pile of dirty dishes and empty bottles and his baby brother
>> is crawling around in garbage. So the eighteen-year-old
>> picks up the baby and puts him in his chair while he starts

to clean up the kitchen and eat dinner. No one is going to eat anyway. The eighteen-year-old will be too tired to study again and he won't have time to write his paper for the only class he thinks he can do good in. What's wrong with this picture? (6)

Even the students who seem the most comfortable are not immune from this culture of chaos and brutality, and teachers are not safe from it either. The admission of mutual implication and of the responsibility we must accept for one another, however, may begin a process of conscious change. *Letters for the Living* is a passionate evocation of writing as a way of describing, absorbing, and surviving what life brings us while remaining aware and reflective. Blitz and Hurlbert describe their students' transformation from being people with stories to tell to also being writers and composers, increasingly concerned with purpose, audience, form, and craft and interested in doing important work in the world.

Like the authors we reviewed in Chapter 1—Sirc, Owens, Romano, and Weathers—Blitz and Hurlbert are critics of the limited forms and superficial purposes of composition delineated within the academy. They suggest that to broaden our practice we must first know that we compose our lives, as well as occasional texts. They write:

We compose and we are the composing. Then why haven't teachers across the profession used the word "composition" in more "living" ways? Why do some of us decide in advance of the composition class, before Monday morning, before any single student's composing, which compositions are permissible and which are not, which are possible and which are not? Why do some of us limit the forms of living at this time in human history? (15)

When writing is the key to surviving or staying intellectually or spiritually alive, we need instead to be open to multiple forms, any of which may be the right way to tell the story, make the point, or follow the question. Blitz and Hurlbert suggest a fuller palette for textual composition that includes creative genres:

In *Letters for the Living*, we choose to invoke the word "composing" as comprehensively as we can: to make, craft, build, write, organize, soothe, comfort, pull together. Students in our composition classes can meaningfully make essays and demonstrate academically acceptable prose, but then can as meaningfully make fictions, poetry, and talk. James Berlin suggested we can act from a confluence of poetics and rhetoric. We can recognize the social function—and functioning—of the imagination. We can observe the collapsing of the personal and social realms of our compositions as we make visions and plans for better ways of living, as we look and work for political inspiration. (16)

At the crossroads of rhetoric and poetics, we find the tools or method that will suffice. This is like a focused form of the de-centering, centrifugal forces of discourse, theorized by M. M. Bakhtin, and described by readers such as Saul Morson and Caryl Emerson as central to what they term "prosaics." Calling these forces by any shared name, Morson and Emerson argue, may be misleading, for they are "a panoply of the most divergent elements," that may have no relation to each other beyond divergence from the monologism of official culture. However, this multiplicity makes such forces useful and inventive in the every day:

> Centrifugal forces register and respond to the most diverse events of daily life, to the prosaic facts that never quite fit any official or unofficial definition. They are an essential part of our moment-to-moment lives, and our responses to them record their effect on all cultural institutions, on language, and on ourselves. (30)

Heteroglossia, defined by Morson and Emerson as linguistic centrifugal forces and their products, "continually translates the minute alterations of and re-evaluations of everyday life into new meanings and tones, which, in sum and over time, always threaten the wholeness of any language" (30). For a consciousness carefully tracing these effects, the unity or meaning of life is continually problematized, and the rules of ethical or linguistic systems applied from on high are deceptive or dangerous. However, a complex unity, which no overarching principle fully captures but several may comment upon, is worth constant consideration and textual orchestration. It is a position further explained by the term *emergent system*, as described by Steven Johnson, where the parts of a whole that may seem out of sync or pointless when seen in isolation contribute to a complicated pattern of work or life that perpetuates itself through a collaborative intelligence, without direction from a mind "above."[4]

As one text spins into others, Blitz and Hurlbert also see the multiplicity returning to its center of gravity on the street or in the home or classroom, where lives are lived, stories are told, and conversations keep us going. Teachers encourage this variegated narration by broadening available discourses while helping students to deepen and complicate their understandings of how language can keep us awake in the world. Research writing can be part of this broadening palette and deepening reflection. Elsewhere, we have reviewed alternative forms of research writing.[5] These include the persuasive research paper, introduced to correct the original research form of only explication by rhetoricians including Wayne Booth, Gregory G. Colomb, and Joseph M. Williams; the personal research paper, or I-Search, practiced by Ken Macrorie and others, where the writer searches for answers to a pressing personal question; the multi-genre research project introduced by Tom Romano but practiced in more structured ways by other teachers and writers including David Joliffe, John Trimbur, Cheryl Johnson, and Diane Thiel; and the discursive, exploratory research essay, explicated by Bruce Ballenger. All these methods are important and potentially useful, and none should be excluded from a versatile pedagogy. Instead, in the method we imagine and work toward, writers are prepared to use any of these, as well as the additional forms, genres, or media, to meet the question at hand, sustain their thinking, or construct the emanation of self that the occasion or the need to survive demands.

As Blitz and Hurlbert have seen and credit James Berlin with pointing out to them, working with students does not mean directing them to "the good life." It means helping them keep going in lives that include pain and often violence and also can involve the search for an expanded understanding. We have found that the most shattered students are often the ones most willing, perhaps in desperation, to begin imagining a different life. We give students the option of not telling us anything about their lives but instead describing the life they should lead, or dream of leading, through papers or projects we have called the Ought-to- or Want-to-biography. Here, for instance, a student who feels abandoned by his father might imagine himself as the founder of the ideal orphanage, ruled by children under his helpful guidance as a benevolent father to all. Another student who was the victim of assault or lived in a climate of fear may reimagine herself as a famous martial artist, able to protect herself while becoming one with the energies flowing around her. Other students find more direct ways to give voice to their darkest stories and then convert this trauma into something else. Several students who have been victimized and sought help at the local domestic violence shelter eventually changed their lives enough to become volunteers at the shelter and then wrote multifaceted projects that included narratives of their experiences, research-based essays about the roots of violence and the difficulties of breaking its hold on our lives, and interviews with or stories of the others they have listened to and aided.

Research writing is or should be a process of change. At the crossroads, the changing notions of the past are always present, but the present is full of possibility, and the future can be imagined as we look down roads we have not yet traversed. We want our courses to be occasions upon which people add new layers of experience and meaning to their lives. Further, we would like our students to recognize that this travel into discovery renews human life and is both continuous and repeatable. In the entry for "Curiosity" in *Milosz's ABC's*, a traditional Polish genre, Czeslaw Milosz speaks of curiosity as both a singular journey and a common experience that carries on through a lifetime:

> The world is so organized that it is endlessly interesting; there is no limit to the discovery of ever newer layers and strata. It is like a journey through a maze which is pulsating, changing, growing as one moves through it. We make this journey by ourselves, but also as participants in the common undertaking of all humanity, with its myths, religions, philosophies, art, and the perfection of science. The curiosity which drives us cannot be sated and since it does not lessen with the passage of time, that is a sufficient argument against dying. Although, to be sure, many of us enter the gates of death immensely curious, expectant, eager to learn what it is like on the other side. (92)

While such curiosity refers all experience back to an emerging self, it can be the grounds for a new way of public living, in which our inquiries and communiqués help others find their routes and inquiry often comes to be held in common. Research-based writing does not belong solely to those who produce it but belongs to all who recognize the sojourner in themselves through this writing of the other. Each project marks a trail for the audience to trace, though a process where change is possible, just as travel to new cultures may recast our views of the world or even a walk through town can alter us for the day. Further, students with truly flexible selves that continue to change are most open to collaboration and to creating projects made as a group rather than a composite of individuals. A senior art show at our university recently illustrated this point, as a metal sculptor and cabinet of wonder artist and two photographers made a body of cross-referenced work filled with the detritus and wonder of rural life (which is also filled with postindustrial objects and forms). Although these students did not originally plot the show to function so beautifully as one, their work, built on years of interacting, spoke of their common experience. We saw in this a deeper version of the already complex interactions and tributes that characterize a class full of projects in our courses.

Freed from its diminished forms, recast as an open act of discursive questioning, research writing enacts what anthropologist Gregory

Bateson calls an ecology of mind, a manner of thinking or being that reintegrates us with a world of history, in flux. In a speech given at the Naropa Institute, Bateson glosses this key term in his thought:

> In the last few days, people have asked me, "What do you mean, ecology of mind?" Approximately what I mean is the various kinds of stuff that goes on in one's head and in one's behavior and in dealing with other people, and walking up mountains, and getting sick, and getting well. All that stuff interlocks, and, in fact, constitutes a network which, in the local language, is called mandala. I'm more comfortable with the word "ecology," but they're very closely overlapping ideas. At the root, it is the notion that ideas are interdependent, interacting, that ideas live and die. The ideas that die do so because they don't fit with the others. You've got the sort of complicated, living, struggling, cooperating tangle like what you'll find on any mountainside with the trees, various plants and animals that live there—in fact, an ecology (265).

Similarly, anthropologist Keith Basso's studies of the Western Apache, which we began to describe in Chapter 1 and often use as course readings, show how an evolving knowledge of landscape shapes the culture and the lives of its members. This knowing of the land includes observation of plants, animals, and landforms and a growing awareness of history as it is connected to the land. Place names become the nexus of landscape and memory and a shorthand for remembering what transpired there. Part of becoming a person in such a culture means constructing an ecology of mind that rises from this palimpsest of story and environment, with the land always there in memory or physical presence, speaking of lessons learned long ago by others that are now retold through the landscape and the observing mind.

Our students practice ecologies of mind that can plumb the depths of their own histories. Earlier we briefly referred to a project on Nez Perce Chief Joseph, which arose from local experience, as its author, Rosemary Day, raised Appaloosa horses descended from the Chief's own stock. Another student, Jennifer Pambrun, traced her family history, which included *metis* (French and American Indian) fur trappers and Dr. John McLoughlin, one of Oregon's first white settlers. In two related projects, Jerred Hermann first showed the necessity of "green" building, then designed his own green house. The first project centered upon a persuasive essay on the environmental degradation caused by buildings and the systems and people within them. It included statistics on the raw materials that make up buildings in America and continue to feed them, and on the wastes that emerge, including trash, sewage, chemicals, and carbon dioxide. It also traced the recent history of building innovations, including new processes and materials, which remain underfunded and little used. The second project, an exploration and plan for the author's dream house, emerged from this context not as a lark or high-end architectural fantasy but as a moral imperative to do things differently.

Researching how to live consciously in a certain locale has often included travel, as education occurs in an eventful journey or quest. Martin Luther King Jr. was changed forever by his trip to India, where nonviolent resistance had achieved results. Jane Addams was inspired toward social action by her encounters with the poor of Europe. Malcolm X's trip to Mecca changed his thought as he saw that people of all races could join together in a single spirit to worship Allah. The Princes of Serendip in the Sri Lankan folktale offer a paradigmatic example. They can free the seas around their home island of dragons only if they journey to the mainland to find a wise man with a secret script detailing a plan of action. On the trip, they quickly get off course and experience what English author Horace Walpole called "serendipity" as they performed marvelous deeds by helping others in distress. Later, they discover that the empathy that called them to action is the very quality needed to banish the threat of dragons.

The tension and collaboration between home and wandering is especially focused in Native American literature. Many "native authors" have a rich heritage of straddling several cultures or ethnic groups. For example, Paula Gunn-Allen's father was the Lebanese-American sheriff of Albuquerque, while her mother was from Pueblo culture in New Mexico. Similarly, Leslie Silko's mother was from Laguna Pueblo, while her father was Mexican. In her novel, *Ceremony*, Silko's character Tayo must rejuvenate his tribal roots partly by realizing his dream of raising longhorn cattle, which are good at braving drought but need more grazing land than the fenced ranches allow. The longhorns lead Tayo, literally and metaphorically, into a landscape inhabited by myth and the lore of shape-changing between people and animals, as they learn to cohabit the world.

Travel is also the process of letting go of control of both the landscape and other people. Creative nonfiction in America—especially in American Studies—frequently explores the way we have tried to "tame" an unruly and complex landscape, often leading to catastrophe. Poet-farmer Wendell Berry's *The Unsettling of America* resists the earlier mythos of westward expansion by refusing to look away from the harm and displacement "settlers" caused to indigenous peoples. John McPhee's *The Control of Nature* and *Encounters with the Archdruid* show the compulsive need—out of a fear masked by anger—to shape the landscape to our desires, rather than learn to live from observing its lessons. In the latter book, David Brower (known as the former head of The Sierra Club and Friends of the Earth, and here playing the role of archdruid) and Floyd Dominy (a world-famous dam builder) look at the same landscape around Lake Powell. Brower can see only the demise of a once-powerful river in order to produce electricity, while Dominy sees only a future with electric power and a recreational body of water. Neither really sees the present as a mix of past and future, this moment—the only time available for action or response.

"Travel" has often been a metaphor in our teaching, as we want students to expand their range of experience and move to different places in their thoughts. Touring different communicative strategies, including genres, media, and forms, can also open doors as students begin to conceive how to approach their subjects in a new way—as the term paper gives way to talk performance, a blog updated throughout the term, or, in emulation of Blitz and Hurlbert, a book of letters between two authors concerned with the same subject. We invite this kind of work in part by beginning the project with a dream of destination, so the point is not displaying what writers already know (although is can be part of the work) but thinking about where they want to head or what can be learned.

We also describe a shared destination: the class is headed toward a great group of projects, perhaps with a public component such as a poster display, art installation, mini-symposium, or community service learning project. Such a class is a happening ala Geoffrey Sirc: something is occurring that cannot be repeated and is taking on a life of its own. The invitation is collective, but it is accepted individually. We often speak to each other of seeing the moment when a student "lights up" and begins to find a great project. This illumination—often the opposite of the traditional "enlightenment" that ends a journey—may come as an analogy, where students connect their work to that of another: an author whose work they have read or examined; an earlier student who has returned as part of a panel presentation on the process; or a professor from another course who shows how she approaches research or creative work.

In other cases, a particular form functions analogically, suggesting or evoking further work. A project on gardening becomes the construction of a discursive mini-garden. Randy Kromwall's project on Houdini, described above, connects magic to writing where illusions are made. Sometimes the form is a suggestive mystery that leads to a project. Michael McClure began an autobiography project with a roughly hewn box with an ornate design on its lid that he found in the basement of the furniture store where he worked as a mover. He liked the box and found that it spoke to him if he listened intently. Making his project was a dialogue as he found the emanations of himself the box wanted or could use. His project became a strangely distanced autobiography as archaeological relic, found by a fictional, perhaps misguided, researcher who saw it in the remnants of a lost civilization. It was then a natural step to a research project on another box artist, Joseph Cornell, whose work evokes a similar feeling of melancholic remembrance through intricate designs and assemblages.

At other times, the key lies hidden in students' experiences, sometimes long suppressed or forgotten. Some of our favorite prompts have to do with recovering childhood through remembering toys the writer liked to play with, games they enjoyed, or items they collected, as well as the problems or questions that occupied, inspired, or scared them. Through a great many activities—including those at the end of this chapter—we help students understand and achieve what Edith Cobb defines in the title of her book *The Ecology of the Imagination in Childhood*—an overview of the curiosity of unselfconscious children.

Even students with the most troubled lives have often found a powerful mechanism for living that explains their interests into adulthood. Student Christy Soto, who has continued creative work in writing, music, and dance, explained that the only "toys" that interested her as a child and the ones she could afford were a pen and notebook. She made up elaborate stories and narrated her life continually, as no one else would do it for her.

Although we prompt students in many ways, the project assignments we have used most often are quite open, asking and allowing people to write as they will: "This term, you will make a Multiwriting Research Project on a subject of your choosing. We will work together to find protocols and parameters of the project, but the main rule is that through doing this, you must learn about the subject (even if you know something about it already), about the processes of inquiry and writing, and about the many possible forms for composition." This is the architecture for a term-long happening, or Sircian "hacienda," as students improvise together to fill in the prompt's open structure.

It is also an invitation for extended travel in the world of thought and ideas. It is a chance for students to begin to set an intellectual agenda for themselves that can continue and change through time. We think of Michelle Skow, who did a series of projects on Japanese American experience that were each unique but also connected to the others in complicated patterns like origami and sushi (subjects she used). Earlier projects lead to research on the Japanese American internment during World War II, which she presented at the National Undergraduate Literature Conference. Bryan Suereth's interest in avant-garde art, shown in his multimedia project on the intergalactic jazz musician Sun Ra, is reflected in his ongoing work in the arts in Portland, Oregon, where his gallery Dysjecta was known for leading edge, cross-media work, and where he joined with others to produce the gigantic "Modern Zoo" show.

While for many students the idea of thought, inquiry, or writing as travel remains metaphoric, others include actual travel as part of their research. Student Linda Ediger followed up her biography project on journalist and National Public Radio commentator Linda Ellerbee by meeting Ellerbee for coffee in New York City. Impressed by his study of the Museum of Jurassic Technology (which we discuss in Chapter 4), Chris Asla journeyed to Los Angeles to tour the museum and interview its director, David Wilson. This visit and the video of it, in turn, inspired Mark to visit the museum this year. Christy Soto's long interest in voodoo and the occult, often reflected in her writing, led to her move to New Orleans, where she lived in a house said to be haunted by a spirit from the 1700s. After careful research about publishing, Frank Kaminski moved to New York to break into the industry. Chris Hatton moved from writing screenplays in college to making films in Los Angeles and other locations, while Skye Fitzgerald moved to Portland and is now finishing a documentary film on disarming bombs and landmines in Laos, Cambodia, and Viet Nam, for which he received a Fulbright award.

While not every student will study abroad or tour the world, an infectious spirit of intrepid adventure often spreads once it begins. At the freshman level, we seek to inspire it through pedagogy based upon travel and research, which includes "Dream Trips," the subject of the pedagogic materials below. We encourage students who research and plan these trips to go to the places they study, and some do, frequently sending back postcards addressed to students currently taking the Exploratory Writing class where the dream trip work occurs. We believe that even students who remain in rural Oregon are led into new routes of thought and glimpse new possibilities for experience through this research and writing. They experience the world as a bigger place, which necessitates learning many avenues for expression and communication. Perhaps, too, they begin to think beyond the day-to-day survival and begin to consider other departures. The key to the highway is always within, in the end.

Musing: Being Moved by the Open Road of Inquiry

If time and money are no objects, most people like to travel. But travel is a key concern for students, who often feel intensely the tension and collaboration between "home" and "wandering." Many are getting out of the nest of a childhood home but have not yet established their own family in a new place. Consequently, some students may not be able to listen to Ralph Waldo Emerson, who once claimed that only those who truly have and appreciate a home can enjoy travel. Instead, such students need to travel to test their knowledge and values and to peek into entirely new worlds.

Travel may also bring home the boon of concepts, talismans, and relationships that are more than a postmodern pastiche or hasty collage. In *Late Night Reflections on Listening to Mahler's Ninth Symphony*, written at the end of the superpower opposition between America and Russia, Lewis Thomas facetiously suggested that each country should have half a million troops in each other's country, circulating on random train schedules. While he pretends that the importance of this idea is as deterrent (neither country would bomb the other, afraid of killing its own citizens), he implies that what would happen is a deeper connection between the two countries, including intermarriage and communication. While the ongoing conflicts in the Middle East or Ireland show that familiarity can indeed breed contempt, it can also give birth to understanding, compassion, and connection. Most people return from travel or study abroad excited and transformed.

Many colleges and universities now have "cornerstone" requirements beyond the classroom in research, internship, community service, and study abroad or with another ethnic group. This latter one is the most difficult, as it costs more and demands that students leave the safety of family and friends. Author Norman Mailer once said that "safe sex" is an oxymoron, and we would add that "safe travel" is another one. While the world is more itinerant than ever, it is not necessarily safer in this Age of Malpractice, and the financial cost of studying abroad is rising.

However, such study is crucial. It has traditionally been driven by language requirements, as most people learn a language best by being immersed in a culture that speaks it. Anthropology also has long sent students into other cultures, presumably to learn about others' customs and traditions before they vanish. However, in both cases, students learn as much or more about their own language and culture by studying abroad. Studying Spanish helps us realize that English has similar verb conjugations that are hidden when we learn it as a native language, without such conscious effort. Similarly, someone horrified by drinking a concoction of blood and milk with Massai hosts in Africa may realize that for Africans the branding of animals done in the American West is just as peculiar or (initially) gross.

So travel is like the number twenty-two in world mythology, which symbolizes breakthrough or impasse. Either way, the breakthroughs, questions, and curiosities travel can bring begin—as the exercises and project below demonstrate—at home, which is usually only a continual-but-temporary retreat from other people and places. The chaotic diversity of exploration dances with the ordered retreat of home, where reflection leads to adaptation through the adoption of new ways of being.

In spite of any and all obstacles, travel and study abroad or with another ethnic group gets the student in any of us excited about learning. Imagine for a minute Caribbean sophomores from the University of the West Indies spending a semester in Montana, riding horses into the Bob Marshall Wilderness during the late summer, or sophomores from the University of Montana escaping the harsh winter to study on the beaches and reefs of a Caribbean island. Students with such travel to look forward to are likely to stay in college. More importantly, such travel and interchange makes us all hungry for discourse and often leaves us eager to see even more of the world. Travel can lead to self-direction and responsibility; many discover a major or vocation through their journeys and experience of the world. Because the open road often allows us to brush up against the best and worst of what it means to be a human being, travel also provides great stories that can make conversation a deep pleasure.

The exercises below begin with telling a story of travel. Even with so many books and films and the Internet, many countries provide too little information for any traveler to feel confident or safe; and much of the information travelers exchange on the road is anecdotal, passed along through powerful but fragile conversation. Often the best way to gain courage toward travel is to recall a favorite trip and write about it. As you write about such a trip, your rhetoric and style will reveal how you approach the world. Similarly, you may also find that you travel in your mind, both to places you have been and those you have never seen but want to. Such imaginative thought can open more of the world to us, even if sometimes we want to escape some of the places that follow us.

Once warmed up with storytelling and acts of memory and imagination, it is time for you to plan a Multiwriting Dream Trip, where you are free to mix multiple genres, disciplines, media, and cultures in ways you find satisfying. The form of your project will help others share your passions and understand your reasons and methods of travel. With luck you will actually take the trip you plan, or a similar one.

Exercise 2.1: Bending an Ear—Retelling and Rewriting a Favorite Trip

Travel writing is the easiest of ways to begin writing, especially when you are allowed to "talk yourself into it." An easy exercise is to write a list of stories about your travels or those of members of your family or of friends. If you prefer not to be too personal, you can recount famous journeys from history you know of, like a part of the trip of Lewis and

Clark as they explored the land acquired in the Louisiana Purchase. You may want to remember a school trip taken with classmates. For example, volunteer chaperone Eric Nelson joined Mr. Carson, the fifth-grade teacher in La Grande, Oregon, at Willow Elementary School in the spring of 2005 for the annual field trip by bus for the fifth- and sixth-graders. They visited the powerful Multnomah Falls in the scenic Columbia Gorge, as well as the Devil's Punchbowl State Park, a beach on the Oregon coast. At the state capitol in Salem, they happened to meet the Governor, and they visited the Marine Science Center in Newport. In Portland, Oregon's large city, they took the Max light rail downtown to Pioneer Square and visited the massive Powell's Books. But it was the most elemental experience—being knocked flat by a massive wave at the Oregon coast—that most impressed these students. What most impressed you as a child on a trip you recall? Remember that even local journeys to another neighborhood, a friend's apartment, or a local landmark can expand our sense of the world.

Think about your travel stories for a day or so, then choose one to briefly retell to the class or a small group within the class. Recall those key aspects of rhetoric: writer, audience, occasion, message, and purpose. What does the audience need to know about you, the storyteller? Is there any special way that the audience needs to be prepared a bit to understand the telling of the chosen story on this occasion? Is there a message embedded in the story? For example, is it a cautionary one that ends by warning the audience of the dangers of dabbling in the occult with a ouija board? Is there any clear purpose? Do you hope the audience will appreciate the teller's position? Is the story supposed to change their behavior?

The stories students tell often include predictable events, like a family vacation during the summer or travel with a sports team to a championship game. To gather more interesting materials, we suggest trying the three-column list prewriting exercise located on the Web site for another publication of ours. This list asks you to list the ten most unusual things that have happened to you and link these (when possible) to habits/hobbies and personality traits. Here is the URL: www.boyntoncook.com/researchwritingrevisited

After you have practiced speaking and listening to your stories of travel and those of your classmates, you are ready to begin the process of writing about some travel more carefully. At this stage you are revealing not only your patterns of error with writing conventions but also your insistences. That is, you have to care about the destination and/or process of this trip enough to write and revise a paper on it. These papers should be brief enough to read aloud in class, as the key is for you to learn a new kind of listening where you are the angel's advocate for other's stories but also able to be reminded of your own by listening to those of others. Teachers can guide you in this endeavor by using personal stories of travel to expand or redirect your ideas. For instance, if you recount a story of your constant trips to the principal's office, the teacher may tell a story of being trapped in a cave while spelunking or being locked in an outhouse that was tipped over during a Halloween prank. This, in turn, may help you rewrite a story about being cramped with siblings in the family minivan during a vacation. All these stories are about being in a confining or unpleasant place. These interactions remind you that all your classes should really be thought of as places where you are trying to integrate listening, speaking, reading, writing, and thinking.

Exercise 2.2: Roaming in the Mind

While we cannot always travel in a physical sense, we can roam through memory and imagination. U.S. Supreme Course Justice William O. Douglas writes in his book of memory and the outdoors, *Of Men and Mountains*, of daydreaming while listening to a predictable argument during a court case. He imagined himself fishing the riffles and pools of the Klickitat River in the state of Washington, near where he had grown up, and landing a large trout after trying a series of flies. This fantasy allowed Douglas to escape the captivity of his current circumstances of being trapped on the bench and journey more freely. Many people have dreamed of returning to a home long left behind, while others have imagined places that are important to them even when they have never been there. Think, for instance, of the generations of immigrants who dreamed of America, while their descendants, and the children of slaves, often wonder what it would be like to return to the lands of their ancestry. Sometimes, too, the place of a trauma, tragedy, or failure can continue to haunt us, shadowing our daily lives.

Where does your mind go when it roams?

1. Make a list of about three places, then "draw" each by using descriptive words or by making an image with a pencil, paints, or some other method.

2. Next, consider each place as open to further learning and research. For instance, Justice Douglas learned the Klickitat by repeatedly exploring it and contrasting it with the other rivers he knew. He also loved to learn about rivers from others, especially his boyhood friends and older people who knew more. How would you go about learning more? Make a list of questions you would like to explore and write a plan for finding out the answers. Are there questions on your list that cannot be answered?

3. Finally, write a short essay of a page or two for your classmates that describes one of the places you have chosen and explains why your mind roams to it. Did you learn anything new about yourself or the place?

4. You and your classmates may want to research and discuss the term *symbolic landscape* as it relates to the places you are thinking about.

Project: Winning an Imaginary Lottery, the Multiwriting Dream Trip

Allowing you to create a multiwriting dream trip project is like handing you the keys to a shiny new sports car, or you may feel like the cabbie who has waited all his life for someone to jump into his cab and say, "Follow that car!"—except the car you are following is being driven by your disappearing dreams. The idea of a spring break vacation on a beach of white sand devoid of other people and a constant beer supply—like the slo-mo Corona beer TV commercials—quickly evaporates when you think about how rare this chance to discover your real desires is. Yet even a single travel brochure may be enough to start you moving. In *The Art of Travel*, Alain De Botton says:

> Those responsible for the brochure had darkly intuited how easily their audience might be turned into prey by photographs whose power insulted the intelligence and contravened any notions of free will: overexposed photographs of palm trees, clear skies and white beaches. Readers who would have been capable of skepticism and prudence in other areas of their lives reverted, in contact with these elements, to a primordial innocence and optimism. The longing provoked by the brochure was an example, at once touching and bathetic, of how projects (and even whole lives) might be influenced by the simplest and most unexamined images of happiness; of how a lengthy and ruinously expensive journey might be set into motion by nothing more than the sight of a photograph of a palm tree gently inclining in a tropical breeze.
>
> I resolved to travel to the island of Barbados. (9)

The only thing more frightening than being the happy drone of a traditional term paper is the real freedom of using the imagination to critique and move through cultural assumptions. The utopian imagination is often the fastest route to the real or practical, as fantasies reveal assumptions that we have adopted, sometimes without much reflection.

The best way to help you dream a transformative trip is to bring in other faculty, students, or citizens who have traveled passionately. During the term when we wrote this part of the book, Mark brought in April Curtis, a professor from the Theatre department, who had taught mask-making last year in Athens, Greece, to speak to students in his first-year Exploratory Writing course. Her bulging journal—full of notes, photographs, screenplay ideas, sketches, pasted-in labels, memorabilia, and more—was an accompaniment to her stories about meeting and attempting to understand not only Greeks and Turks but also the citizens of Czechoslovakia and Costa Rica, the other countries she visited during her Sabbatical.

Besides writing to or about photographs and music from the destination students choose, many get momentum from their projects by including maps from the library or mapquest.com; a packing list of things they will take; mock passports; itineraries and plane tickets; reviews of movies or books about their chosen destination; a fact sheet; mini-research essays about the history or politics of the country; a description and explanation of travel companions and means of transportation; and illustrations of customs and sports.

Perhaps the most powerful motivation to begin creating genres and shaping the form of the project is the knowledge that you will perform your project for about fifteen minutes during the last third of the quarter or semester. You might want to begin a PowerPoint as an overview of the trip, easily intertwining texts and photos and maps, or you might settle upon some microcosm or synecdoche or epitome of what your trip was or is about. For example, David Newport—whose trip investigated and relived Japan's most famous haiku poet, Basho, in the travel that became his collection of poems, the *Narrow Road to the North*—focused upon a single, nearly untranslatable poem. With increasing clarity and with the help of Japanese students, he demonstrated the ambiguities and difficulties of Basho's poem, especially for an American audience.

As you think about performing your project, you consider not only additional media but also which disciplines you want to explore. Sometimes this involves remembering or discovering a major. A student in biology followed the migration of monarch butterflies back and forth between Mexico and America, while one in agriculture doing a tour of the world's greatest golf courses included research about different kinds of grasses and their role in this sport. Many art majors have planned trips to places famous for art, including Russia, France, Italy, and Mexico. Chemistry majors interested in eating and cooking often make good use of how taste works, studying the food in microscopic detail.

The most complicated projects may involve dozens of genres, many disciplines and media, and several cultures. Neva Sanders's amazing project on the Mexican Days of the Dead included a screenplay (a hybrid that combined the work of individual playwrights and the collective plays put on by Mexican American farm workers), a corrido (ballad), poems, reflections, a letter, and more. The project was housed in a large coffin that opened to reveal a painted gallery of art and writings (in both English and Spanish). Besides America and Mexico, the project connected the Mexican Days of the Dead with the *Tibetan Book of the Dead*. She continues to add to this and other multiwriting projects.

You may do a dream trip that is vacation and later take it, sending postcards back to your family, your teacher, or us along the way. Perhaps you will use your project as a warm-up for planning study abroad in your junior year, which you will make a reality. With or without your classmates, you may decide to display your project in an art gallery, coffeehouse, museum, or business.

Readings: Travel as the Passion, Art, and Theory of Pilgrimage

Phil Cousineau, in *The Art of Pilgrimage: The Seeker's Guide to Making Travel Sacred*, lists several forms of travel: tourism, business travel, scientific or scholarly exploration, touring to add to one's social status or for the sake of one's education, and "drifting for the sake of drifting." Each of these forms has its purposes: scholarly exploration may lead to new discoveries, tourism to relaxation and entertainment, business travel to global commerce. But Cousineau is most interested in using his own life and travel to explain how to make secular travel sacred—a journey of risk, but renewal. Like Alain De Botton in *The Art of Travel*, Cousineau is interested more in the *why* and *how* of travel than the *where*; however, both authors would agree that all three must be discovered through the kind of steady reflection that reveals personal insistences.

Early nomads may have "vacated" a site because they had used up the resources there, but no doubt for a long time people have traveled with the seasons for, among other things, better weather. Even the business adventures of the spice routes are, in the account of Evan Connell, a part of what the French call—the title of his book about Marco Polo—*A Long Desire*. There are endless manuscripts involving travel for scientific research, whether they are the journal kept by flashlight in an underground cave in Antarctica or Deborah Gordon's careful accounts of insects in the Arizona desert in *Ants at Work*. Another set of books involve travel that charts and revisits the history and philosophy of science. Jacob Bronowski's book *The Ascent of Man* has the author standing wherever the history took place or the scientific breakthrough occurred. Dava Sobel chronicles the melodramatic discovery in finding a twin for latitude in navigation in *Longitude*, just as Amir D. Aczel demonstrates the slow development of navigation as observation of currents, tides, and bird migration in *The Riddle of the Compass*.

Outside travel as tourism, business, or scientific research, the sacred pilgrimages Cousineau is interested in transforming for secular travel were perhaps expected or inevitable in the past—a cultural imperative. Flagellants who whipped themselves as they walked long distances to shrines in Medieval Europe had little to lose in a materialistic way and much to gain spiritually, according to the Christianity they subscribed to. The religion was also an emotional shield to endure physical and psychological hardship; it was an end in itself, even if the pilgrim was accruing rewards in the afterlife. In Islam, every Muslim hopes to make a trip to Mecca in Arabia, where the Prophet Mohammed fled. When African-American writer and activist Malcolm X finally went on this pilgrimage, it changed him; only when he was surrounded by Muslims of every color and nationality from all over the world did he realize the importance of cooperation and diversity.

In other cultures, traditional sacred journeys were often a matter more of philosophy than religious practice. For example, a *sunyata*—the leave-taking of man in late middle age from his job, family, and community—was a Hindu ceremony that had implications for his family, whose members now may sometimes object to it. Similar journeys of readjustment in middle age occur in Buddhist culture. In Spain there is the *despedida*, a trip arranged by family and friends. Many students still find the traveler's philosophical quest in Herman Hesse's *Sidhartha* as interesting as J. R. R. Tolkien's spiritual war in *Lord of the Rings*. The self-reflection of characters in Jack Kerouac's *On the Road* or J. R. Salinger's *Catcher in the Rye* are updated in books like Jon Krakauer's *Into the Wild*, where a young Alex drops out of college and travels to Alaska, where he dies from lack of wilderness preparation in, ironically, a school bus in the forest.

The Journey Is the Destination: The Journals of Dan Eldon is edited by Kathy Eldon, Dan's mother. It is a compressed palimpsest and running collage of photographs, paintings, words, drawings, maps, clippings, scraps, shards, and more by photojournalist Dan Eldon. When he was stoned to death at the age of twenty-two by a mob in Somalia while investigating a UN bombing in 1993, Eldon left behind seventeen volumes of fascinating journals. Dan, with a British father and American mother, studied in a variety of diverse schools in four continents. At the heart of this book is the "Safari of Desire," where Dan, his sister Amy, and friends take two old vehicles across Africa. This trip is an attempt to discover the difference between exploring and being lost. The title is the answer, for the journey itself is the destination. Beneath the bravado—as when the crew says they have nothing to lose but their lives—there is a serious consideration of the political and physical dangers of this rough travel. The travelers discuss the consequences of the abuse of both people and animals along their route. But there is plenty of parody when the texts and graphics transform the journal entry of Livingston or talk about "Clarence" of Arabia. Eldon's life is a compressed invitation to explore and link the worlds both inside and beyond us.

Guillermo Gómez-Peña and Coco Fusco's *Dangerous Border Crossers: The Artist Talks Back* also develops autobiographically to dramatize the outsider consciousness that enables Gloria Anzaldúa's vision of a *mestiza* or crossblood world through the performance art of Gómez-Peña, who is the leader, with Roberto Sifuentes, of the troupe *La Pocha Nostra*. The group's performance pieces include the famed *Temple of Confessions*, a "pagan temple" housing figures that were at once caged "cultural specimens" and holy people taking the audience's confessions of fears and desires concerning America, Mexico, globalization, and "the other." They also radically extend the television idea of "the makeover" by changing the clothes, hair, mannerisms, and even skin color of people they then release into an only partly controlled world. People who experience this have a hard time getting back into their old world, and talk about having a "cultural hangover."

Some other researchers exploring the world believe that instead of reflecting upon the purposes of travel it's best to just do it. Certainly one process strong enough to get people moving is romance. Nick Bantock's *The Gryphon: In Which the Extraordinary Correspondence of Griffin and Sabine Is Rediscovered* consists of the colorful postcards of lovers across the globe. The senses may also beckon the traveler, as they do in *The Secrets of Pistoulet: A Fable of Food, Magic, and Love*, which is written and illustrated by Jann Fayne Kolpen and designed by Mary Tiegreen. This book is centered upon the cuisine of southern France. Barbara Hodgson's *The Tattooed Map* is similar, using the analogy of tattooing for the imprint travel in Africa leaves upon the visitor. She uses colorful maps, charts, photos, journals, drawings, money, postcards, Arabic script, tables, notes, newspaper clippings, plane ticket stubs, ads, and more to pull the reader through this square-shaped book of wonder.

Most students who go to college are encouraged in a thousand untraceable ways by family who expect them to arrive there. Curious adults often develop their interest in the world's questions with the help of family and friends. So you may want to read about family members studying the world or traveling together. A good update to Robert Persig's father-son journey in *Zen and the Art of Motorcycle Maintenance* is William McKeen's trip with his son down the length of a legendary road, from Bob Dylan's hometown in Minnesota through the Mississippi Delta to New Orleans, in *Highway 61*.

Travel can also stand in for obsession, as it does for Red O'Hanlon in his *No Mercy!: Journey to the Heart of the Congo*. Like a Monty Python parody of the famous early explorers, like Sir Richard Burton, O'Hanlon is determined to see the rumored dinosaur in a remote lake in the Congo. He braves disease, insects, hostile soldiers, chiefs, and politicians, as well as melodramatic sidekicks, as he moves upon the rivers and through the jungles, with the help of pygmies. A bizarre irony ensues when O'Hanlon, having sent his American sidekick home, becomes the surrogate "mother" for a baby gorilla that clings to him as fiercely as his dreams.

O'Hanlon's obsession is sometimes mirrored by the involvement of anthropologists who "go native." Colin Turnbull's rather romantic account of his life with the Babenzele pygmies in the rainforests of central Africa in *The Forest People* comes to a climax when he has to decide whether to receive the traditional scarification. In the interest of telling the truth about their struggles, anthropologists have written about not only their academic successes but also their catastrophes. Examples would be *Ants, Indians and Little Dinosaurs*, edited by Alan Ternes, or *The Naked Anthropologist: Tales from Around the World*, edited by Phillip DeVita.

Some researchers find new things to research within the familiar. Wendell Berry talks about how his daily walk in the same place always changes in his *Traveling at Home*. Witold Rysbynski tracks the way even our idea of home and what it means changes in *Home: The History of the Idea of Comfort*. In this sense, architect Frank Lloyd Wright lets the world come to the dweller in his most famous house, Falling Water, where a stream moves through the house, bringing small water-born treasures and sound. Chris Anderson, our Oregon colleague, turns the lemons of discovering his house was inside an experimental forest that was to be clear-cut into the lemonade of *Edge Effects*, where he borrows the scientific idea that the richest biodiversity is where the forest and a clearing meet. His self-enlightenment grows from traveling into even the enemy camp of loggers and forestry officials and learning from them.

For a long time, people have reflected upon their continuing urge to travel. Joseph Campbell's structuralism in *The Hero Has a Thousand Faces* argues that all quests are comparable; the hero leaves home, faces trials and tribulations, and brings the wisdom she gains in the process back to transform and/or protect her home. Author Carlos Fuentes explains this sort of approach in "Indian Mexico," a chapter in *A New Time for Mexico*:

> Travel is the original movement of literature. Words are the origin of myth; myth is the first name of home, forebears, and tombs. The word of movement tears us from the hearth. Its name is epic, and it throws us into the arms of the world, of the different, of the voyage. During this trip from mythic hearth to epic strangeness, we discover

our tragic fissure. We then return to the land of the origin, there to tell our tale and renew our dialogue with the myth of the origin, asking it to have pity on us.

Just as there is not yet a consensus on open-field physics, it may be too soon to find an overarching theory of travel. Philosopher J. Glenn Gray keeps a phenomenological journal that charts the tragic destruction of not only people but also plants and animals, during World War II in Europe in *The Warriors*. There may be no way to comprehend the postcards and bullets that fly along their separate tracks in the War in Iraq, yet researching and understanding the experience of that tragedy surely lives along both trajectories, and their consequences. It may be impossible to unravel the conspiracy of the kind of media spin doctors, government spooks, esoteric stamp collectors, and underground artists portrayed in Thomas Pynchon's novel *The Crying of Lot 49*. Yet in the simple act of licking a stamp, we nurture and envelope our words, sending them on an adventure beyond our knowing. Like the blood inside us, we have been moving along the blue-veined highways and embattled arteries of commerce for a long time.

Film: Travel as (Self-)Exploration

Many people travel as part of their work or scholarly research, not expecting the kind of change that comes when they discover they must adapt to their surroundings in order to do their job effectively. For example, in Kurosawa's classic film *Dersu Uzala*, a group of Russian soldiers are sent, at the beginning of the twentieth century, to map Siberia. The Captain and leader is befriended by Dersu, a Goldie tribesman, who guides them through the forest and arctic tundra, eventually saving their lives. While the Captain has learned to love Dersu and his world, he makes a second trip and tries to take the aging trapper and hunter to live with him and his family in the city. This fails.

Marc Salzman, a martial artist and musician, takes a job in China tutoring medical students in English. He is humbled both by his mistakes with the language, and by competitive and highly skilled martial arts teachers, in *Iron and Silk*. Similarly, a white dam builder in Brazil fails to spend enough time with his son, who is kidnapped by a tribe that believes him to be sad, in *The Emerald Forest*. The son becomes a shaman, who travels to the city to encourage his father to stop building the dam. In this struggle between father/civilization/dam and son/forest/river, there is no reconciliation. At the other extreme, the white girls from a nineteenth-century boarding school, in *Picnic at Hanging Rock*, have no idea about the Australian outback, where they mysteriously disappear.

Sometimes travel is about preserving or celebrating a nomadic or traditional way of life, as it is in the Lap-Lander legend that is turned into *The Pathfinder.* A young boy must lose his innocence and become a shaman when violent outsiders attack. Sometimes an outsider or refugee appears to help a culture understand a threat, as when the German soldier Heinrich Herrer escapes from a British prison in India and makes his way to Tibet, where he tutors the Dalai Lama, explaining Western culture to Tibetans, in *Seven Years in Tibet.* In *Il Postino,* the exiled Chilean poet Pablo Neruda helps his mailman appreciate the Italian fishing village from which he is attempting to escape by revealing a sensual world or nature. The mailman returns the favor. When Neruda returns to Chile, he receives a tape—lovingly made by the mailman—of all the sounds of the Italian village he has left behind.

Travel can also be a quest to revitalize life in the face of divorce, death, or political upheaval. In *Under the Tuscan Sun,* Frances Mayes needs a change after divorce and on a trip to Italy surprises herself by buying and restoring an old villa. She fixes herself along with the house, whose problems let her into the life of her neighbors. Paul Bowles, who was a member of the Beat Generation of writers who moved to Morocco and stayed, chronicles the travel of a troubled couple in Africa. They are neither as superficial as tourists nor as dedicated as anthropologists, and the landscape (the main character) gives them enough room to ironically disassemble under *The Sheltering Sky.*

Some individuals must assemble or pick up other travelers on their quest to remake themselves. This is true of the seeker in *Pow-Wow Highway* who is the sidekick-become-leader. Slowly he heads toward his friend's emergency, with some important spiritual side trips to sacred Native American places, which make the problems encountered upon arrival understandable. A young brother and sister sneak out of the hostile environment of their Central American home in *El Norte.* Their journey north to America is fraught with danger, from Mexican grifters to rat-infested tunnels, and they struggle to fit into a language and world they are not fully allowed to comprehend. A happier and more intentional collaboration is the result of guitarist Ry Cooder's love of Cuban music. In *The Buena Vista Social Club,* he travels to Cuba to assemble the best traditional musicians into a band that will take a world tour and release a CD to go with this documentary.

3   THE LOOSE TALK OF PERSUASION

Ideology is a "club," like never before—in two senses of the word:

a dull instrument to bludgeon the other without subtlety, a crudely
violent way of relating to the world and the others in it

a social association with its own rites, rituals, and predictable responses

Bill O'Reilly vibrates like a cell phone nightly on Fox TV, with guests
invited to confirm his rightness or reveal their errors. In the occasional
simulation of doubt, our host looks down at a script that may have gone
blurry (put on your specs, O'Reilly) and says, "You may be right," or "I'll
have to think about it." It is then time to move on: "You are a passionate
advocate and I appreciate that." The perfect vacuum of spinlessness came
on National Public Radio's *Fresh Air*, when O'Reilly, fed up with the
host, the "unfair" Terry Gross, vacated the sound studio in outrage. It
was a perfect gesture of "debate" for a Jerry Springer world, a spectacle
that, while unseen, we can picture.

This chapter aims to move us away from this discourse of simulation
and forced disagreement toward a "loose talk" where persuasion occurs
as ongoing dialogue through which all parties may be transformed. We
trace selected contemporary theories of rhetoric that reread the long history of this ancient tradition to discover that rhetoric has been the study
of change, by which societies and their members seek out otherness in
themselves and the world and follow uncertainties and open questions
toward altered understandings. While Chapter 2 suggested a more open
approach to research writing as wandering, this chapter follows with an
evocation of loose talk as persuasion that forestalls violence and quietly or provocatively counters the rhetoric of certainty that has risen to
prominence and is now being codified in the world.

Like the terrorists they hate, George W. Bush and his operatives stay
the course, while the wrongness of others is never in doubt, no matter
what events may suggest. No one said the right is easy, the thinking appears to be; the right is difficult, and the more difficult it is, the more
steadfast we must be. The engine of justification includes simulations

of diversity of views, reason, and—in the occasional leaked Rumsfeld memo—worry. But this hand wringing reifies steadfast linearity. We know the dangers and study the options. But we will not be dissuaded. For right is right.

Virtual worlds are tightening up along with real ones, as part of Homeland Security, with its Orwellian doublespeak. In his recent book, *The Future of Ideas: The Fate of the Commons in a Connected World*, Stanford law professor Lawrence Lessig warns of the chokehold corporate America has on the Internet. Even Howard Rheingold—who has argued that the gap is closing between virtual and actual communities in his books, and as editor of *The Millennium Whole Earth Catalog*—urges some caution about the evolving notions of online communities, in *Smart Mobs: The Next Social Revolution*. Responses to this book have included the notion that cyber communities exhibit many people preaching to the champions of their prejudices, instead of the more complicated give and take of actual communities, where members must debate toward consensus and test, live with, and celebrate or enjoy differences.

Meanwhile, on repeat-o-TV, the ritual of alteration is continual and circular. A character on MTV's *The Real World* is often confronted with others' views that he is an unfeeling, selfish jerk. He is: the protocol of the show is that everyone must be at their worst and all slights, tensions, bad days, and weak moments shall be magnified and commented upon. So, in the "private" televised asides that constitute reflection, the other characters simulate pain and anger to mount their charges against Sky. He is conceited, doesn't listen, won't do the dishes, and holds a malicious view of others. Sky's aside is tearful, enraged, poignant, and big of him: he is misunderstood; he is trying; they are against him; it is hard; he is learning. Gina, his current dalliance, understands.

In their formulaic style and content, the arguments that now populate both popular culture and politics, in which the deliberations of legislative bodies become mere recitations of the given, are parodied in the brilliant skit on arguments by the Monty Python troupe. Here a man seeking an argument goes to an office where arguments are administered (another in the line of bizarre bureaucratic establishments in the Python world, including the Ministry of Funny Walks). As often happens when one goes to such an office, our hero is at first misdirected, sent to an office of abuse where he is called, among other things, a "snotty-faced heap of parrot droppings," then redirected by the abuse-clerk down the hall, to arguments. Here, in apparently the right place, the man has a less-than-satisfying experience as he "argues" with the argument-official about whether or not the office was properly identified by this employee when the customer walked in. You did not [say this was the place for arguments]; I did so; the two go back and forth, until the costumer points out that this is not an argument but simply a contradiction. "Argument is an intellectual process," the customer finally says. "Contradiction is just the automatic gainsaying of any statement the other person makes."

The clerk—perhaps interested in keeping things simple, as this is, after all, the five-minute argument rather than the whole hour one (a course of ten arguments is also available)—replies, "No, it isn't." When the customer wants to complain about this reductive treatment, he accidentally ends up in the office where being hit in the head lessons are administered. Complaints are next door.[1] The skit reminds us not only that arguments can easily be templated in their most reductive forms but also that they should emerge from reflective thinking and living in a world of others, not by going to the right office or tuning into the Argue-media in its many diminished manifestations.

Despite the waves of repetitious contradiction that greet the flat-lined curiosity of channel surfing, another social life emerges, largely untracked. The world is coming together in a variety of ways that over-arching processes such as economic globalization and the "War on Terror" cannot contain. Wildman Adams, who, with his brother Patch (once played in a movie by Robin Williams), leads the Gesundheit! Institute's cadre of clowns, who travels to war zones and cultures billed as dangerous in the West. The film *Clownin' Kabul* follows the clowns into the Hindu Kush of Afghanistan, where they were perhaps the first Westerners to perform in thirty years. In a presentation at our university, also often termed *remote*, Wildman Adams shared these observations:

> The leaders of violent movements are insane but cagily use ideology to gain personal power.
> The soldiers of such movements are children.
> Most people worldwide want to live in peace, raise nonsoldier children, and have safe, plentiful, and tasty food, as well as reliable shelter and some laughs.

The group's clowning displaces the singularity of forced ideology and creates ambiguity. At times, their desired effect is distraction, as in a heartbreaking scene in *Clownin' Kabul*, when a clown's sight gags fascinate a terribly burned child, so that her bandages may be changed without anesthetic. The clowns' performances also remind people—including the audiences, who often come from miles away to see the clowns live, and Westerners watching film footage—that human relations extend beyond and even contradict war. The performances in Afghanistan are rife with the irony of a tragic history. Now that the Russians have left, the civil war has gone latent, the Taliban have been shoved toward the borders or gone underground, and the Americans' "shock and awe" is sporadic and fitful, it is apparently time to send in the clowns. Cheer up, people!

Although Americans lead them, the clowns have acted for years as free agents, willing to go where they are invited as a purposeful edge of a complexly connected worldwide culture of resistance. The clowns pull people away from their entrenchment in dominant ideologies and the violent pathologies thrust upon them by revealing an extra share of identity that is beyond loyalty to nation, race, or creed. In his presentation, Adams described clowning for a line of children with machine guns in a Central American country. It took a series of gags, but when one began to laugh, they all did—at their comrades, the clowns, and themselves. Were they changed? Does this moment remain an uncanny singularity that they still remember? Is there space for such memories in their lives? Are these kids alive today?

Georges Bataille writes of "the accursed share," the energy left to us when our most basic needs are met. The share is a gift we have made into a curse by our choices of how to deploy this energy in the world. The energy itself is essentially ambiguous, as useful for clowning or healing as it is for killing or producing consumer goods. As teachers of persuasive writing, we want to uncover this ambiguity, for doubt, reflection, and the disarming conversations that are needed to counter the culture of mutual and multiple *jihads* that polarize the world and terrorize its peoples.

Writing in the *New York Times*, Amy Harmon reports that the Internet "democracy" of the 2004 presidential campaign, initially cited for reaching "the grass roots," became another series of havens for true believers, as candidates' bouncers patrolled their discussion forums and chat rooms, encouraging the like minded and ignoring "trolls"—supporters of other candidates—looking for trouble. Valdis Krebs's study of purchase patterns of ideological texts, from authors such as Al Franken, Molly Ivins, Ann Coulter, and Michael Savage, shows that consumers buy titles on the right or left exclusively, with only a few texts, such as Bob Woodward's *Bush at War* and Robert Baer's *Sleeping with the Devil: How Washington Sold Our Soul for Saudi Crude*, bridging the sides.[2] Harmon cites Eli Pariser, campaign director for Moveon.org (a group denied a Super Bowl ad spot for espousing anti-Bush views), who suggests that the purpose of Internet activism is not persuasion but mobilization: "'Changing people's minds is overrated,' Mr. Pariser said" (16).

Education, however, is often about change. Through it, we have been changed ourselves and have watched enough people convince themselves of some new idea, life plan, or value to know that change happens for many during their time in college. Despite the shattering revelations that follow from world events, change for most people comes more personally, through life crises, intellectual inquiry, or conversations with others who are different. Perhaps the cumulative mission of college, and of teachers of rhetoric and composition, is to find and enact the structures, forms, theories, and pedagogies needed to facilitate, invite, and encourage such change. Like many teachers, we have taught students to stay the course and limit their doubt. They learn to list the other side's best arguments so that the strength of these may be admitted while their message is countered. At its best, this is a graceful Tai Chi Chuan move, where the opposition is welcomed and absorbed. But Tai Chi also teaches that if we step either into or away from the dance of Push Hands, a new question will arise that will require a set of movements we have not yet learned or anticipated. This chapter describes and enacts a theory of persuasion as change that searches for such questions. It is informed by these arguments/assumptions:

- Persuasion works not through airtight arguments that others must honor because they cannot be denied but through "loose" exchanges and ongoing conversations that leave room for responses, pauses, and questions.
- Around and within each argument is an "accursed" or blessed share of doubt, which is an invitation to new thoughts, encounters, actions, and forms.
- As a pedagogy, loose talk operates through analysis of current positions and arguments at hand; overturning of these, often through entry into the world of those who don't agree; reclamations of questions to explore; and collaborative discussion and action, with room and need for continuing dissent or doubt.

In *Rhetoric: The Wit of Persuasion*, Walter Nash suggests that rhetoric involves external and internal relations. It is a social act, in which speakers or writers reach toward the audience. However, it is also a personal and inquisitive art, socially constituted, in which we listen to the world, decide what we think of its messages, and respond. Its dialogic quality contrasts with dialectic reasoning, as Nash illustrates through an image used by Zeno of Citium, founder of Stoicism, who represented the two styles of thought and communication, respectively, by a closed first and open palm:

> The closed first is dialectic reasoning, operating in the intimate world of the mind, insisting on the necessary consequences of necessary premises. The open hand is rhetoric, operating in the social world, dealing with the probable or negotiable outcome of generally agreed conditions. Zeno's imagery is very concrete and vivid; we can see the logician's fist as he clinches point after inescapable point, and

the orator's palm, turned outward to his audience, as he appeals to them to agree that such-and-such a thing might arguably be the case in this particular social or ethical instance. (201)

The palm holds the various possibilities for thought and action we find in the search for the good. Nietzsche theorized that the memory of pain and fear were regulators of human conduct. But he imagined himself as the prophet of another method of conduct, in which free humans, after shedding superstitions, would create an earthly home. The open palm and loose talk are not manifestations of the will to power but instead are the quieter modes of operation through which such shedding and mutual creation find chances to occur and take hold. Wildman Adams spoke of times when certain clowns in the group were overcome by the violence, pain, and death they witnessed. Such clowns, in his view, had to be removed from the audience until they had regained the clown's perspective, which allows for bottomless sadness but mixed in a well of life and joy. After all, Adams reasoned, we are clowns, and what people need from us is clowning, not more anger or grief. Their job, as he sees it, is to delve into the layers of misery and tease out the being that is not dead, or inhuman, yet.

Loose talk, then, unties the moorings to which we have become tied and sets us, at least for a moment, on a course toward other, often unseen, possibilities, including recoveries of altered versions of earlier selves we thought had been killed by our corruptions, resignations, compromises, and tragedies. It is related to Luba understandings of memory, encoded in stories and forms such as statues, ceremonial stools, and memory boards, but also experiences in daily life. The Luba have a nuanced vocabulary of memory that includes terms such as *bulanda*, the memory of suffering and hardship, and *kilàndà*, an outstanding debt, but also *milandu*, an unresolved dispute to which one is likely to return. As Mary and Allen Roberts note, in each case, "At issue are *connections*, sometimes salubrious, sometimes not, and the relationships that are accordingly presumed or posited. This idea of memory as connection is imaged by the related dialect of the Tawba, for whom '*mulando*' is a tree bridging a stream" (31).

Theodore Zeldin, the British philosopher and theorist of conversation, has traced loose talk as a historical principle enacting changes in societies by transforming personal relationships. In *An Intimate History of Humanity*, he retells the Western story of historical progress, but the hero this time is not technological progress, the utopian dream of transcendent reason that Stephen Toulmin traces in *Cosmopolis: The Hidden Agenda of Modernity*, nor is it the leveling of difference in the service of corporate capitalism that Bushites have called the fight for freedom. Instead, Zeldin traces the rise of more intimate and free-ranging ways of talking and knowing. He views the mindsets that limit how we relate to others and recognize ourselves as vestiges of earlier ways of existing.

However, the past also holds rich possibilities for being. He argues, for instance, that the hospitality of welcoming strangers into the home has been sadly diminished as "entertaining" acquaintances. The recovery and remaking of hospitality is essential to change:

> A new phase in history begins when this ancient and simple hospital-ity is succeeded by a deeper hospitality, which alters the direction of human ambition. That happens when people become hospitable to strange ideas, to opinions they have never heard before, to tradi-tions that seem totally alien to them, and when encounters with the unknown modify their view of themselves. (438–39)

He lists some of the cases and conditions that allow or encourage these modifications of views, including foreign travel, especially when seen as a necessity, rather than a lark; media coverage, when extended to a global condition, in which we hear more about famines and wars in other lands than we do the latest celebrity scandals from the United States; and the heightening of powers of empathy so that we want to know the points of view of the people we meet (439). He looks forward to a global "talk" where the real issues of life and how to live it can be addressed in an atmosphere of respect and learning.

In *Conversation: How Talk Can Change Our Lives*, Zeldin dis-tills his message by tracing historical change to transformations in conversation.

> Humans have already changed the world several times by the way they had conversations. There have been conversational revolutions which have been as important as wars and riots and famine. When problems have appeared insoluble, when life has seemed to be mean-ingless, when governments have been powerless, people have some-times found a way out by changing the subject of their conversation or the way they talked, or persons they talked to. (7)

He recounts profound changes in human talking, including the dialectic of Socrates, which called others into a process of questioning that could be so uncomfortable that it was judged corruption of youth; the man-nered but sociable discussions in the Renaissance salon, as modeled by Madame de Rambouillet; and the sparse language of science and plain speech philosophies that gave many people a shared language for work-ing toward truth. More recently, women's movements have changed the subjects of conversation and helped new understandings to emerge by showing how private and family life can reshape our ways of knowing and talking to include connections that span body and mind. As discussed below, the expanding circle of teachers and scholars of rhetoric have begun to reshape this conversation by considering how human ways of talk stem from culture and how the discourses of "mixed" cultures are now the norm.

Zeldin says that we are ready to loosen our tongues in a conversation that can go wherever the parties want or need it to in order to better appreciate each other and understand a complicated world. Many forces drive us toward division—besides culture, economics, religion, and race, Zeldin hones in on the separations foisted upon us by vocation. Work, he notes, increasingly consists of talk: We are all at a meeting. The danger, however, is that our talk will be narrowly concerned with the specific topics of a field or the urgencies of the problem at hand. Specialization is often unsatisfying. In isolation, each of us is boring, but others are potentially interesting. It is useless to defer to a fixed set of emotions, beliefs, and memories that constitute "an individual" or to a base of knowledge that constitutes "expertise." Instead we discover and create our selves through our actions in a changing, demanding, and uncertain world of others, where the concerns of the here and now find their meanings in relation to larger wholes. The accursed share, sign of plenty, which hegemonic ideologies and reductive theories have sought to kill, returns as a Potlatch of full and variegated talk we give to one another.

Loose talk is also part of the action of the blues in the lives of musicians and listeners. In *Blues Legacies and Black Feminism: Gertrude "Ma" Rainey, Bessie Smith, and Billie Holiday*, Angela Y. Davis shows how blues lyrics and performance that celebrated sexual power, the right to choose partners, and the freedom to struggle toward a self-directed life were among the ways black women announced their emancipation. Albert Murray's *Stomping the Blues* shows how the "Saturday night" culture built around the blues and the juke joint became a second way of living, different from both the church culture of Sunday and the restraints, violence, boredom, and back-breaking work that continued to characterize black experience after slavery. The blues on the loose could roam, as musicians often did, but even for a more place-bound audience, the blues spoke of getting through life's travails and heading toward freedom.

In the field of composition and rhetoric, different understandings of loose talk are also growing prominent. A myriad of writers have redescribed rhetorical practices as ways to rethink history and bring altered realities into being. These works are many and varied, but we would point especially to those falling into broad categories.

Theories of Rhetoric as the Nomadic Art of Wonder and Invention

Richard McKeon identified rhetoric as "an architectonic productive art" that brings into being new devices and methods for thought and action. In an introduction to McKeon's rhetorical thought, Mark Backman notes that the term *architectonic*, as used by McKeon, shares meanings with modern usage, where it refers to skill in structural design of architecture but also retains the ancient sense of a "master craftsman" who makes objects for use while envisioning these objects and how to make them (xxi). Rhetoric for McKeon not only is an intellectual tradition reaching back to the ancients—occasionally dismissed by the latest principles of knowing that claim universality—but also is the perennial contender that reemerges when claims to universal knowing subside.

In a technological age, rhetoric emerges as a conditional method for humanizing the effect of machines and helping humans to direct them. In a multicultural world, rhetoric is a practice of understanding that uses differences to generate more inclusive forms. Rhetoric thinks beyond disciplines and "interdisciplinarity"—itself a product of a culture of specialization—by arranging and connecting diverse elements in the pursuit of theoretical questions and practical actions. Rhetoric is a syncretic and generative practice that creates new knowledge by posing questions differently and uncovering connections that have gone unseen. Its creativity does not exclude or bracket history but often comes from recasting traditional forms and commonplaces in new contexts and questions.

While McKeon boldly imagines an architectonic rhetoric designing and crafting human thought and action, William Covino recasts rhetorical discourse as a collection of "forms of wondering" rife with generative "magic." Rather than studying rhetoric as a way to complete finished arguments, Covino rocks the lens to view it as "an art of wondering, and writing as a mode of avoiding rather than intending closure" (*The Art of Wondering* 9). He reclaims Plato as a rhetorician who wondered by pressing difficult questions through a range of assertions. Thinkers traditionally aligned with rhetoric are also seen in altered ways. Aristotle is no longer the forebear of Scholastic chop-logic and cloistered proofs but a restless wanderer in the world of rhetorical devices, searching for all the forms of persuasion and thought the world had produced. Cicero appears not as the progenitor of ornate speeches but as the philosopher who suggests that rhetoric must be an art of everything for which all the knowledge of humans is significant.

Covino's study of magic in rhetoric is also inventively contrary. While others have sought to demystify rhetorical processes, he returns to the opaque power of the rhetor, who through the magic of the word, brings new forms of thought and action into being and alters situations that seemed without recourse. He divides magic into two kinds. In its first sense, it is a "program of spells for arresting discourse" by which the powerful use shock, awe, guns, and money to constrain and paralyze the world (*Magic, Rhetoric, and Literacy* 8). The second, less common but more powerful, is a generative magic that disrupts official power and stratified situations, often by using multiple perspectives or ways of being, like a trickster changing shapes (9). This magic is akin to the carnival, as described by M. M. Bakhtin, which overturns established hierarchies and once unleashed is a threat to continue, even when its time assigned by the king's calendar is done.[3]

Intellectual Life and Social Consciousness Permeated by Rhetoric

Everything's an Argument is the title of Andrea Lunsford and John Ruskiewicz's textbook, and lately the title seems true to life in academe. Rhetorical thinking is omnipresent, practiced not only as a discipline or tradition but as a yeast fermenting within other disciplines or a space probe sending back pictures from their surfaces. Hayden White has brought rhetoric to history. Deidre N. McCloskey is a leading scholar of economics as rhetoric, while Mary Lay and others are part of the burgeoning study of medical rhetoric. Clifford Geertz, Mary Louise Pratt, and James Clifford study anthropology from the rhetorical point of view, while Dorothy Winsor has written on the rhetorical education, which is often painful, of engineers. Charles Bazerman has written on subjects including the codification of the experimental research article and the rhetorical and representational history of Edison's invention of the incandescent light bulb.

Rhetoric is not always a welcome guest in the American university's Germanic system, fed by research dollars to be a knowledge-machine with a culture valuing demonstrative truth. For the rhetorical gadfly, however, this very focus makes the American academy an easy mark. In *Laboratory Life: The Construction of Scientific Facts*, an anthropological study of the work and culture of the Jonas Salk Institute, Bruno Latour and Steve Woolgar show experimental science as obsessively devoted to textual production. At times, this book's descriptions of work in the lab are reminiscent of those of sweatshops seen in investigative reports on international capitalism or of the high pressure, breakdown-inducing, real estate office in David Mamet's *Glengarry, Glen Ross*. Latour and Woolgar find other metaphors as well:

> In a successful laboratory, there is likely to be constant excitement about finding new statements, proving them, extending their influence, setting up new instruments, chasing credibility, and reinvesting

it. The tension of a battalion headquarters at war, or of an executive
room in a period of crisis does not compare with the atmosphere of
a laboratory on a normal day! The tension is directed toward the
secretaries in efforts to persuade them to type manuscripts in time
and towards the technicians to affect the rapid order of animals and
supplies and to careful execution of routine assay work. (229)

Latour and Woolgar show scientific facts as constructed, typically
through a long process of argument. Scientists' activities and energies,
they suggest, are directed not toward an objective reality they are attempting to uncover but into the space where claims are made and countered
and possible facts inscribed and often rejected or overturned. Following
Jean Francois Lyotard's evocation of the "agonistic," Latour and Woolgar
term this site of contestation "the agonistic field," which they describe
as follows:

> An agonistic field is in many ways similar to any other political field
> of contention. Papers are launched which transform statement types.
> But the many positions which already make up the field influence that
> likelihood that any argument will have an effect. An operation may
> or may not be successful depending on the number of people in the
> field, the unexpectedness of the point, the personality and institutional
> attachment of the authors, the stakes, and the style of the paper. This
> is why scientific fields do not display the orderly pattern with which
> some analysts of science like to contrast the disorderly tremors of
> political life. The field of neuroendocrinology thus comprises a mul-
> titude of claims and many substances that exist only locally. (237)

Latour and Woolgar's provocative rendering points out that from
the detached viewpoint of anthropological observation, science's claims
to objectivity and universality may be a more comforting fiction or organizing myth than verifiable truth. However, this is not to devalue
such claims but only to shift them into a different register. Latour and
Woolgar see their study as another fiction, not likely to be truer than
others. Instead, their text expands the field of meaning and helps us to
see more of what is within it.

Identity as Similarly Permeated

Ever a social text, rhetoric cuts inward to begin to show how we are part
of the many arguments and discourses around us as we gradually craft
a mix of our own. Another work relating rhetoric to a field of inquiry,
Michael Billig's *Arguing and Thinking: A Rhetorical Approach to Social
Psychology*, evokes the social self as a loose set of shaggy, variegated

debates. Billig finds the metaphor "life is an argument" both accurate and liberating when compared with the others he entertains: "life is theatre" or "life is a game." Theatre and games frequently exceed their labels, run over their boundaries, and take on greater complexity as they wash into other parts of life. Is *Hamlet* just a play or something more as we use it as an occasion for debating if life is, after all, worth it? Games, too, are about more than they seem. Billig cites C. L. R. James's maxim from his study of cricket, *Beyond a Boundary*: "'[H]e who only knows of cricket, knows nothing of cricket'" (Billig 20). The metaphor of argument, conversely, easily expands. If social life is indeed an argument, even the scripts and codes we use to guide us are open to debate, agreement, dissent, revision, and invention.

Billig's master example is the Talmud, an ancient history of argument over right conduct and Godly living that must continually be discussed, sifted, and fought over as Jewish experience evolves. Other cultures and religions have similar experiences of debate and inquiry. In *Wisdom Sits in Places*, Keith Basso reports how the Western Apaches use traditional and more recent stories connected to places to regulate behaviors. In black Baptist churches, the fluid mix of scripture, sermon, prayer, and song is a collaborative mediation, mourning, and celebration that can change directions when a single member sends the right call. Irshad Manji's *The Trouble with Islam, a Muslim's Call for Reform in Her Faith* rehabilitates the Islamic practice of *ijtihad*, defined as questioning, talking, thinking, and relating. Buddhism, with its quiet meditative practice, asks its devotees to reflect upon their masters' wise world. As Lama Tarthang Tulku relays in *Openness Mind*, meditation integrates us with the richness of the world rather than isolating us from it or from other people.

Secular theories and practices of the self similarly include rhetoric. Freud originated a talking cure, while Tommy Wilhelm of Saul Bellow's *Seize the Day*, like many other modern characters, displays the anxiety of a discursive soul:

> You had to translate and translate, explain and explain, back and forth, and it was the punishment of hell itself not to understand or be understood, not to know the crazy from the sane, the wise from the fools, the young from the old or the sick from the well. The fathers were no fathers and the sons no sons. You had to talk with yourself in the daytime and reason with yourself at night. Who else was there to talk to in a city like New York? (91)

In a postmodern world, internal discourses fragment, blend, and morph into spectacular oddities. For instance, the astounding parodic novel *Et Tu, Babe*, by Mark Leyner, which seems increasingly realistic as times grow more strange, mixes discourses of self-help, voyeurism, celebrity super-ego, paranoia, and media scandal to create the distorted view of its narrator, the pumped-up megalomaniac "Mark Leyner," who plans to rule the world through hype, intimidation, and best-selling novels.

Rhetoric Seen as Necessarily "Mixed" and Plural

As rhetoric occupies all internal and external space, it also changes in form, generating new possibilities and including many voices. The emerging fields of multicultural, global, and comparative rhetoric are especially exciting. Groups and individuals once hidden, disrespected, denied, or silenced are changing the way discourse, persuasion, debate, composition, and conversation are understood and practiced in the academy and the wider world. These are among the writers who have studied the relations between language and culture and in some cases "traditional" academic discourse and others: bell hooks, Geneva Smitherman, Henry Louis Gates Jr., Juan Guerra, Victor Villanueva, Scott Lyons, Malea Powell, Danling Fu, LuMing Mao, Paul Matsuda, Laura Lai Long, Keith Gilyard, Gesa Kirsch, Helen Fox, Shirley Brice Heath, Anthony Petrosky, Andrea Fishman, Toni Morrison, Maxine Hong Kingston, Gloria Anzaldúa, Mark Salzman, Michael Blitz and C. Mark Hurlbert, and Denny Taylor and Catherine Dorsey-Gaines. Their studies often create a middle space between the cultures where an inclusive, sometimes conflicted, but also potentially syncretic discourse is the "native" tongue. During her Chair's Address at the 1995 Conference on College Composition and Communication, Jacqueline Jones Royster recounted how some people seemed to believe that her "black woman's" voice was real but her academician's was affected. "All my voices are authentic," she said.[4]

In *Rhetoric in Ancient China Fifth to Third Century B.C.E.: A Comparison with Classical Greek Rhetoric*, Xing Lu discusses a possible future for rhetorical study:

> The challenge that rhetorical studies will face in the twenty-first century is not simply to dismantle the notion that only Greek rhetoric legitimately belongs with the rhetorical canon, but, more importantly, to produce unpolarized, subtly nuanced, postethnocentric intellectual discourse and multicultural modes of intellectual inquiry. (308)

Lu practices such discourse, gliding between the ancient rhetorics of China and Greece. While she often organizes her thinking through comparison and contrast, her work suggests that the poles of difference and similarity are not adequate to describe these intermeshed but not entirely overlapping rhetorics. For instance, both provide traditions of inquiry and argument, which value analytical reasoning. However, while the

Western tradition tends to favor logic and deductive and inductive reasoning, Chinese rhetoric developed a sophisticated practice of persuasion and inquiry through analogy, which often served to open one's thinking through association, rather than narrow it with the precision of the Greek strategy called "hypothesis." Thus, "[w]hile Greek logic prioritized essence and certainty in the deductive and inductive processes, the Chinese made allowances for flexibility and probability . . . arguing that one's conclusion does not necessarily derive or depend upon one's premises and examples" (301).

While *ALT Dis: Alternative Discourses and the Academy* is also useful for building an understanding of rhetoric across cultures, its chapters often address our failures to find good ways to describe rhetorics that do not fit into singular cultures. Several contributors question and critique categories such as "alternative" and "hybrid," which still assume that only certain academic forms can be "traditional" and that culturally specific discourses are fundamental, even to discourses that fit no one culture. Laura Lai Long's "Full (dis)Course Meal" discusses the work using Hawaiian language and the discourse of her student Jacinta, who says, "The term 'alternative' is a bit problematic for me because I don't see my voice as alternative. It is my voice and therefore it can't be alternative for me" (144). Even Sidney I. Dobrin's critique of the concepts of alternative and hybrid discourse argues that all discourse is a mix of discourses, without the initial purity that the process of hybridization implies.[5]

The monovocal facade of rhetorical traditions has also been exposed by recent work. Cheryl Glenn's work rereads the classical Greek and Roman rhetorical traditions as a gendered text, showing how women have been ignored, patronized, and erased not only among the ancients but also by many of the scholars of rhetoric who followed. As Glenn tells it, her work on women in ancient Greek rhetoric, including Aspasia and Diotima, began as she stopped heeding what she had long heard:

> I began writing about Aspasia only when I began resisting the paternal narrative that assured me that she was either apocryphal or a glorified prostitute, that she could not be legitimized because her words appeared only in secondary sources, that she could not and did not represent an entire community of rhetorical women in ancient Greece. How could I write a map of rhetorical history if I did not have "proof," if I had instead only an angle, if Aspasia provided only a fragmented view rather than a panoramic vision of rhetoric? (5)

She proceeds with cautious imagination, using the available evidence to reanimate these intriguing figures. Her sketches appear in the spaces opened by her critiques of the dismissive opinions of the past, such as the sanctimonious views that as "virtuous woman," Sappho could not have been a lesbian, despite what the poems obviously say (21). Glenn notes with irony that Socrates' existence, like Aspasia's, is evidenced only in secondary sources (5), and his morality, too, was once impugned. Socrates, however, has overcome his demise and the shaky grounds of our knowledge of him to guide centuries of searchers. What about Aspasia? While Socrates resigned a role of potential power as a male and citizen to beckon others from the edge of the culture, Aspasia, a foreign-born "stranger" and a woman, made her way from the margins to the core. As a recognized member of the Athenian intelligentsia, she taught the skills of speech at her famous salon and, with her partner Pericles, spread democratic values. She also lived unconventionally, loving and cohabitating with Pericles, despite not being married, as well as taking part in the conversations of the men who ruled. Glenn quotes Marie Delcourt: "Aspasia was so brilliant she could not possibly be respectable" (*Rhetoric* 38).

This expansion and reanimation of the texts and traditions of rhetoric, performed by Glenn, Lu, and others, is mirrored by a similar reformation of academic discourse. In her essay in the *ALT Dis* collection, Jacqueline Jones Royster stresses that such discourses are socially constructed, plural, and connected to the discourse of the wider world (75). Malea Powell maps her own literacy, using the figure of the crossroads, where no discourse tells the sum of the story:

> One thing I know for sure. My own scholarly practices are firmly rooted at the crossroads between what Gerald Vizenor calls "trickster hermeneutics" ("the uncertain humor and shimmer of survivance") and "narrative chance" ("the counter causes in language games") (1994, 15;66). This crossroads offers points of entry into discourses, language games, meant to discipline me and those like me. A signpost reads "look for other ways of being here." (14)

Taken together, these three manifestations of the new rhetorical consciousness reveal a world where discourse is inescapable but never pure, singular, or fixed. Instead, the world's discourses are always coming into being and sweeping its creatures along with them. Inquiry and writing in such a world may begin locally and individually, with the problems presented by one's own life or experience, but they take on additional meanings and resonance as they extend to include a variety of others. Writers prepare for such a world by building their collections of cultural and discursive strategies. In *Writing the New Ethnography*, H. L. (Bud) Goodall Jr. argues that the best writing also finds patterns of connection that allow others to follow the writer's path:

Great writing is naturally *dialogic*. It is a medium, a message, that furthers our journey. Writers write to discover, and to further themselves, *and* they write for audiences *outside* of themselves. They have stories borne of personal experience that don't end with just retelling the personal experience, but instead are designed—through conscious, stylistic deployments of language—to connect readers to larger patterns of lived experience and cultural meaning. Writers learn to find storylines by paying attention to their selves in relation to the details and patterns of everyday life, and reading large the potential for connection. It is through the process of writing that we connect those details and patterns back to our selves and, through the magic of language, to something else. Which is to say, we connect our accounts to the larger story, to the bigger plot, to the discovery of our part in the nature and purpose of persons and things. That is the mystery, and that is the quest, that for a writer is always *there*. (41–42)

Goodall's message to experienced writers concerning the constant mystery of connection is also important for students to hear. As writers including Paul Heilker and Bruce Ballenger have suggested, students may learn best if thesis-driven writing is supplanted with an inquisitive essayistic approach. Rather than showcasing their expertise or arguing a fixed position, students persuading via exploration practice writing as a process of connection, through which old understandings and versions of the self yield to those made in the world, through inquiry and writing. For the audience, persuasion comes via the journey that moves them toward an understanding they have not reached before and invites them to think with the text, forming their own connections in relation to those the writer presents. This empathy between reader and writer, while seldom leading to full agreement, builds a commonality of experience and humanizes the argument, making its legitimacy hard to deny. Such dialogic writing helps to span cultures by allowing the inclusion of multiple viewpoints and welcoming disagreement as it becomes conversation, understanding, or renewed questioning.

In "Contrastive Rhetoric: A Must in Cross-cultural Inquiries," Haixia Lan stresses the difference in understandings of being between Chinese and Western philosophy and rhetoric. For instance, in a Western way of thinking, the being of an object—Lan uses a table as an example—derives from the idealized form of "table" as a pure form. Any particular table resides a few steps away from this form as a peculiar, or common, example of how the form takes its earthbound shape. The Chinese idea of table, however, fixes the particular in a pattern of interrelationships that inscribes the room or dwelling as a whole. Bruno Snell, in *The Discovery of Mind in the Poetry and Philosophy of Ancient Greece*, notes that language was similarly unfixed in pre-Socratic Greece and that we might be able to approach middle ground in an ancient world. Processes of invention, persuasion, and rhetorical education also enact such differences. Lan particularly examines the rendering of "creativity" in Chinese tradition. "According to the Confucian tradition," she notes, "[a] sage is consummate communicator. The character sage in Chinese consists of the graphs for ear, mouth, and king." Becoming a sage is a social process: "By observing, mimicking, reflecting upon ritualistic communication behaviors, we gradually become more and more fully participating members of our cultural/discursive communities." Eventually, fluent improvisation and purposeful invention characterizes the wisdom of the sage: "As cultural ideals, which embody the Tao, become natural to us, we interpret these cultural norms for each given situation, thus becoming creative ourselves" (71).

As a teacher of writing in the multicultural United States, Lan seeks to find her improvisational sage-hood through acts of questioning, invention, and reflection that include "fostering students' sensitivity to their own dissonance/puzzlement" and "assisting them in braving the unknown, in refining their judgment, and in creating new possibilities." This pedagogy includes the perspective of Chinese rhetoric:

> Reflecting upon my own practice of teaching writing as inquiry, I've realized how the process is compatible with my own culture's propensity for correlative thinking, correlative learning, and correlative teaching. In other words, although writing as inquiry is indeed very Western, in a rather important way, it is also Chinese. (76)

We find that using an inquisitive approach to composition and inviting students to do the same can help us to advance toward a more inclusive and dialogic method of learning. As this chapter turns more directly to practical considerations, we point to and will explicate two overall strategies that guide our teaching of persuasion:

Fostering a flexible and reflective approach to multi-persuasion
Recasting "courses" and "the academy" as problem-centered collaborations

One of our ongoing efforts is to find pedagogies of difference and connection, where students learn to persuade diverse audiences as they write multiple but linked texts. Students writing multi-argument projects— we've included a prompt for such work as "A Palette for Persuasion" in the pedagogic materials below—orchestrate different opinions and worldviews within multiple genres and forms and often blend argument and inquiry.

Judy Cornish's "What Comes after Death: A Consideration of the Arguments" combines argument and analysis to persuade others, as Cornish finds out for herself. The project includes dialogues with a Catholic priest and several Mormon women; a research essay on views of death from other religions; and interdisciplinary analysis of cyclical life that describes a painting by M. C. Escher in relation to various natural processes, such as photosynthesis and cellular respiration. She adds a personal narrative on a series of odd recognitions and premonitions involving an acquaintance. How are these to be explained? In a formal argument late in the project that anchors the rest, she writes:

> I can't say that through this exploration I've reached a conclusion and settled for myself the question of what comes after death. To me, it seems rash and foolhardy to claim to know beyond a doubt what follows life on this planet. However, we can look at what is more likely, and can evaluate our own experiences to formulate a hypothesis. My own belief is that reincarnation is more probable than one life/one death, because of the cyclical nature of the world around us; because I see patterning of the whole in the smaller part, and because I see all living organisms following seasonal and daily rhythms.

Nadine Galinsky's project on the future of the women's movement performs a similar provisional, in-process persuasion. She retraces many strands of the movement as she has known it and reweaves them into a form she finds inclusive and empowering. In her analysis of her project, she writes, "The process of developing this argument was really one of clarifying some of my own ideas as I plan for my future." However, the feminism she discovers has the potential to touch everyone in the culture. Galinsky enacts this collaboration in a formal argument drawing upon Judith Posner, Rene Denfeld, Gloria Steinem, and Susan Estrich, as well as a collection of pop culture sources ranging from the hip-hop star Queen Latifah to the Pepsi-executive-turned-full-time-homemaker Brenda Barnes. Galinsky writes an imaginative dialogue in which a group of friends on a back porch discuss the problems of the misogyny encountered in the workplace, at home, and with politicians and doctors. However, the group also sees that the women's movement has made a difference. Without it, such conversations would not occur. The group concludes support for women, by men and other women, is needed even in cases where agreement about issues is not reached. Galinsky writes:

We can make choices, and choose again if those choices don't work.
We can achieve as much or as little as we want, and we are not
responsible for the choices our fellow women make. We can work
to educate women and resolve problems such as domestic violence
and sexual assault, but with a balanced approach that encourages
women to be strong and empowered. We can disagree and debate,
but still maintain respect for each other.

Such work supports Sidney I. Dobrin's contention that discourse contains both vestiges of the theories and tongues we carry with us into new
situations and "passing theories," which we may adopt or dispense with,
that show the possibilities of who we are becoming (53). Students can
begin to participate in such dialogic loose talk by inventing and revising
their projects with partners or in small groups, where interlocutors play
both "devil's" and "angel's" advocate as they take turns supporting and
speaking against the arguments posed by others. Students can then work
together to research the best evidence to support various sides of a particular debate and stretch the conceptual limits with which their debate
began. We have structured this collaboration by: pairing students; asking
each to write an argument on or exploration of an issue; and then asking
the partner both to play both Angel's and Devil's advocate for this work
by restating it differently or amplifying it, asking questions, sharing experiences, or providing additional evidence or other lines of reasoning.

Part of the enjoyment students have with rhetoric comes from finding,
studying, and reusing the cornucopia of forms for persuasion. Using a
strategy we call "tiny interventions," for instance, students use the form
of the post-it note to implant small thoughts in the minds of unsuspecting
others. This has led, for instance, to the posting of philosophic questions
in the staff break room of our local McDonald's, where those making
burgers and fries later reportedly continued the multifaceted discussion
of subjects such as "If there is a God, how do you know?" and "Why
do people deny their faults?" Another student combated problematic
roommates not with nagging ("PLEASE clean up after yourselves") but
with kindness: "Hey, hope you are okay and your test went well. Please
do these dishes so we can use them tonight. I'm cooking."

Persuasive interventions also occur through performance. The theatre
troupe led by Marc D. Rich from California State University, Long Beach,
makes audience members into actors through scenarios regarding issues
of diversity and racism. For instance, audience members take turns playing the part of an apartment-dweller who hears her roommate's old friend
espouse a racist view in the midst of a long story about a failure to land a
high-paying job. The friend says that he is "working like a Mexican," as

a landscaper. The beer-drinking roommate and the racist friend answer admonishments from the audience-member-turned-actor with calls to "lighten up." It was only a joke. Pushing harder to show why the remark was offensive leads the friend to leave the room and the roommate to say that while the friend is a jerk at times, he is still a friend and should be made to feel welcome. Do you want to risk alienating the roommate, who you need to pay rent and whose company you have enjoyed? Will any arguments you make be convincing? Must these arguments be made regardless, as a moral purpose is at stake? What strategies can be invented to make a productive difference? This performance leads us to review our repertoires and leaves us with questions about our roles in fighting or tolerating racism.[6]

The work of performance artists Guillermo Gómez-Peña and Roberto Sifuentes similarly works to bring racist views, stereotyping, and fears about cultural crossing into the open. Their *Temple of Confessions* installation and performance used the cultural form of diorama, popular in both museums and Mexican churches, to "display" subjects of cultural fear, especially for white Americans. Sifuentes posed as a "holy gang member" in a chamber with the equally ambiguous label, "The Chapel of Desire," which included a pre-Columbian temple made from Styrofoam. In the "Temple of Fears," meanwhile, Gómez-Peña sat on a toilet and was disguised as a curio shop salesman marketing spiritual talismans. The image again points out its construction:

> Just as in Roberto's case, I looked "authentic." (I could have been an indigenous shaman in a diorama sponsored by *National Geographic*). But as viewers got closer to my box, they began to be aware of the artifice, and I started to look like a generic Benneton primitive—a designer shaman created by the wizardry of MTV. (38)

Perhaps because of the confessional intent of the project, members of the audience seemed to want to regard the holy figure as real:

> Visitors attempted to establish a personal "spiritual" connection with me. Their eyes looked desperately for mine. If I decided to engage in a personalized relation with them (mainly through eye contact, symbolic hand motions or subvocalizing), emotions began to pour from both sides: sadness, vulnerability, guilt, anger, tenderness. Some people cried, and, in doing so, they made me cry. Some expressed their sexual desire for me, and I discreetly reciprocated. Others spewed their hatred, their contempt and their fear, and I willingly took it. At least a third of the visitors eventually decided to kneel and confess. (38)

Confessions were also recorded using microphones and tape recorders, written on cards and deposited in an urn, or called in on an 800 number. Those collected in *Dangerous Border Crossers* show fear: "When I go on vacation to the Yucatan this winter, I don't want to get kidnapped or killed." They also performed loathing: "I hate you because I understand you." Sometimes they modeled judgment: "You people treat your women like slaves and your pets like shit." At other times there was desire: "I want to be seen as true advocate of your culture; as righteous and not as a 'white liberal' and to make love to a Latina with a firm body" (41–42).

Such confessions may reify old views, but they may also make room for passing theories, dialogue, and change by beginning to clear out the views, experiences, and inherited biases that prevent us from seeing for ourselves and from hearing and coming to know others. In a multicultural world that threatens at times to move past the contact zone of cultural difference and become a place of polarization and entrenchment, strategies for restarting the process of community are sorely needed.

In *Bowling Alone: The Collapse and Revival of American Community*, Robert D. Putnam reveals another potential loss of community. He reports that volunteerism and other forms of social interaction that cut across class and racial divides, such as participation in service organizations and bowling leagues, declined sharply in the last third of the twentieth century. The result has been a loss in "social capital," a term that, he notes, has been independently invented at least six times by different theorists. He defines it as follows:

> Whereas physical capital refers to physical objects and human capital refers to properties of individuals, social capital refers to connections among individuals—social networks and the norms of reciprocity and trustworthiness that arise from them. In that sense social capital is closely related to what some have called "civic virtue." The difference is that "social capital" calls attention to the fact that civic virtue is most powerful when embedded in a dense network of reciprocal social relations. A society of many virtuous but isolated individuals is not necessarily rich in social capital. (19)

It will take a society-wide effort to reverse this trend toward isolationism, build social capital, and create a common culture in which all people are included. Structural changes are needed, even in the forms and structures of communication. For teachers, even the usual classroom dynamics must be called into question. This is why we have been experimenting increasingly with a Study Circle approach.

Study Circles are loose structures that bring people together to form creative responses to social problems. Used either in place of or as an enhancement to traditional class structures, they allow teachers, students, and community partners to work together and find a common purpose based upon mutual learning and positive action. While Study Circles often include a facilitator or guide, they are notably nonhierarchical and make use of the expertise and interest of all members. While the group may form with a particular problem in mind, its members work together to set an agenda, plan a course of study, and decide on appropriate actions. Although the group should be focused, it must also be open to purposeful wandering as one problem merges with others and the ambiguity of proposed actions and "solutions" begins to show itself. The goal is to find and perform actions that all can agree to, even when the group begins with a broad base of opinions. While the roles (teacher and student) and structures (grades, credit hours, term limits, tuitions, and fees) of academic culture may keep college courses from becoming Study Circles, similar open approaches can be used to connect experts and learners from inside and outside higher education to study complex problems with political, economic, social, and environmental dimensions. A class with a sense of shared inquiry may emulate a Study Circle without being supplanted by one.

Similar approaches have also been used in several of the communities and projects Putnam discusses in his follow-up to *Bowling Alone*, entitled *Better Together: Restoring the American Community*. The bowling team may not be making a comeback, but new forms for friendship across political lines, volunteerism, and collective action are (re-) emerging. Putnam reports on new patterns for collaborative engagement, including Internet job boards, public art projects, and political actions of various kinds.

In the academy, this trend can be traced by the rise of community service learning and national initiatives such as the American Democracy Project, designed to foster civic engagement. The metaphor of the "Ivory Tower" is giving way, but the next master image is not yet clear. Perhaps it will be the expanding circle, like the magic circles envisioned by some cultures that mark the local as the site of focused care but through concentric rings or spirals connect to the rest of the world as well. George Venn's *Marking the Magic Circle* is a multi-text combining imaginative and analytic writing focused upon this theme. As a young person, Venn grew to understand that even as he ventured further into the world, the Northwest of the Unites States was his home. He then added to this awareness through study of the circle as cartographic form:

> Later, I learned that people universally scribe a similar sacred circle with their lives and homes at the center, a circle with a meaningful series of concentric rings spiraling outward from that center toward

an edge—an opening, a passageway to the infinite, the unknown. Though often hidden from us, that magic circle and its positions have long given centuries of arrangement and expression to human life. (4–5)

Venn sees his work as a poet, novelist, essayist, and editor as the marking of the circle of his region, which extends concentrically outside the Northwest and into the wider world. This region is not a province or an outpost on the far edge of a world but a microcosm that includes or samples the whole.

Teaching within a microcosm may similarly entail joining with others to inscribe the circle as a home placed within a region and world. For instance, students at our university, like many on campuses around the country, are participating in service learning projects through which they study and act upon the local manifestations of global issues. Some are working on a Community Garden that is part of an interdisciplinary study of community food systems. This, in turn, connects with a statewide initiative begun by Oregon Campus Compact to address the many issues that have made this by some measures one of the hungriest of states.[7] The Garden arose from a Leadership in Service Study Circle for students experienced or keenly interested in community service. The Garden provides better food than much of that collected in food drives and distributed in the food baskets upon which people increasingly depend as governmental programs such as the one for food stamps are cut. In a related project, students participated in a large food gleaning from area farms and stores that again gathered fresh local produce for people who needed it.

A Study Circle that includes undergraduates (including international students), high school teachers, university faculty, and community members is also at the heart of the oral history and public art project in Eastern Oregon called the People's History of the Wallowas (referring to the Wallowa Mountains). The group has studied "The Hen Party," a legendary but real local group of women who rode trails and horse-camped in the mountains each summer, starting during World War I and extending into the 1960s. The Hen Party was known for "roughing it"; for instance, they never used a tent and often took their horses into tight spots. Party members developed and enacted a core philosophy of self-reliance, freewheeling conversation, and intrepid adventure—mixed with a sense of humor—that helped to set the ecological ethic of the region, insisting that the mountains they roamed were kept pristine and tracking those who littered. The project's products, so far, have included a large bronze bell commemorating the Hen Party, now mounted at the place where they entered the mountains each year, and an oral history with one of their surviving members. The group filmed a documentary about the Hen Party that included a pack trip into the mountains.

While such circles do not alleviate conflicts among people or necessarily make us see difference as beneficial, they do help to provide a sense of provisional community by asking people of different views and background to work together for the common good. A project like the Community Garden comes into being when a core of people agree that is the right thing to do and are willing to collaboratively and creatively make it happen. Such practices also build community by establishing networks of relations that span the usual bounds, as faculty, students, staff, and community members come to converse and create. Susan Wells suggests in "Rogue Cops and Health Care: What Do We Want from Public Writing?" that preexistent public discourses and spaces may not exist. She says of the ready-made *polis* that waits for us in our minds, "That space is so intently imagined that we think it must be real—just like live theatre or downtown department stores" (326). Writing teachers and students interested in working within public space need to create it through reflection upon rhetorical purposes, audiences, and occasions. She writes, "Public speech is a performance in time, located at specific historical junctions, temporary and unstable, even though it is imagined as a location in space, always available, with secure and discernible borders" (326–327).

The Hen Party project and the Community Garden make use of existing spaces, including museums and greenhouses, and structures of support, from the expertise of botany and agriculture faculty and community food bank directors in the case of the Garden to the resources of a countywide history project for the Hen Party work. However, new forms are also being created, and an audience, interlocutors, and collaborators are being found. The Garden, for instance, has literally made a common space of turned dirt and plants in rows where weedy grass was growing. The Hen Party project has spawned continuing interest in the community, from old and young, and uncovered memories and materials from people in the region who know of or were changed by this group. Their film showing will feature a memory board for audience members to add to the wealth of information about the Hen Party and the mountains.

While these circles are special cases within the curriculum, their practices of community need to be transported to other college courses. Service learning offers many possibilities. Students in our English-Writing program complete service projects with a variety of agencies as course projects in an upper-division technical writing course. However, even more traditional "academic" courses can also form collaborative connections through the processes of research, reflection, and action. A course in expository writing can find a center through the open study of "academic discourse" and its engagements with the world, while a literature course focused on a famous writer can do the same by asking all participants to gather research together and create a common display or installation rather than or in addition to individual essays.

Open structures for collaboration and reflection can also be brought to the study of persuasion. Our 200-level Argumentation course complicates the concept of argument by considering the critiques of thinkers including Theodore Zeldin, William Covino, and the celebrity lawyer Gerry Spence, whose *How to Argue and Win Every Time* unwinds the terms *argue* and *win* as they have been practiced in the culture and argues for measures of success that include learning to unlock one's voice while learning to better hear others. Meanwhile, the upper-division seminar in Interdisciplinary Rhetoric practices loose talk by stretching the limits of academic discourse in a project in which students consider the limits, blind spots, and exclusions of an example of academic discourse, then rewrite it using new forms to bring in additional dimensions or viewpoints. A writing prompt for this project is on the Web.

We close this chapter with musings, exercises, and readings for enacting persuasion as conversation leading to change.

Musing: Practicing an "Either/And" Consciousness

Many students find courses in argumentation immediately off-putting, partly because the arguments they have witnessed in the culture involve attacking others or defending positions that seem far too simplistic to apply to real life. However, involvement in public debates is vital if a spirit of participatory democracy is to grow in the world. The planet and its people face difficult problems: finite resources, many mouths to feed, a complex environment to understand and interact with. Perhaps we can enter into these issues and overcome the attack mode of persuasion first by attempting not to argue but to find out. For instance, how much do you know about the basic resources and environmental effects of the community or campus in which you live? Where does its water come from? What watershed do you live in? How is the water you use treated? How is power generated? What are the sources of fuel for transportation, heating, and other needs? How does the design of the community lead to their use or misuse? What are the community's sources of food? What locally produced food can be found and who can access it? Who goes hungry and why?

What kinds of waste does the community generate? How are these processed? Where do they go? What is the community putting into the air and water? Why? What recycling options are available? Where does hazardous waste go?

You may also want to turn this research toward a list of people to contact or interview. Who is in charge of environmental policy or compliance in the community? Most city governments have such a person, and many campuses do as well. What federal, state, or local agencies do environmental work in your area? How can you contact them with questions? What citizens groups, organizations, or clubs are active around you? Does your university have an Environmental Club?

Who are the major polluters in your area? You may think here of large industries, but do not forget that in most places private citizens driving each day are the leading cause of air pollution. Similarly, in arid places, especially, people who overwater their lawns or cut their grass to short may use more water than any other group.

When working through such an agenda, it can be wise not to try immediately to put forth an argument for change, even as you begin to see that change may be necessary or desirable. Be sure to speak with others you meet along the way about options they see to make the community healthier and more sustainable and to search especially for groups of people you would like to work with. You will find that the most viable solutions often arise from dialogue, group action, and awareness-raising in the community. Often it helps even to know what people who oppose you are thinking and what they value so that you can eventually reach out to them using ways of thinking they will appreciate. Through such dialogue and ongoing research, you will develop an "either/and consciousness" that is able both to see why various viewpoints conflict and to look for areas of agreement that hold potential for building relationships between people and finding solutions that many can support in good conscience.

Here are some materials to turn argument into inquiry by reintroducing the complexity of issues and ideas in the world. The first exercise, Turning Commonplaces to Conversations, is both critical and creative as we stop listening to the muzak that permeates the culture and begin to compose more valid viewpoints. The second, Requests for a Study Circle, presumes an alternative course structure but can also be used in smaller ways to craft a more democratic approach to conventional courses or can be used in non-course contexts, wherever a good start is needed for a group.

The writing project, the Palette of Persuasion, can be used as it is written, as a prompt for generating multi-genre, multimedia arguments that use both the forms that dominate cultural debates and some more suitable for the steady conversation where change is more likely to occur. It can also be used as a list, to add to or shorten, to help us reply rhetorically to the problems we engage. For instance, one group or Study Circle in a course structured upon issues in the community or culture may find a documentary film the best product for their work, while others may concentrate on a letter-writing campaign, a petition drive or an anthology of essays.

Exercise 3.1: Turning Commonplaces to Conversations

Ideological commonplaces are shared beliefs that often color our thoughts or inspire our actions. Some Americans hang flags from their windows or porches on national holidays or when signs of trouble surface because they believe in the commonplace that citizenship means showing their patriotism and pride in the flag of our country, which has been through so much. Our national anthem, a song valorizing the flag, may be one of the sources of this commonplace. As you know, the song tells a story about the bombing of Fort McHenry by the British during the War of 1812. The flag makes it through the fierce bombardment, just as you hope your flag will survive any contemporary disaster.

Other commonplaces also affect the lives of Americans. For instance, the nation's work ethic, often traced to the Puritans, says that if you work hard, you will succeed. We admire people who are "self-made," but we also like the "underdog," who is still scrapping, as well as those who have overcome reversals and adversity. We are often a forgiving people and believe in giving others a second chance. For us, starting over may be painful, but it is also a new opportunity.

Many commonplaces help to define not the culture as a whole but groups within it. For instance, people in Paris are said to value solitude and chances for reflection and the company of those who do as well. More than half the population of the city lives alone. Smaller groups, such as circles of friends and families, also share beliefs, which sometimes become "inside jokes." For instance, your friends and family may share certain beliefs about you—that you are high-strung, a neat freak, or an amazing procrastinator—and these may lead to frequent teasing. Occasionally, too, we develop personal commonplaces that set us apart. Perhaps, for instance, you believe that no one should marry or that money should be kept crumpled in your pocket as a sign of your disrespect for it. The blanket-toting Linus in the old *Peanuts* comic strip and TV specials believed with all his heart in The Great Pumpkin, who would rise out of the most sincere and well-meaning pumpkin patch to deliver his toys.

Whether commonplaces are silly, serious, personal, or shared, they all come from somewhere. This is sometimes hard to believe, as some commonplaces are so deeply buried in us we can no longer see their sources. Rhetorical education necessitates digging these out for examination and helping others, upon occasion, to do the same. Here is an exercise for beginning:

1. Identify a commonplace that has been significant to you. It may be one you believe in or one you have rejected. It may be shared by many in your culture, prevalent among your family or friends, or shared by you and a few others.

2. Consider these questions, working first by yourself and then with a partner or group:
   • How do you see this commonplace reflected in your life or those around you?
   • What are the sources of this commonplace, as you see them?
   • What sorts of actions or arguments do the commonplaces allow, encourage, or support?
   • What actions or arguments do they resist or repress?
   • What can be said against this commonplace?

3. Think of a story that shows your involvement with the commonplace. Tell it to the group.

4. In a piece of writing of one or two pages, consider the following:
   • Describe the commonplace and the way you see it being used.
   • Describe the sources of your interest in it.
   • List some of the reasons for believing in it.
   • List reasons for doubting it or disagreeing with it.
   • Describe your own current relation to it. Are you a doubter or a believer? Would you like to change the commonplace? Get others to adopt it? Ask everyone to question it?
   • Consider the function of the commonplace for you or the culture or group. What does it inspire? What does it prevent? Who does it help or hurt? What does it bring to light? What does it hide or keep out?

5. Share your results in a group or with the whole class.

Exercise 3.2: Requests for a Study Circle

Study Circles are structures for bringing people together to form creative responses to community problems. Although they often include a facilitator, they are notably nonhierarchical and make use of the expertise and interest of all members. In a better future, when the college experience is freed from the scaffolding of grades, credit hours, majors, and requirements, which have often distracted us from a focus on learning, flexible structures for common inquiry, such as Study Circles, may remain.

As well as an alternative way to study content and take action, Study Circles are experiments in self-governance and collaboration. While the experience of a Study Circle is nonrepeatable, its lessons about working with others to find and structure a project can carry over to the rest of your life. The exercise below is one we have used with Study Circles, but it also should be useful to other collaborations in college courses.

While our experiences this term may focus on intellectual study or the building of skills, we should also consider our work an exercise in collaborative decision making and governance. Rather than listing pre-set rules of behavior, let's work to agree on what we expect from each other and ourselves. We can begin with a series of requests suggesting how members of the group should behave toward one another and work together. Here are some sample requests from other courses:

- Please do the reading and come prepared with questions and comments.
- Don't disregard the views of others just because you disagree. Use disagreement as an invitation to learn more.
- Look for pleasure in the fact that sometimes others know more about a subject than you do.
- Remember that you have a responsibility to share your knowledge and understanding with others. Don't be afraid to speak.
- Let's make this more than a class, with work that connects us as humans rather than separates us as teachers and students.

You may want to begin such a list now, then continue to modify it as your circle continues to round into form. Do you want to limit the requests to a certain number in order to make sure that they don't become diluted by volume?

For more on how and why to use Study Circles, see www.study-circles.org.

Project: A Palette for Persuasion

A painter's palette is not only for separating colors but also for mixing them into unusual but often appropriate combinations and colors. As rhetoricians and writers, we also need an ability to mix and match different strategies, depending upon our purposes, the needs and disposition of the audience or others in the debate, and the nature of the occasion and the issue at hand. Often, arguing a single position involves many shifts in style and method as the situation around us changes or new contexts arise. The Greek term *kairos*, roughly translated as "timing," has long been a key but puzzling term for rhetoricians, since it suggests that some arguments and ways of making arguments become more palatable at certain times—and can go out of favor as well.

The sections that follow offer alternative ways of arguing that can be used in your project to build a persuasive project that functions in flexible ways.

A Formal Argument in the Academic Style

The old standby of academic culture remains an important intellectual strategy for developing a reasoned, clear, and well-supported argument. In this piece, you should state a position and use a range of evidence to support it. You may include support from your personal experience, but you should also bring other support to bear, including information gathered through research. You should anticipate some of the counters or criticisms other thinking people might think of in response to your argument and try to answer their claims. You should show that you understand both your argument and its counters well enough to see the strongest and weakest points of each. In the end, you should show why you believe your position is the right or best one. Make clear what you see as the determining factors.

A Dialogue

Often, persuasion occurs best through conversations, discussions, or debates among people who respect one another. In this piece, you will project yourself explaining, defending, and arguing on behalf of your views to another person or a group of other people. You can create a scenario that interests you. For example, it might be:

> a relaxed dinner conversation with a friend
>
> a conversation with a child who is hard to convince
>
> an internal argument where different parts of you argue different positions or you defend a view against your internal critic
>
> a public or private meeting of a group where you have been invited to speak or put yourself on a speakers' list
>
> a formal debate staged by an interested group
>
> a wilderness camp where you are in the company of people with various opinions or who do not agree with you

Other scenarios would also be fine, but no matter what, it is important that you are talking with a person or group who doesn't completely agree with you. They don't have to be fully against you, either. For instance, a friend might not have a strong opinion about the issue but might be interested in finding out why you think as you do. If you are debating in front of a group, you might have supporters in the crowd making comments and asking questions, as well as people who don't agree with you criticizing your views and arguing other positions.

When you write this piece, be clear about the scenario. Set the scene for us. Then, write the actual dialogue as a playscript. You can use physical descriptions instead of names if the scenario has you speaking to people you don't know well. If you want to, you can make up a character to state your views, rather than imagining doing it yourself.

You should try to show, however, that you can state your opinion clearly, perhaps in different ways as the discussion goes on, and that you can support it with a range of evidence and rhetorical strategies. Also, show how you might handle challenges to your position.

Do you have to convince everyone in the end? Not necessarily. Convincing people is hard to do. But see if you can get them to think. And think about what they are saying. One possible outcome for this piece is to use it to further develop your position, understand it better, and state why you support it. Another possible outcome is to find a middle ground or at least a new respect for the positions of others. See where your scenario and characters take you.

A Sound Bite

While a dialogue or discussion often allows you to develop your views in length, the media culture we live in tends to chop arguments into very small chunks that are easily digested by a busy and sometimes scanning audience. The "soundbite" is often criticized for "dumbing down" public discourse by changing nuanced positions into catchy slogans and simplifying complicated debates into two opposed positions, but it remains an omnipresent form in an accelerating culture. Describe a scenario where you or a spokesperson you create has only about twenty seconds to say something convincing. Perhaps it is at the end of a TV debate show where the host gives the participants one last chance to persuade the audience. Perhaps it is at the end of a meeting that has run late where you are given only a chance to preview your views, which will be featured at the next meeting. Perhaps it is a TV talk show about to go to a commercial or a radio commercial where only words and sound can be used. What would you or your worthy character say that would stick in people's minds as they think more about the issue?

A Persuasive Image

Pictures, as they say, speak louder than words, and many times this is shown even by words that paint a picture. In the 1960s, for instance, Rachel Carson's *Silent Spring* inspired many people to join the environmental movement by showing us a world dead from toxic pollutants; a few years later, television images of American dead and wounded from the Vietnam War convinced viewers that the United States should pull out. What images have made an impact on your life and the positions you hold? Now think about a persuasive image related to this project or the position you are arguing. What do you see? Where do you see it presented? Are words needed to complement the image? Or should words create it? Write, draw, paint, or otherwise create a persuasive image. Then, in paragraph form, write about the scenario you imagine for its use and describe the audience who you hope it engages.

Additional Arguments

Arguments come in many genres of writing, media, and forms in our culture. Here is a list of possibilities for you to consider or develop for your project:

post-it note	quotation	documentary
postcard	parable	TV commercial
poem	flash-mob	e-mail
bumper sticker	blog	campaign speech
T-shirt	song	brochure
letter to the editor	picket sign	newsletter
voter's pamphlet	chant	testimonial
cartoon	question	

What items would you add? Which two or three would you like to develop for your project? You may want to try several to find those that work the best. Again, include a scenario that sets the scene for the use of the forms you select.

An Analysis of Your Work

Here is a chance to think about the choices you have made and methods you have used to construct your argument. Analyze your work, considering some of the following questions:

- What purpose or purposes did you set out to fulfill? Did your purpose change along the way? If so, how is this change reflected in your final project?
- What attitudes in the audience or ideas about your subject did you wish to change? How did you go about doing this? What attitudes or ideas about the subject did you wish to affirm?
- Did you try to appeal to the powers of reason of your audience? If so, how?

- Did you try to arouse emotions? If so, which emotions? What strategies did you use to inspire an emotional response?
- Did you construct an ethical argument that appealed to the audience's sense of right and wrong? Or was your argument more rooted in more practical questions, such as those related to procedure or how to get things done?
- What changes do you wish your project could make in the thoughts and actions of others? Once your audience has considered your project, what would you like them to see and do?
- How could you have made your project even more effective? What would you do differently, or how would you expand or alter your arguments if you have the time, expertise, or budget?

A List of Works Cited

Such a list also has a persuasive quality, showing you have done your research and are knowledgeable about the issue at hand.

A Regathering of Mystery

Some of the most important work we do as thinkers and rhetoricians is often hidden from the world and sometimes even from ourselves. Others may hear us making arguments, but few see us rethinking or altering our positions or mulling the possibilities and problems presented by the argument of others. Sometimes it seems as if the changes in our mindsets emerge all at once, but in truth they are usually the result of long mental processing. Here is a chance to make this process visible by "regathering the mystery" of your argument and its issues. You may have seemed rather sure in making the various portions of your argument, but why not end by allowing yourself the luxury of doubt?

Try some or all of the following to open a route for continued thinking:

- Create a list of questions that remain unanswered for you about your issue or argument. These may be questions that you have wondered about before or ones your argument tries to answer. They may also be new for you, perhaps having arisen as you worked on the assignment.
- Reconsider the arguments of those who don't agree with the position you've taken in this assignment. What are the best arguments that can be raised against you? Are there any that you don't know an immediate answer to? List these arguments.
- Write an agenda of things you can do to further your thinking about the issue. Discuss with friends an agenda for continuing to think about the issue you've raised. What questions do you most

want to think about? Is there additional research you'd like to do? Are there books you'd like to read or people to talk to? What other kinds of writing might be interesting to try?

Readings: Texts for Transformational Conversations

Persuasion is finally about transformation, changing our lives and those of others. In a culture dominated by ready-made arguments, reading remains one of the ways of suggesting the complexity of global issues and the need for hearing "alternative" views. Some works are useful in focusing attention upon certain locales or events where global dramas are enacted. Joe Kane's *Savages* illustrates the destructive nature of the capitalist carbon economy through the story of the Huaorani, once the most "untouched" of South American tribes, as they face the pressures of "development." Similarly, William Langewiesche's *American Ground: Unbuilding the World Trade Center* provides a useful synecdoche of the 9/11 tragedy and Americans' responses to it by focusing upon the actual site in the hours, days, weeks, and months after the attack.

Other works enact global visions by fusing large amounts of material in a piercing vision. In *One World: The Ethics of Globalization*, Peter Singer rewrites all of history into the few sentences of a single progression of perspectival thought and action:

> The fifteenth and sixteenth centuries are celebrated for voyages of discovery that proved the world is round. The eighteenth century saw the first proclamations of universal human rights. The twentieth century's conquest of space made it possible for a human being to look at our planet from a point not on it, and to see it, literally, as one world. Now the twenty-first century faces the task of developing a single form of government. (200–201)

Chris Hedges's *War Is a Force That Gives Us Meaning* also brings the miscellany of human actions and motives into a pattern. A correspondent who has seen war all over the world, Hedges sees that humans crave war and miss it even when it has caused them great suffering because it provides a singularity of purpose, heightening of emotion, and narrowing of vision that scattered, mundane, "normal" life does not easily gain.

The following list of additional works of multi-argumentation that may reopen for students a world of issues requiring conversation, conversion, and commitment.

Patriotism, Democracy, and Law after 9/11

David Cole, *Enemy Aliens*. Cole argues that the many foreign nationals held by the United States since 9/11 is an illegal act in itself and also a harbinger of further actions, including detentions of United States citizens. He traces the history of such detentions and denials of rights, including the internments of Japanese Americans during World War II and the black lists of the McCarthy era.

Cass R. Sunstein, *Why Societies Need Dissent*. This reasoned defense of dissent is also eminently practical and accessible for students. Sunstein shows how dissent leads to alternative possibilities that can increase a society's options and give its citizens choices they wouldn't otherwise have.

Genocide

Samantha Power, *A Problem from Hell: America and the Age of Genocide*. Power reveals the pattern of American inaction during the many episodes of genocide in the twentieth century. She takes on the commonplace that America comes to the aid of those in danger while showing how some Americans have cut through public apathy and political maneuvering and deceit to call for American involvement. For shorter related pieces, see also Nicolaus Mills and Kira Bruner, eds. *The New Killing Fields: Massacre and the Politics of Intervention*.

War Culture

Brigadier General Smedly D. Butler, *War Is a Racket*. This is the timely republication of a famously tough and heroic soldier's scathing attack upon war as the defense of business interests. The ethos of the author gives it special authority for students raised to believe that we should support the military no matter the circumstances or cause.

Arundhati Roy, *War Talk*. Arundhati links the "war against terror" to the continued rise of corporate culture worldwide. The subjects of her critique include hydroelectric dams in India, the nuclear showdowns between India and Pakistan, and the squelching of dissent, home and abroad, by "patriotic" America.

Globalization

Saskia Sassen, *Globalization and Its Discontents: Essays on the New Mobility of People and Money*. Sassen sees both the disastrous injustices and synergistic potentials of globalization in the world's great cities, where the disparity between the wealthy and poor is greater than ever but the population now typically includes people from all over the world. Will the presence of the historically disadvantaged and coalition building among people who were once apart lead to radical change?

Joe Kane, *Savages*. What happens when the oil companies come to the rainforest of Ecuador? Kane focuses on the Huaorani, once the most "untouched" of South American tribes, as they face the pressures of "development." It's a great source for showing students how the West's need for resources dismantles other cultures.

Crime and "Security"

Angela Y. Davis, *Are Prisons Obsolete?* With two million Americans now behind bars, a disproportionate share of people of color among them, Davis asks the overlooked questions about the efficacy, cost effectiveness, and justice of incarceration. Are prisons the right response to crime, or have they become a system of political violence and corporate profiteering that threatens democracy?

Christian Parenti, *The Soft Cage: Surveillance in America from Slave Passes to the War on Terror.* Parenti details the history of American surveillance from the search for runaway slaves to airport security and the credit report. With new technologies for surveillance coming online, and the political will to resist their use waning in the "War on Terrorism," this study is a timely wake-up call. Use your GPS to find fellow readers.

Scott Turow, *Ultimate Punishment: A Lawyer's Reflections on the Death Penalty.* Turow has experience with the death penalty, as a prosecutor, defense lawyer, and part of the group that eventually recommended suspending the death penalty in Illinois. Turow's stance, as one in the middle between the passionate extremes, is useful for helping readers move to a more nuanced view of the issue.

Water

Bernadette McDonald and Douglas Jehl, eds., *Whose Water Is It? The Unquenchable Thirst of a Water-Hungry World.* Consider a coming world crisis with this collection of essays about the future of water; topics include pollution, desalination, and ownership of this essential commodity.

Marc Reisner, *Cadillac Desert: The American West and Its Disappearing Water.* This regional history of the politics and mythos of water is also significant to others outside the American West as population growth in this dry region puts additional strain on water supplies elsewhere. Reisner traces the "messianic" quest to make dry land inhabitable that has created the West we know.

Film: The Persuasion of a Complex World

Listen to Me follows the budding romance of two members of a college debate team. Jamie Geertz's character complicates the topic of abortion by having to take a philosophical stand that does not match her personal experience. Conversation is sometimes dependent upon equal time for speakers. But in Sherman Alexie's *Smoke Signals*, the quiet, angry, and worldly Viktor finds out he needs his nerdy storyteller and childhood companion, Thomas Builds A Fire. Together they go upon a pilgrimage to retrieve the effects of Viktor's estranged father, who has deserted them and affected both their lives.

Erin Brockovich follows the paralegal who gets lucky enough to find evidence against a major polluter in California. However, her message is also that justice can be a matter of persistence, that people can collaborate, and that group action can be powerful. This lesson is also part of the struggle of farm workers in *The Milagro Beanfield War*. Sometimes an outsider must help others whose voices have no power in their home place. This is true of Eastern Oregon University alumni Skye Fitzgerald, whose *Bombhunters*—made with a Fulbright grant—follows the dangerous lives of Cambodians and their neighbors who disarm overwhelming numbers of unexploded ordnance. *Hotel Rwanda* shows the breakdown of both rational discussion and toleration for others while some of its characters are able to stay alive in part through the wiles of persuasive talk.

It can be difficult to prove corporate pollution, and the lawyer in *Civil Action*, played by John Travolta, exhausts both his patience and money to achieve a conviction. Sometimes we can only be articulate or persuasive when the arguing is a moot point, as in *Dead Man Walking*, where Sean Penn is on death row. In *Mystic River*, Tim Robbins is unable or unwilling to argue his case effectively, and others have already mistakenly judged him of murdering and possibly molesting a friend's daughter. Other times people reach a denial so deep they cannot see a part of themselves. Their internal argument is transferred to a split personality, as it is in *Fight Club*, the disturbing film about the tension between freedom and routine.

Tide pool on the Washington coast. This tide pool is a comfortably limited but ever-changing world, where starfish cling to rocks yet point in every imaginable direction. The ocean is muted and calls to children and our childlike nature, begging us to investigate the creatures that float in like messages. Photo by Rob Davis.

"Messages in a Bottle," a multiwriting project by Patricia Hansen. The beautifully stacked bottles of Patricia's project could float into the tide pool and, like tiny bells, clink against the rocks. Featuring historical and imaginary stories launched into the roiling sea, the epistles sing the past and the future, seeking to be the present for someone who will rescue and use them. Photo by Kerry Loewen; used with permission of Patricia Hansen.

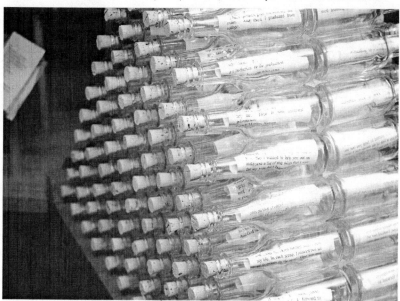

Close-up view of bottled messages in the "Messages in a Bottle" project.
Photo by Kerry Loewen; used with permission of Patricia Hansen.

Eagle Creek, in the Wallowa Mountains of Oregon. Those lost in the wilderness of eastern Oregon know enough to follow the rivers to safety. But there is more than survival in the allure of this stream that fishes for anglers and beckons to those who will twist with it. Beyond the hypnotic, colored rocks of its sunny bed, the shady path alongside the stream rewards travelers with a new view at each bend and the urge to defy gravity and head upstream. Photo by Rob Davis.

"Stanley, I Presume?," a multiwriting project by Jim Benton. A former private investigator, Jim follows his ancestors' name, Stanley, to the headwaters of his genealogical Nile. A battered doctor's bag contains his trek through history toward the mythology of reporter David Stanley, who searched for Livingston in Africa. He found that his relatives had renamed the family after Stanley, leading to genres centered on self-identity. Photo by Kerry Loewen; used with permission of Jim Benton.

Wind-eroded, inhabited caves in Goreme, Turkey. Like oceans and rivers, the earth can call us to explore it and turn the small cave where we survive a cold night into these glorious rooms of carved and painted rock, inhabited by refugees from many religions for thousands of years. Tribes are layered like rock, just as the Toloy and Tellem live as remains beneath the Dogon in the caves and cliff dwellings of Mali. Photo by Mark Shadle.

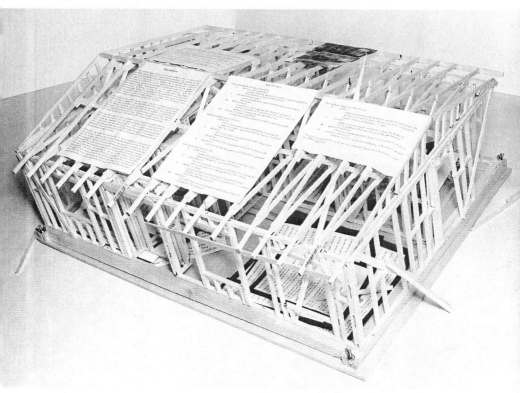

"Shotgun: History as a Scattered (De/Re-)Construction," a multi-writing project by Cydney Topping. The frame of Cydney's composite shotgun house stands between reconstruction of the traditional shotgun houses and the vulnerability of homes in the Delta to both the hurricanes of nature and the shotguns aimed at slaves. Each room contains different genres (e.g., journals, poems, and fables), and meditations on beauty and comfort incorporate platform construction and deconstruction theory, as well as autobiographical information.

Photo by Kerry Loewen; used with permission of Cydney Topping.

Lotus pond in rural China. This lotus pond reminds us of the attempts, in Buddhism and other religions and philosophies, to transcend—in the beauty of the present moment that unfolds like the lotus blossom—the barriers of time and space that hide in the ghosts of the past and future. Control of nature is abandoned by the self who chooses to experience it, whether as a flower or as a hurricane. Photo by Mark Shadle.

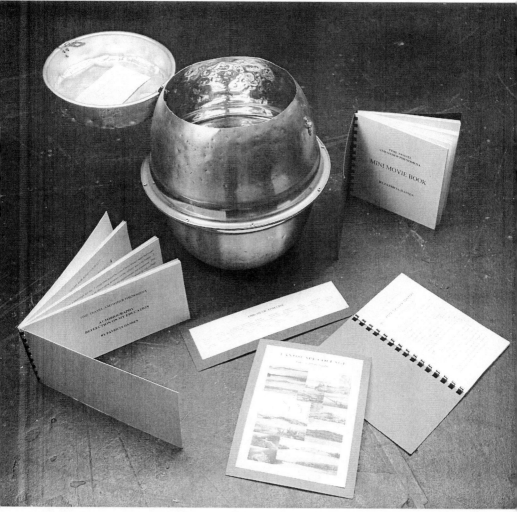

"Tic Tok: Autobiography as Time Travel," a multiwriting project
by Patricia Hansen. Meditation shakes hands with fantasy here.
The metal on the outside of Patricia's Time Machine is dented and
tarnished by experience, but inside it's shiny and protected, like
her dreams and interpretations. Movie reviews, a collage, a music
timeline, and a biography of a composer for film are used to link
theories of time travel across disciplines toward autobiographical and
retrospective reflection on the trajectory of learning from childhood
through college. Photo by Kerry Loewen; used with permission of Patricia Hansen.

Rope coiled on the deck of a schooner in Maine. Strands of natural
fibers woven into rope hold up sails and even a sailor's pants. When
a ship is anchored by rope to the ocean floor or a dock, the coils rest
neatly on the deck. They are beautiful but ready, as in the interspersed
circles of a ballantine (three rotating circles inside a bigger coil), to
fly into action without becoming entangled with each other or the
crew—human strands working carefully together, often to songs, as
they move their cargo. Even knots are an image of cooperation.
Photo by Mark Shadle.

"The Woven Thread of Time," a multiwriting project by Connie Berry. Like rope, our clothes and papers are woven of fibers carefully entwined. Connie's elaborate multiproject contains samples, artifacts, and tools of weaving that fit into an enormous woven box. A glossary, pictures, miniresearch essays, and literary excerpts persuade us of the omnipresent power of the metaphor of weaving throughout history, mythology, and literature all over the world. Experiencing this, we begin to warp the loom of our identity. Photo by Kerry Loewen; used with permission of Connie Berry.

Giant Buddha in the Bamiyan Valley in Afghanistan. Formerly the
world's largest statue, the gigantic Buddha of the Bamiyan Valley
in Afghanistan had its face chiseled off by former Islamic invaders.
Recently the Taliban blew up the statue. Early in its existence, the
sculpture had a face that was a stage lit by lanterns and voices for the
citizens and pilgrims below. Can history survive only with the power
of the mythology that inspired it? Director Christian Frei explores this
question in his film *The Giant Buddhas.* Photo by Mark Shadle.

"Viva la Muerte!," a multiwriting project by Neva Sanders. Like
the Buddha in the cliff, Neva's black coffin rises up and opens to
reveal a colorful series of collages. The lid becomes a path toward
the shrine that shows us how to use the Mexican Days of the Dead
to celebrate life. Writings of many genres, from poems and songs
to miniresearch essays, are tucked into the sides of the coffin, as
if they were its skin. Like the dead, they come alive when read
and remembered. Death becomes life remembered and embraced.

Photo by Kerry Loewen; used with permission of Neva L. Sanders.

View of "Viva la Muerte!" with
the coffin open and the collages,
poems, essays, and so forth
visible. Photo by Kerry Loewen; used with
permission of Neva L. Sanders.

"Hen Party Bronze Bell, a Collaborative Remembrance" by students at Eastern Oregon University. Safer than a statue, the bronze bell, created by sculptor Doug Kaigler and the students he and Rob Davis taught as a team, was placed at a trailhead, where it rings in commemoration of the horsewomen of the Hen Party, who roamed the rugged Wallowa Mountains. It is a microcosm and synecdoche of the way nature invites culture into its abode. These women knew the pull of headwaters and pools, as well as ropes that reigned and hobbled their horses while they wrote about their travel. Photo by Rob Davis.

Front and back of a *lukasa*, or memory board, of the Luba people of
central Africa. This totem and tool, in the shape of a thumb piano that
implies a sound track, incorporates the wood and beads of a natural
world to promote memory of culture as migration routes, secret
clan information, and the sacred layout of the chief's abode. Some

versions animate it with a head. We want to reach for it as something
beautiful that can slowly reveal its magic, like the worn and grooved
axe handle that tells the stories of the trees it has transformed.
Nature. Nurture. Culture. Photos used with permission of Susanne Bennet.

4 THE ESSAY AS CABINET OF WONDER

In her introduction to *The Art of the Essay*, Lydia Fakundiny compares the act of writing an essay to wandering, a spontaneous manner of travel that may appear to be purposeless but leads to knowledge:

> Say you are wandering—without a map, because no satisfactory one comes to hand—in what you believe to be a neighborhood. Wandering about, you come to know it and locate yourself in it only as you keep on traversing it. Here is a fire station, a corner drugstore, a spot of green space, a row of turreted Victorian homes, a canal. As you pass and repass any one of these landmarks, you see where you are in relation to all the others; you map the place out as a neighborhood. Note: it is your own movement that brings you into being the map that tells you what kind of terrain you are in. Your orientation is of your own making. You know where you are by having gone there. (4–5)

Other theorists and writers of essays have used similar metaphors of motion and transport, as Paul Heilker notes in a chapter of his *The Essay: Theory and Pedagogy for an Active Form*, aptly entitled "Kineticism Incarnate: Motion/Movement and the Form of the Essay." The subtitle— "Moving Violation: These Boots Were Made for Walking"—reminds us that motion is the essay's ubiquitous trope, cast "as flying, slithering, flowing, journeying, walking, rambling, wandering, following, tracking, hunting, and transgressing" (168). Identifying the Protean essay with action and motion suggests new ways to describe it as a form. The motion metaphor suggests, for instance, that the essay may be best viewed not as a genre or as an, at times radical, mix of genres but as an impulse within discourse and a mode of operating in the world. All discourse becomes essayistic when it begins to move into country unknown even to the author.

Heilker points in particular to two implications of the travel trope. First, by viewing "the essay" as a verb—as in the French "essayer" meaning "to attempt"—we release essaying as an action of intellectual freedom, an "unhindered, unregulated, untrammeled mental mobility" that becomes "an active movement across intellectual boundaries and borders" (180). Second, the essay as motion overturns Plato's privileging of speech over writing by encoding in text the mutable dialectic of oral dialogue.

Thought and emotion and text are set in motion and enacted when voiced through the resonance and reverberation of the body and shared airspace of public debate. Poet Charles Olson tracks speech to the Sanskrit "Mu," or first utterance: "Down through your own throat / to that place where all drama comes from . . ." (22). Olson, like so many other scholars of the late twentieth century, tries to "get behind the Greek" of Plato, who we have often blamed for taming the voices of conversation into a tightly linear argument that mocks the dead ends and great discoveries of debate by taking the reader along a path that can lead to only one outcome. From this point of view, "Socratic dialogue" is an oxymoron, where Socrates and his students are Plato's marionettes, merely advancing the logic of the puppet master. Olson points this out in "Apollonius of Tyana," where he creates a dance-drama that lets Apollonius (as a figure of the male, Apollonian principle of advance, and a stand-in for thought) dance with Tyana (who is place, shaping the enactment of thought and the emotions that she guides as Earth Mother).

In a world still torn with war in Iraq and America's exploitations of people and resources, it is again important to see how we must learn from the longevity of what we can no longer call "primitive" cultures. In *The Pale Fox*, Marcelle Griaule examines the way the Dogon in Africa use the fox as oracle. Sand is meticulously prepared, and the fox moves through it at night. Then the signs are read by those trained to interpret the tracks. Like the fox's motion, tribal sculptures in Africa—in the shapes of gods, and with a hollow core—are sometimes "tuned" to the wind that "plays" them. The essay can be like this: played and attuned to its environment and writer.

A related if converse way of viewing the essay is as a provisional homecoming that involves welcoming travelers and learning by reflecting upon tales, information, and viewpoints that are initially unfamiliar. While Chapter 2 took up the theme of research writing as travel that changes writer and audience, and Chapter 3 finds a similar kind of journey in the transformational dialogues of loose talk, this chapter looks to the essay as a way of bringing the world to oneself to create a primordial, shifting sense of order that is also a way of preparation for the next voyage, metaphoric or literal, into a world where nothing is settled and about which little is permanently known.

Michel de Montaigne, the French nobleman and writer, was often credited with originating the essay. As a courtier, soldier, and gallstone-sufferer, he journeyed to Italy in search of good health; however, he spent most of his writing life in his home, with its library tower, where his vista spanned the world:

> At home I slip off to my library a little more often; it is easy for me to oversee my household from there. I am above my gateway and have a view of my garden, my chicken run, my backyard and most parts of my house. There I can turn over the leaves of this book, or that, a bit at a time without order or design. Sometimes my mind wanders off, at others, I walk to and fro, noting down and dictating these whims of mine. (258)

From this perch, Montaigne is both a global learner with an eagle's overview and an analytic thinker who can scurry forth, like a mouse, into any part of his familiar world, or wander from it. His pacings make the exotic more familiar, without closing off difference or explaining away the odd. Instead, the curious case or strange story becomes the impetus for rethinking and recasting matters once thought known or understood. He is comfortable moving us into spaces where only questions reside. While his writing is credited with opening new internal space for reflection and confession, it is also a social act connecting self to other. Even his most personal revelations are made with readers in mind. In "On Three Kinds of Social Intercourse," he writes, "The proper essence of my own form lies in imparting things and in putting them forth: I am all in evidence, all of me is exposed; I was born for company and loving relationship" (253). He desires escape from the clatter of petty affairs but not import of experience.

He accepts the world and all that is in it. He finds nobility in unexpected places while reserving his harshest judgments for himself and those with whom he is most familiar. His wonder-work holds itself open to experience and avoids the anxious desire to eliminate the other through "civilization" or "salvation"—terms he finds dubious. As Alain de Botton notes in his tour of Montaigne's library in *The Consolations of Philosophy*, the tower room's ceiling beams are inscribed with quotations filled with reservations about human claims to knowledge and understanding, such as "There is nothing certain but uncertainty, nothing more miserable and more proud than man" from Pliny and "Everything is too complicated for men to be able to understand" from Ecclesiastes (118).

For an opposite take on this, John Kennedy Toole's *A Confederacy of Dunces* is a parodic novel whose main character, Ignatius, is attempting to critique the modern world by adhering to his Bible, *The Consolation of Philosophy*. In contemporary America, Wendell Berry has this kind of openness to a familiar world in his essays and poems. As he says in his poem "Traveling at Home": "Even in a country you know by heart / it's hard to go the same way twice" (23).

The early rush to judgment is evidence of the foolish pride Montaigne's essays attempt to suspend. In "On the Cannibals," for instance, he avoids enthusiasms or conceits in attempting to see what or who is actually present in the New World. The cannibals of whom he writes live by a moral code that includes both the eating of their enemies and being eaten, as the circumstances demand. Such outrages shock pious Europeans, who think nothing of torturing others or setting the dogs to eat them, even though these sins are forbidden by their own morality. Particularly galling are their delusional justifications in the name of Christ. Compared to these hypocrites, the "cannibals" are civilized. He ironically concludes, "But they wear no breeches . . ." (92).

Montaigne's attitude of openness is especially commendable given the uncertainties of the times. The high anxiety of a time of societal and intellectual breakdown led to a quest for first principles, such as Descartes's "I think, therefore I am." Montaigne's starting point is broader and more enigmatic: I am, here, with you and all others, in this world that is larger, wilder, more magnificent, and more frightful than we had imagined. As Michael Hall argues in "The Emergence of the Essay and the Idea of Discovery," the early essayists like Montaigne and Francis Bacon—and later John Donne and Sir Thomas Browne—share "a common attitude, a spirit of exploration" that emerged as part of and in response to the Renaissance idea of discovery:

> In an age fascinated by the implications of the new philosophy and the discovery of the New World, the essay provided a kind of prose composition particularly suited to the examination of conventional wisdom, the exploration of received opinion, and the discovery of new ideas and insights—a kind of written discourse which allowed the author to think freely outside of established authority and traditional rhetorical forms. (78)

Paraphrasing the work of Steven Greenblatt and others, Lawrence Weschler, in *Mr. Wilson's Cabinet of Wonder*, boldly states the effect of those times: "*Europe's mind was blown*" [italics Weschler's]. He quotes Greenblatt: "'The expression of wonder stands for all that cannot be understood, that can scarcely be believed. It calls attention to the problem of credibility and at the same time insists upon the undeniability, the exigency of experience'" (Weschler 79). As exploration quickly turned to conquest, wonder at an unknown world gave way to the desire for possession. As James Elkins says in *The Object Stares Back: On The Nature of Seeing*, the thought of possessing is always implicit in our encounters with the other: it does not accompany looking, it is looking itself (22). Further, what we desire to see or own is often our narcissistic selves.

This self-looking is paralleled by the possession Werner Muensterberger sees in "the unruly passion" of collecting:

> I have followed the trail of these emotional conditions in the life histories of many collectors . . . They like to pose or make a spectacle of their possessions. But one soon realizes that these possessions, regardless of their value or significance, are but stand-ins for themselves. And while they use their objects for inner security and outer applause, their deep inner function is to screen off self-doubt and unassimilated memories. (13)

In the "new world," this desire to observe and collect became a similar act of self-reference that led to the related desires to eliminate others, who were not human, or turn them into a mock version of ourselves: simpletons, but Christians. Otherness was also reified as a Eurocentric hierarchy was imposed: the "cannibals" and their like were animals, or nearly so, and a portion of our burden, as the rational stewards of the world. The land also became a scene of such delusional exploitations: it was there to be used for those who saw in it their own providential rise to wealth and glory.

Literary criticism used this definition of the essay in trying to understand the westward migration from Europe. The myth and symbol treatments in American Studies followed the willful conquest of the New World with Henry Nash Smith's *The Virgin Land* in 1955. Smith saw the images of the land in literature as a virgin territory. Leo Marx's *The Machine in the Garden*, R. W. B. Lewis's *An American Adam* and Annette Kolodny's *The Lay of the Land* were just a few of the books that researched this rape of the New World by men and their machinery. Richard Slotkin's *Regeneration through Violence* addressed this pattern beyond the confines of highbrow literature with a look at folk culture from the Puritans' arrival until the end of the Civil War, and Wendell Berry's *The Unsettling of America* charted the way the Jeffersonian dream of the immigrant yeoman farmer unsettled the tribes who were displaced.

The academic essay, too, has lived its own minor version of this history of conquest and commodification, through the codification and valorization of what Heilker terms the "thesis/support" form. The target of so much of our teaching, this form has become the currency of academic rhetoric, which students trade for good grades. Heilker cites the research of Russell Durst, who has shown how students use the thesis/support form—which they have internalized as real and valuable—on almost any occasion (2–3). For scholars and teachers of language, however, the original Montaignian essay remains a discursive practice not based on narrow arguments or objectification of positions with which the author disagrees. Instead, this dialogic, multifaceted essay reveals and relies upon the seductions of the unknown and the uncanny ability of language to lead us into a curiously altered world. As Susan Griffin puts it in her meta-essay, "The Red Shoes," in *The Eros of Everyday Life*:

> The extent of the unknown borders all language. One's relationship with it is erotic. One has a passion to know. But one can never entirely know what is other. Telling a story, no matter how much you know, you are very soon pulled into unexplored territory. Even the familiar is filled with unexpected blank spaces. The usual Sunday drive is all of a sudden a wild ride into terra incognita. You are glad to be going, but there is a vague feeling of discomfort. Where are you? (170)

As it draws us into the unfamiliar, revealing the strangeness of the world—while also becoming a means of reintegrating with it—the essay is akin to those nearly forgotten objects of art and collection, Renaissance cabinets of curiosity and wonder. These *Wunderkammern*, forebears of museums of both natural history and art, collected the marvelous of all kinds, often without the categorical differentiations we now see as natural. Weschler cites a 1673 monograph by Edward Brown, its title itself something of a Cabinet of Wonder: *A Brief Account of Some Travels in Hungaria, Serbia, Bulgaria, Macedonia, Thessaly, Austria, Syria, Carinthia, Carniola and Friuli. As also some observations on the silver, copper, quick-silver mines, baths and mineral waters in those parts: With the figures of some Habits and Remarkable place.* In Leipzig, Brown visited Burgomeister von Adlershelme and his Chamber of Rarities. The items on Brown's list are remarkable in their oddity and diversity, and he claims this list is far from complete:

> An Elephant's Head with the dentes molars in it. An animal like an Armadillo, but the scales are much larger and the Tail broader. Very large flying Fishes. A seahorse. Bread of Mount Libanus. A Cedar-branch with the Fruit upon it. Large Granates as they grow in the Mine. A Siren's hand. A Chameleon. A piece of Iron, which seems to be the head of a Spear, found in the tooth of an Elephant, the Tooth being grown about it. The Isle of Jersey drawn by our King Charles the Second. A piece of wood with the Blood of the King Charles the First upon it. A Greenland Lance with a large Bell at the end of it. Much Japan painting, wherein their manner of hunting and working may be observed. A Picture of our Saviour [upon] the Hatches [of]

which . . . are . . . written . . . the story of his Passion. Bevers taken in the River Elbe. A Picture of the murther of the Innocents, done by Albrecht Drurer. Pictures of divers strange Fowls. A Greenland Boat. The skins of white Bears, Tigres, Wolves, and other Beasts. And I must not omit the Garter of an English Bride, with the story of it; of the Fashion in England for the Bridemen to take it off and wear it in their Hat, which seemed so strange to the Germans, that I was obliged to confirm to them, by assuring them that I had divers times wore such a Garter myself. (Weschler 118–19; Weschler's additions, deletions, and corrections)

Brown's list and von Adlershelme's cabinet freely mix objects of art and natural artifacts, and items from afar and those from closer to home. The collection renders the strange more familiar—an elephant's head is there to be observed and handled—while the familiar regains its wonder: the passion of Christ becomes another example of the marvelous. This recontextualization is reminiscent of the collector's dream described by Walter Benjamin, which transports us to not only a distant or past world "but a better one," where ordinary objects, needed for everyday life, are "free of the drudgery of being useful" (155). In such a collection, we encounter the strangeness of objects we once knew in the company of those we can begin to know now.

This collection of the wonderful is reminiscent of another mnemonic device of the Renaissance, the "memory theatre" of Guillo Camillo Deminio. He imagined a giant cabinet marked with carvings and filled with boxes, containing images symbolizing different aspects of existence or figures of the imagination, that would grow to encode all that humans could find or conceive. While this would be a theatre without performance, where the gestures of the stage were captured in fixed images, the audience peering into drawers or examining the surface would provide a theatre of reactions as they began to recognize all that was hidden in the world and themselves.[1]

In her reading of the memory culture of the Luba and the initiation rites of the Mbudye, the secret society who are the ultimate keepers of tribal memory, Mary Nooter Roberts suggests that Western Renaissance and Luba mnemonic systems are related by a quest to represent the order of the eternal through architectural forms such as the memory theatre or *lukasa* memory board, which are configured to contain abundant knowledge. For the Luba, writing, when it was introduced, could not capture the infinite combinations or nuances of lived experience or personal or societal histories. For this, talismans, statues, ceremonial stools, and *lukasa* remain more flexible forms, especially when used in ritual, political discourse, proverbial instruction, and cultural storytelling.[2]

While striving toward order, Cabinets of Wonder became experiments in classification that called the collector to consider the relationship between the objects on earth. As Barbara Maria Stafford and Francis Terpak argue in their history of devices of wonder from cabinets to motion pictures, classification of the macrocosm took on a new material form as collectors handled and arranged their treasured objects. Schemes of order in the cabinets were charmingly homespun; fish skeletons hung from ceilings over drawers filled with rocks, while figures from classical sculpture looked on, bemused. Often, the items were arranged to tell a moral story. Weschler recounts how the Theatrum Anatomicum in Leiden combined elements of a Natural History Museum and a morality play, with displays of executed criminals posed in the action of their crimes. (The skeleton of a cattle thief, for instance, was mounted astride the skeleton of an ox.) At the center of the amphitheater, a skeletal Eve handed Adam an apple, while a pennant exclaimed the consequences of original sin for "any dim souls who might still have been missing the point" (84). But it was in these cabinets that modern taxonomies began to take hold. By 1679 the collection of Jacob Swammerdom was catalogued by his son Jan, the famous entomologist, into categories such as "items from mines," "growing things," "animals," and "works of art," similar to those used to divide earthly matter today (Muensterberger, 213–14).

In a relativistic and postmodern universe given to chaotic patterns, when the fertile nature of doubt and fascination supplant the assuredness of modern knowledge, the Cabinet of Wonder appeals once again and appears in new forms. Writing of the Museum of Jurassic Technology (MTJ), in Los Angeles, which mixes bizarre facts with fictions that seem believable, Weschler sees that this is a crossroads of the pre- and post-modern, as well as the parodic and serious. One of the functions of such a museum is to re-historicize museums as places of the muses, where inventive thought occurs. It is a partial cure for Ishmael Reed's idea of the museum as imperialist safe. In *Mumbo Jumbo*, Reed depicts the Metropolitan Museum of Art as an "art detention center," where sacred tribal art is kept from the cultures that created and still need it. Conversely, another stated purpose of the Museum of Jurassic Technology's founder, David Wilson, is "to reintegrate people to wonder." This kind of wonder, Weschler responds, is metastable, shimmering between "wondering at (the marvels of nature) and wondering whether (any of this could possibly be true)" (60).

This "delicious confusion," as Weschler calls it, is one of the joys offered by an ambiguous world. Patrick Mauries ends his tour of cabinets of curiosities with the proclamation of ours as a new age of curiosity, then lists evidence from art and aesthetics, including the container or cabinet art of Joseph Cornell, Mark Dion, and Robert Williams and the eclecticism of contemporary design, including the interiors of Françoise de Nobèle, who sets, side by side, artifacts and detritus as different and connected, as toy stuffed animals and the mummy of an Egyptian cat (241). The collection, design, and artistic use of *curiosa* come together in spaces such as the Parisian workshop and residence of Miquel Barceló, where animal skulls, heads, and carcasses from Majorca, Mali, and other parts of Africa surround him. These become subjects for his paintings, which are "deeply impregnated with Mediterranean memories, themes, and motives of ancient painting" (239).

A direct reference to cabinets of wonder appeared at the Getty Museum in Los Angeles in 1989, in a diminutive version of a *Wunderkammern*, with an intricate cabinet made in Germany in the early 1600s, containing objects of wonder including miniature carvings "patterned into a complex iconic program of biblical, mythological, and historical subjects." The project was finished and recycled as a postmodern work by the contemporary American artist Sumiya Swoboda Nichols, who added to the top of the cabinet a crown of beautiful shells, minerals, crystals and coral (Stafford and Terpak 158, illustrations 159–62). In 2003, our university gallery exhibited works by Wade Eldean that presented wondrous objects more comically, through a "traveling exhibit" mounted in a series of old suitcases and illuminated from within by lights in bright colors and containing plastic toys, such as animals, beads, "lite brite" pegs and "furbies," and detritus, as well as vacuum cleaner hoses, toothbrushes, and fake fur.

Stafford and Terpak also see *Wunderkammern* in cyberspace:

> Consider the universal flea market of eBay, an Internet swap meet hosting two million-plus on-line auctions per day, listing some four million items organized into over three thousand categories of mostly nonstandardized goods. Today, the collectible is everywhere. As the science-fiction writer William Gibson observed, this obsession with thrift-shop hunting and picking may be a sign of "some desperate instinctive reconfiguring of the post-industrial flow, some basic mammalian response to the bewildering flood of sheer *stuff* we produce" (Gibson 102). Most of our contemporary objects of obscure desire are composed not of rare woods, expensive metals, and variegated minerals but of plastic and Styrofoam. Yet this morass of deracinated junk can still be analogically transformed into something personal. A fuzzy scan on a computer monitor can be miraculously transformed into a cherished desktop item to be integrated with other meaningful items at home or in the workplace. After surfing, browsing, searching, and

downloading comes mapping—not only of our vintage past but also of the engineered future toward which we are heading. That lengthening prospect is littered with obsolete technologies, with hardware and software that no longer talk to each other. The *Wunderschrank*, then, represents, the revenge of multisensory media. The combinatorial cabinet reminds us of the long cultural conversation objects have had, and will continue to have, with one another, and with us. (20)

Hypertext and electronic multimedia may constitute a similar revenge of the multisensory, revealing print to be, as Richard Lanham once called it, "an act of perceptual self-denial" (74). The essay, however, may also move the senses, recollect cultural artifacts and rearrange pieces of knowledge into striking new patterns. In *A Natural History of the Senses*, Diane Ackerman writes of synesthesia, the grafting of one sense onto another, as a cross-cultural tour of expressions, attitudes, and enigmatic facts. She cites research showing that synesthesiacs from different cultures tend to assign the same colors to their experience of certain sounds. Train whistles may simply be blue.

Blues music, too, has its uses for wonder, although the use of the word *wonder* in lyrics often connotes suspicion, worry, and impending doom. Louis Armstrong claimed that the problem was not the world but what humans had done to it. It would be a wonderful world if we'd give it a chance by loving it and each other. Similarly, the blues often starts with trouble and sings its way past coping, pride in survival, and the will to overcome to arrive at a foot-stomping celebration of life, good and bad. The fact that the music was there at all must have been a wonder to the people who heard it at the tiny juke joints of the Mississippi Delta, where laborers could at last begin to enjoy their freedom by playing as well as listening and dancing to a music that spoke of travels, travails, loss, and getting through. This spirit of wonder and gratitude occasionally still reigns, even in upscale clubs like Chicago's subterranean Underground Wonder Bar and in remaining blues dives and juke joints, like Tabby's Blues Box in Baton Rouge, Louisiana, or The Meeting Place in Greeneville, Mississippi.[3]

Placing the essay—as writers, scholars, and authors are resuscitating it in its discursive, multifaceted Montaignian form—in this blues song of wonder allows us to further its transformation into a nonpossessive form of world exploration and hospitable welcome. Essays bring the world's curious bounty into a space of reflection and communication, where what we thought we knew meets what we seem to have discovered. Essays trace trails of understanding, where final knowledge is never achieved. Their forms emerge in relation to their messages, but they are not fully transportable to other situations or occasions. Just as a new trouble requires an altered blues, new objects can change the appearance of the cabinet. Even their authors can never entirely "own" or master such texts, since the writing often leads into new territory. Writing an essay entails loosening preconceptions so that a "cannibal" may reteach us the world. Here we think of Phil Hartman's character on *Saturday Night Live*, the Caveman Lawyer, who wins the case by abrogating careful, factual, scientific reasoning to make vicious use of the emotions of "logical fallacies" that for a "caveman" are presumably the *modus operandi*.

Engaging the essay, for our students and ourselves, may begin by reading published essays that move us from ignorance to understanding without closing off questions or claiming expertise. Although such texts may be more ambitious projects than students can complete in a term, their open styles and intellectual but conversational voices invite readers to add to the meanings they make and consider how other or related subjects may be written about in a similar way. The tradition of natural history writing, which is as old as the Greeks but popular again today, is a possible approach. Contemporary natural histories typically show how a single subject—whether the senses, pencils, tulips, or transsexuality—may gather meaning in at least three dimensions: personal meaning made by exploring one's history with the subject; shared and debated meanings, including the views of sources on the subject; and global meanings, in which the subject becomes a route to a new understanding of culture, history, nature, or the cosmos. This chapter's list of readings is selected natural histories. Any of these or another such text may prove the right resource to open students' thinking.

Popular writing on science is another route to the essay. It conventionally operates through a sense of ongoing mystery, in which the leading edge of discovery reveals, time and again, a cosmos that is stranger still. Works such as James Gleik's *Chaos*, Bill Bryson's *A Short History of Almost Everything*, or Brian Greene's *The Elegant Universe* can help students to like English, humanities, and art. In turn, this can help them overcome their fear of the other spheres of academia while leading them to think associatively about how cosmologies may enable or revise their emerging worldviews. Each of these works reveals the physical earth and universe as its own box of wonders, governed by nearly inexplicable forces and patterned in ways that seem at once accidental and contingent, as well as fateful and necessary. Bryson, for instance, describes the "goldilocks effect," in which the universe exists as it does—enabling life and earth—because a number of factors are uncannily "just right." He cites British astronomer Martin Rees, who lists six values that must be as they are for our universe to be as it is. Even a slight change would have a strong effect. Bryson writes:

> For example, for the universe to exist as it does requires that hydrogen be converted to helium in a precise but comparatively stately manner—specifically, in a way that converts seven one-thousandths of its mass to energy. Lower that value slightly—from 0.007 percent to 0.006 percent, say—and no transformation could take place: the universe would consist of hydrogen and nothing else. Raise the value very slightly—to 0.008 percent—and bonding would be so wildly prolific that the hydrogen would long since have been exhausted. In either case, with the slightest tweaking of the numbers the universe as we know and need it would not be here (16).

Similarly, a slightly stronger force of gravity would cause the universe to collapse in on itself, with all matter melding in a single point of un-imaginable density; whereas a weaker gravity would have prevented the interactions of primordial elements, such as the conversion of hydrogen to helium, and led to a lifeless and increasingly vast universe, with all matter heading further and further apart. Whether we are studying the goldilocks effect, the "butterfly effect" Gleik discusses (in which the motion of a single butterfly's wings changes climate worldwide), or the subatomic "superstrings" (pulsating in multiple dimensions) that Greene envisions as the fundamental substance and energy of matter, such studies present a cosmos that is odder and more contingent than we suspected. They also show students that scientific discoveries are often surprises made through an essayistic spirit of inquiry through which researchers wonder, "what if?"

We have also used other varieties of the essay, including writings on travel, electronic technology and culture, race and gender, and culturally based autobiography to help students find paths for essayistic thinking that connect personal experiences and fascinations with research from multiple sources. "Professional" texts can be daunting models, but es-says tend to inspire talk, rather than suppress it. Montaigne's essay "On Educating Children," for instance, remains a favorite text to use with freshman, despite differences in culture and the passage of time, because the experiences and values it describes remain common to those who have been "educated" as children. Fresh from the high school experience or looking back at it after some years, students can recognize themselves as those who have knowledge poured into them as through a funnel, in Montaigne's metaphor. However, the essay moves beyond this simple recognition, toward a free space where education can be rethought.

Montaigne's metaphor of the bees that find their pollen in many places but make a honey that is their own may empower students beginning their own searches for the stamen of academe.

Shared readings framing the essay writing assignment are often invitations to theory, especially the theory of the essay as a way of writing in the world. As Scott Russell Sanders has aptly put it in "The Singular First Person," the essay is "the amateur's raid in the world of specialists" (660). It brings the esoteric inquiries of others into association with the essayist's evolving language and cosmology to discover common meanings. In a composition course, essays provides adventurous public learning, in which each writer becomes the scout, leading readers into a land that few have seen. In multiwriting, the essay can become part of or turned into an installation, a poster session, a presentation or performance, a photo-essay or mini coffee table book, a Web site or blog, or a project of many textualities residing in a unifying container or form. The sense of audience can come more fully to life as writers begin to conceive of the project as a unity of form and content designed to fascinate others and help them understand.

Such projects also foster collaboration as the audience works with the author to conceive, draft, and revise the project. Kurt Spellmeyer argues that the essay can become a "common ground" that invites us to surrender the safety, and blindness, of localities such as singular disciplines or insular cultures. In the common ground Spellmeyer imagines, differences are not erased but admitted and nurtured as they add meanings to the open path marked by the essay. An offspring of the spirit of heteroglossia, which sheds appropriation at every turn, essays exceed the limited interpretations each reader brings to them. We need each other to explicate the text and to begin to witness the range of responsive discourses it inspires.

As he resists constrained forms of writing in the disciplines, whereby the conventions of discourse communities dictate the writing students may do, Spellmeyer is joined by others who see the essay as a resistant and liberating alternative to discursive forms that may hinder student learning. *In Beyond Note Cards*, Bruce Ballenger casts the research essay as an alternative to the freshman research paper, which he terms "the assignment that would not go away," despite a "long legacy of teacher complaint and student angst" (7). Ballenger finds that the research essay encourages inquiry-based, intentional learning, while also introducing students to academic culture, without voiding the culture and languages they bring to the academy. Similarly, Susan Griffin's "The Red Shoes" displaces public argument as the essay's dominant purpose, to make space for, theorize, and practice an intimate discourse that parallels the novel in its capacity for bringing to light the sensual details and abiding mysteries of private life.

Heilker's critique is broader based still as he casts the essay as a corrective to the overused thesis-support form. The essay as he and others envision it is a free discourse that must be found and made again and again. Lydia Fakundiny draws the distinction between templated discourses, in which forms are predetermined, and the essay, in which form is constructed through reflective unfolding of the rhetorical occasion:

> If you are writing a letter to your boss to ask for a raise or to complain about the conditions of work, or if you are going to write a user's manual, or even a letter to the editors supporting a particular candidate for mayor, you had better think about your audience—that scrutinizing other "I"—from the start; you had better work out your arguments beforehand and know exactly who you are talking to and what for. You had better care, in other words, exactly where and when you are going to come down. But an essayist, disposed as she may be to instruct or convert or entertain, has as her first task coming into being in the wilds of the occasion that sets her writing—her topic, hunch, idea, concern, question, puzzle. (5)

In the space opened by the occasion, the essay presents its objects of wonder. It is a crossroads, where the rhetor (as investigator), reader (as curious other), and content (as the tracing of an open question) exchange meanings and form provisional alliances.

Working within this open zone requires an unlearning or untangling of the restraints that hold questions at bay and keep discourse wound tight. Heilker argues that the academy needs to overturn the essay as we have practiced it if we are to reclaim it as verb and process. "The thesis/support god," he argues, blaspheming, is "not all-powerful, not all-fulfilling. It is, rather, inadequate from developmental, epistemological, ideological, and feminist rhetorical perspectives" (2). If the outcome we have in mind involves learning, he claims, the thesis/support essay is the wrong means, since its function is to close rather than open minds and to "win" arguments by shutting down the opposition.

For Heilker, shutdown begins with topic selection, as students narrow their topics, often repeatedly—not because they are interested in a specific point that encapsulates or stands out within a larger field—but because the form they have come to rely upon and that their teachers require works best in narrow spaces, where a clear thesis can be found and supported. "A" papers in such a world often find their purity of argument through self-isolation; the sloppiness of human debate—where one issue leads to the next and back again—is ignored so that a more perfect form can be achieved:

> The incredibly tight discursive structure of the thesis/support form makes the additional ideological claim that the complexities of the world's problems and issues are not problematic after all—not a complex web of interconnections that need to be addressed from multiple perspectives in a collaborative dialogue—but rather neat, "slottable," and solvable in a very short space using a single point of view and formulaic thinking, a procedure that will leave one with no bothersome loose ends. (6).

This a priori evokes a positivist rhetoric, in which truth predates language. The discursive essay instead makes its truths in its own becoming. In "The Skewed Path: Essaying as Unmethodical Method," Robert Lane Kauffman casts the essay—practiced by writers as different as Walter Benjamin, Theodor W. Adorno, Roland Barthes, and Jacques Derrida—as a counteractive that potentially can undermine philosophic systems that hand down their dictates abstractly from above: "At its most combative, modern philosophical essayism recalls Nietzsche's taunt in *Twilight of the Idols* that the will to system betrays a lack of integrity." (227). The essay's teachings, in contrast, stem from particular experience, which may lead us to question our systems or values. But the essay is not merely deconstructive. It also may constitute a revaluation, subject to continued change.

As Graham Good puts it in *The Observing Self: Rediscovering the Essay*, the essay resides "outside *any* organization of knowledge, whether medieval or modern. In it, an open mind confronts an open reality" (4). The knowledge made by the essay is experiential and idiosyncratic, rather than evidentiary or corroborative; however, this uniqueness also yields a proximate, often intimate, authority. Reading the ancient essayist Herodotus, the English Patient in Michael Ondaatje's novel says:

> I have seen editions of the Histories with a sculptured portrait on the cover. Some statue found in a French museum. But I never imagine Herodotus this way. I see him more as one of those spare men of the desert who travel from oasis to oasis, trading legends as if it is the exchange of seeds, consuming everything without suspicion, piecing together a mirage. "This history of mine," Herodotus says, "has from the beginning sought out the supplementary to the main argument." What you find in him are cul-de-sacs within the sweep of history—how people betray each other for the sake of nations, how people fall in love . . ." (119)

By allowing eddies of private life to enter public history, the essay becomes a way to evoke questions that show more complexity than often-repeated narratives have allowed. Griffin's "The Red Shoes" is eerily similar. The narrator contradicts family stereotypes by remembering that her silent, stoic grandmother also owned a daring pair of shoes. Or is this a projection born of desire on the part of the narrator? We do not know.

"The Red Shoes" operates on two discursive ledgers: the *theoretical*, in which history of the essay is described and bracketed so that its overlooked possibilities can be brought to light; and the *confessional*, where buried memories or dreams come to words. The ledgers parallel one another, as each is concerned with illumination and recovery. The unity of the text is enacted by an uncanny moment, where each text crosses into the other's space and takes on the other's identity, as signaled by the use of italics and plain text. Similarly, Montaigne's form grows from his message as his use of quotations from sources enacts the social intercourse with books that he saw as the most reliable kind of human intercourse. Even his way of quoting—swooping to gather intriguing lines, rather than crafting summaries of entire works—suggests that he sees the source as a friend too complicated to summarize but full of momentary wisdom and occasionally annoying.

By enacting innovative connections of form to content, the essay makes possible a dialogic relationship among author, audience, and source. We read essays as both finished products with intentional forms and experiments to which we may contribute. The essay invites us to enter a collaborative process of inquiry, reflection, and creation. Reading, we may ask: What is this text? Why is it structured as it is? What holds it together? What questions remain? And what can I contribute to the field it has opened?

As Heilker sees, the qualities of the essay—mutability, resistance to hierarchy, matching of content with form, and openness to wondering and dialogue—are also the hallmarks of the desired discourses of feminist rhetorics. He cites Jane Tompkins, who sees contradiction in feminists adopting the impersonal and abstract ways of thinking and writing of patriarchal inscription. Instead, Tompkins joins many other theorists and writers in calling for a woman's language that is fluid, associative, flexible, and mobile. She cites Ursula LeGuin's evocation of a collaborative "mother tongue":

> The mother tongue, spoken or written, expects an answer. It is conversation, a word the root of which means "turning together." The mother tongue is language not as mere communication, but as relation, relationship. It connects. Its power is not in dividing but in binding.[4] (Heilker 11; Tompkins qtd. in Heilker 173–74)

In Maxine Hong Kingston's *The Woman Warrior*, the narrator's mother slices her daughter's frenum so that her tongue may move freely, allowing her to say any word, in English or Chinese. Yet, when the narrator starts English-speaking school, she cannot speak. Later, the narrator/daughter bullies and humiliates a younger child at school whose crime is her silence. The "strategy" backfires: the girl still will not speak, and the narrator immediately falls into a long illness, from which she emerges, once again, silent. Force, even the forcing of forms of discourse upon others, cannot help people to free their tongues. Needed instead are forms that invite speaking. The essay provides such a form because of its openness and its invitation to conversation and inquiry through writing.

This inquisitive conversation often leads to conversion: the essay traces change. Richard Manning describes how researching and writing his essayistic book, *Grasslands*, transformed him: "After a life spent among trees, I now understand that life seems comprehensible only when I place it in the context of grass." (1). As students turn from reading essays to writing them, we find it useful to remember where the essayist started her adventure in learning. For instance, in *Edge Effects: Notes from an Oregon Forest*, Chris Anderson recounts how his understanding of the forest next to his new home quickly changed. At first, the forest seemed a refuge, twelve thousand acres of peace. After only a few months, however, he learned of plans for a clear-cut of the trees by the university that owns the land. The news carried an urgent demand to learn. Anderson is soon caught up in the politics and science of forestry as he comes to see the forest as part of a contested planet and his own involvement as essential:

> I had moved to the forest for silence but found myself immersed in words. I had moved for experience but found myself struggling with competing theories. I had moved for solitude but suddenly was trying to situate myself in a tense, divided community. Interviewing forestry faculty, tromping through the poison oak, or driving the logging roads, I learned over the course of one summer that the forest I live near is a forest of voices, of languages and ideas (13).

Such texts can encourage students by showing them not only that the need for research continues in life but also that even published authors often begin in ignorance. At the meeting in which the clear-cut was first publicly discussed, Anderson found himself lost in the words of the scientists and managers: "gap dynamics," "biodiversity assessment," and "aesthetic viewsheds." They showed the audience computer-enhanced photographs of the "targeted" timber "units" before and after "treatment" (13). Within a few months, however, Anderson had become a member of a forestry study group on campus and accompanied scientists and helped them to do their work in the woods. He was learning quickly, and still nothing seemed to completely alleviate his fear that the University's College of Forestry cut trees for profit more than for science.

Anderson's title, *Edge Effects*, is borrowed from the realm of biologists and others working in the natural world. That is, instead of a "clear-cut" that takes all timber from a section of the forest, selected logging can allow the flow and mixing of plants and animals. Ironically, though, even a clear-cut can be regrown as a meadow that acts as an oasis within the forest, where biodiversity is greatest at the edges, at those points where the meadow and forest meet. Just as Anderson salvages learning from the disaster of the clear-cut that surrounds his home and uses the opportunity to understand the larger occasion of his property and its history, students can use the essay as a form to wander, like coyote, along the fertile perimeter of their observable universe. This essaying and mapping prepares them for the conversation they are then ready to have with those people and creatures whose clearings overlap theirs. This, too, is the best way to explain the way a Boolean computer search overlaps the concentric circles of three topics and finds only those sources that partake in all three.

For some students, the essay becomes a way of updating perennial fascinations or regathering previous ones. Often, a sense of serendipity aids topic selection as an unexpected happening reopens the past. Student Eve Turek's essay "On Feathers" begins with her observant walks on the beaches of the Outer Banks of North Carolina, where she finds fallen feathers. Whose are these, she wonders, knowing that the question is both ornithological and spiritual. While her college biology textbook provides the beginnings of information about feathers and molting, her search takes her to many other sources, on the Web and in print, including the Smithsonian, where she learns of the "feather detectives" called upon to determine the species of birds involved in aircraft-avian collisions, as well as identifying feathers brought to the museum by curious people. Eve has learned the pleasure and danger of what folklorist Kent Ryden explains in his *Invisible Mapping* and elsewhere; he helps us understand that Henry David Thoreau was probably the most "thorough" mapmaker of his generation and that he railed against the bureaucrats who completed maps by guessing from existing ones rather than walking the terrain, where feathers can be found and spills can be taken.

Once feathers have left the bird, however, they sometimes find other uses. For the American Indian cultures Turek researches, feathers are often a symbol of connection and spiritual solidarity between people and birds. Feathers fallen and found are a gift, reminding people of their relation to the kindred beings in the skies. Among Turek's sources is Ted Andrews's *Animal-Speak*, where an understanding of connection and scientific analysis begin to come together as the author stresses the specificity and individuality of birds and their feathers and people and their experiences: "Even though there are general applications for any feather, each individual bird and its feathers must be examined for its own unique qualities, if you are to understand its function within your own life circumstances. You must examine its characteristics and behaviors and draw the connections to your own life" (69).

Turek's essay draws these personal connections as she begins to review her way of living in relation to the feather collection she had as a child and the down couch she loved, and her mother disliked for being formless and never looking neat. A tomboy who collected rocks, preferably fossils, and feathers, Turek remains a curious person who is at times frustrated by the complexity and circularity of life's questions but continues to follow them with persistence, wonder, and, usually, joy. Her original questions remain unanswered. She is not always sure to whom—bird or person—feathers belong. But her feelings of mystery, connection, comfort, and quest remain and deepen.

Like cabinets of wonder, essays are both collections and provisional sortings. Turek gathers her feathers, facts, perspectives, and memories and connects them in the multiple inferences of a single question. Other essays find their pattern of connection through different media or forms. We have had luck teaching the photo-essay, since an image or series of images can help writers find a center or parallel path for their work. For instance, a student project on Bosnia found its route because the writer's photographs—often of the friends he met in his travels—suggested that a human history about the suffering of a triumphant and surviving people was a story he wanted to tell.

Eventually, student essayists need to find the "through-line" that will connect the parts of their vision without forcing linearity on a complicated structure. Lydia Fakundiny compares writing the essay to being suspended in an airplane, "inside the roar and hum." The image is terrifying, but beyond this, there is "freedom, lightness, the sheer irresponsibility of being carried so swiftly, so involuntarily, to one's destination—just" (5). The essay may similarly propel us, but it also may need a navigator to set its direction. An aerial view provided by reflection, theory, and/or form may help us to see how the landscape fits together to form a whole or help us to choose among possible destinations. It is also from this stance, above the work, that we may see new pieces of the essay, connected to what we knew, but also not yet conceived, awaiting our exploration.

Achieving this sense of theory challenges essayists to become outsiders to their own work who can see and reset its boundaries. For students, the writing tutor or peer writing group is often the angel's advocate able to ask the right questions to generate the dissonance between author and work that precedes more elegant understandings. The Cabinet of Wonder as a metaphor offers inventive possibilities for students collecting essays filled with texts that are familiar, wondrous, or both, and for teachers trying to show students the long history and current imperatives of the essay. Such cabinets trace personal narratives about collectors and their world and show how exploration is often collaborative, despite the rivalries, hatreds, and grand illusions of the conquistador that may yet reside as traceries in any of us.

In *Cabinets of Curiosities*, Patrick Mauriès writes of the cabinet called the Kunst-und Nataralienkammer, at Halle, Germany, begun in 1598. This collection survives in an orphanage and must have been a fixture in the memories of the children who grew up there. Many of them traveled the world as missionaries and added to the cabinet through donations of wonders they collected. The cabinet was restored in the 1900s, with its contents carefully organized into categories, such as objects from Asia, which included fans and boxes; shells; minerals, fossils, and corals; and large nuts. The collection resides in several large shelving units, each decorated with images reflecting its contents.

Perhaps this spirit of collecting together should inhabit courses in writing as well. The essay's open form encourages us all to participate in texts we are reading and responding to, as well as those we are writing. However, this open form also makes it hard to know if we need a nut or a fan, or whether a strange skeleton or jeweled crucifix will fit the collection, disrupt it or change it into something new. This sense of mystery and need for experimentation makes the essay both compelling and risky to teach. A class full of distinct essays may require us to use our full bag of invention and revision methods and to create new ones on the spot, often as students show us what works. We are all essayists, filling our cabinets and wondering how to order the world.

Musing: Juke Joint *Lukasa*

Essay writing leads to expanded vision, through which we often take in more than we did before we set out to write. Finding this "essayistic" potential and allowing the work to open new passages for thought and connection can be a problem for writers used to sticking to a preconceived plan or worried about straying off subject. Conversely, without clearly traced connections or visible patterns of association, expansion can easily become diffusion. We believe that the best way for the exercises below to achieve an expanded sense of unity and stay on task while wandering down a crooked path is to come full circle and remind ourselves where we began, with Lydia Fakundiny's idea that we make our own maps, improvising through work and play a way of going in the world.

While David Wilson has transformed the idea of a modern, static museum of trapped or detained artifacts back toward the European Cabinet of Wonder, we would like now to change it further inside the analogy and reality of the lowly but exciting juke joint. You may want to get in the mood for a mixed media or multicultural essay by visiting the photographs, texts, maps, and more of Junior's Juke Joint, which explores real establishments in the Delta and Louisiana at this URL: http://www.deltablues.net/

On a Saturday night, this kind of bar—which Mark has visited on his research jaunts in the Mississippi Delta and Rob knows from his meanderings in rural Louisiana—is usually "jumping." We would like to invite you on a brief visit to this environment. Perhaps it's best to imagine history. The *lukasa*, or memory board, pictured in the photo gallery is associated with both music and dance. Mary and Allen Roberts explain:

> The lukasa not only stimulates recitation, it elicits music. There is a formal and functional relationship between a lukasa and a Luba musical instrument called "kasanji." . . . Luba liken the kasanji [or "thumb piano"] to a lukasa memory board. Sometimes those instruments are embellished with heads and geometric design elements much like those of the lukasa, and their structure must bear symbolic as well as practical significance. (144)

Now let's move forward to the Mississippi Delta. After a long day of plowing fields behind a mule or logging trees or picking cotton, picture yourself as an African-American slave taking your field hollers, humming, murmurs, shouts, curses, and prayers spoken aloud inside. If you are lucky there might be a shack on its way to becoming a still-humble "juke joint" nearby. There not only can you eat, drink white lightening or home-made liquor, and smoke but, more importantly, you can talk and tell stories and sing and dance. In most of Africa, this rhythmic talking and singing is part of daily life. Song and dance not only was for the many annual or seasonal festivals but included, say, the greeting song performed each morning to a neighbor over a fence. Our colleague in English-Writing at Eastern Oregon University, Susan Whitelock, was in the Peace Corps in Togo Land and reminds students that people there may sing a greeting song for over a mile after walking past someone!

In the exercises below, you can begin to see—using the juke joint as model or sample—that there is a cornucopia of interesting topics that range across disciplines and cultures for essays and the makings of your own Cabinet of Wonder close at hand. Remember that complexity comes from flexibility. Shake loose the tensions and again remember the *lukasa* as a collection of layered or simultaneous forms. Mary Roberts writes:

> Paradoxically, lukasa memory devices provide a framework for history, while permitting multiple interpretations of the past. Once again, history and memory are in contest. The lukasa memory board illustrates how Luba organize memory according to a spatial grid. Space is used to remember multilayered bodies of knowledge pertaining to royalty, genealogy, medicine, and other complex and arcane subjects. Mbudye members associate memories with particular loci or *lieux de memoire* on a luskasa. Through a rectangular or hourglass shape that represents the Luba landscape, the royal court, human anatomy and the emblematic royal tortoise all at once, the memory board embodies multiple levels of information simultaneously. A lukasa is a visual rendering of Luba spatiotemporal thought, then, and a kind of memory theater of the Luba mind." (134)

Exercise 4.1: Beyond the Lecture—Interviewing for a Disciplinary View

Maybe it's been a long day of despair as you enter the shack. Right now, while writing this, we're listening to a CD entitled *Blues Juke Box Hits*. Picture and try to hear Bessie Smith comforting your tired spirit as she sings, "Nobody loves you when you're down and out." After awhile, Howlin' Wolf is singing about walking all the way from Dallas, Texas, or Leadbelly talks about being Alabama-bound. Memphis Slim even claims to have "the keys to the highway." Suddenly the world has grown a little larger and more interesting as musicians and patrons tell stories about their escape to other places.

Perhaps an argument erupts after John Lee Hooker sings about wanting a woman who stays home and cooks for him, instead of being a "drugstore woman" who buys lipstick, watches TV, or talks on the telephone. Then maybe the conversation veers off toward alternatives to drugstores and the way slaves used herbal medicine. Suddenly there is the opportunity to see the world through different vocations or disciplines. Writing an essay often requires expanding your base of knowledge and learning different means of expression. You may already see how your essay can include various kinds of writing, including narratives of incidents from your life or others' or summaries or analyses of sources. Perhaps you are also planning to use other media such as drawing, photographs, or film to supplement the written word.

Another way to expand your thinking and composing in relation to a subject is to research and view it from different disciplinary or cultural perspectives. It is interesting that we often experience trouble thinking about research subjects from the perspective of various disciplines, since we gain experience with disciplines through the courses we take in college. However, it may be that while we often learn or memorize the basic content of courses, we don't always practice fluently thinking about a myriad of subjects from the perspective of a chemist, linguist, or psychologist.

Here is chance to gain some insight into the ways these people think while also learning more about your research subject. First, identify a discipline that relates to your research subject or a discipline you think may be useful and that you are curious about applying. Conduct a mini-interview with your "Disciplinary Representative." Ask questions such as:

> What discipline or disciplines is your work related to?
> What would you see as the key questions of your discipline(s)?
> What are the key questions of your own research?
> How did you come to enter this discipline and do this research?
> Is there a text I can read that you would see as particularly helpful in understanding the discipline or inspiring people to join it?
> What makes you unique in the discipline? How does your perspective or work differ from many of those in the field?

These can be tricky questions. Sometimes we are so close to the disciplines we work in that it is hard to step back and see their starting points. You may want to give your interviewee a chance to come back to these later. For now, hone in on your own research subject or questions. Ask about what your interviewee's discipline can tell us about this. Look especially for those pieces of knowledge of perspective that may illuminate the subject in a way that outsiders to the discipline might miss:

> Are there open questions within the discipline that the research subject helps us to see?
> What other disciplines need to be brought to bear to understand this subject?

Suppose you interviewed each of your current instructors. What would you learn about how they view the world and about your research subject?

Exercise 4.2: A Venue and a Menu—Inventory as Gumbo

While sitting at the makeshift bar, you listen to the complaints and dreams of others. Someone is promising to quit her job and leave town and her spouse. Another hopes to make money breeding horses or selling the animals he has trapped. Meanwhile, the menu reflects whatever is available in the way of food. Perhaps there is gumbo, a "stew" capable of mixing whatever fish, meats, or vegetables are available or in season, just as the cast iron skillet or stewpot may contain a trace of every meal cooked in it. When resources are scarce, making an inventory and "re-stocking" is especially important. Making lists and planning ahead lead, of course, to more conversation between suppliers and buyers. Stories are everywhere.

Academic culture has traditionally emphasized linearity by numbering and lettering the points writers plan to make as if one must follow the next station along a straight path. Essayists, however, often need to more compli-cated and unique patterns of organization and association to link the many elements of a work. This, then, is an open-ended exercise, through which you may experiment with different patterns, figures, and forms, searching for those that best match your content, purpose, and desired effects. Here we again want to remind you of the *lukasa*, whose "scarifications" are not only a parallel to identifying tribal scars but borrowed from the history of the tortoise, who stands in for longevity and history. In their book on the art of the Luba, Mary and Allen Roberts remind us that

> [t]he same "scarifications" on the back of a lukasa are also called "lakes" (dijiba), and each is the kitenta spirit capital of an impor-tant king—because kings were buried under the water, people say the Luba note that the patterns on a tortoise shell testify to the animal's longevity; similarly, the striations within a lukasa's "lakes" are the deeds and accomplishments of each king. Lolo Inang' ombe [or turtle], then, is the ultimate metaphor for kingship itself. She is the land that nurtured and sustained a kingship, upon whose plains and fields are etched the duration and deeds of each king, and from whose lakes emerged the various incarnations of power. (139)

So begin swimming by making an inventory of your project. Group the contents that may appear into categories you derive. These categories may include personal narratives; quotations and summaries from print and Web sources; information and quotations from interviews; facts and interpretations from a discipline or disciplines; perspectives from vari-ous cultures; descriptions of key scenes, arresting images, or significant sounds, tastes, or moods; and key questions, theories, and hunches. Use the categories you find appropriate, but be sure to find a place for every-thing that may be in your project.

Next, look at your inventory to begin to see how the elements may relate or fit together. Imagine that you are taking an inventory for a sale. How would you group the material? What goes together in the same displays? What greets customers as they come in the door? What should be positioned near the check out?

Shift metaphors to imagine that you are a guide leading a green party into unfamiliar territory. What would you need to show them before leaving? What would be the first landform they came to, and how would they traverse it? As you consider your list, begin to think about geometric figures. How could these elements be made into a triangle? What would be the three sides or corners? Is your essay more given to be a four-sided square or a many sided figure? Is it best represented as a circle, ellipses, or spiral? How can your materials be plotted along these paths? If you still favor the line, reflect on other ways of describing it. For instance, perhaps this line is a rope you are using to rappel down a sheer rock face. Your materials may form geologic layers: what is the "oldest" or the "youngest"? Why?

Think also of the layered form of the palimpsest, where the most recent compositions are on top and often only partly cover those below. What parts of your project could remain partly hidden or seep through to change our reading of the rest? Another option is to consider your list as features—buildings, trees, roads—at a crossroads. In the tradition of the Delta blues, the crossroads is a charged landscape, where the physical and spiritual words meet. What gathers at your crossroads?

Find and sketch at least two different ways to represent your project; these may be maps, architectural drawings or floor plans, stick figures, geometrical shapes, or other structures you see. Then, plot the items in your inventory within these figures. Are the representations you have chosen related to the contents of your project, the points you want to get across, or the effects you hope to have? Write reflectively about the connections you see between structure, content, and purpose.

Project: Cabinet of Wonder—Opening the Mystery through Objects and Artifacts

Renaissance cabinets of wonder housed collections of intriguing objects and artifacts, often gathered from far-flung places during this age of exploration. They are often cited as forebears of museums, but these early cabinets often were not specialized, or even organized, but instead collected. They commingled objects and art forms ranging from paintings to the skeletons of unusual animals or examples of exotic nuts. In this way they kept a prescience that was "pre-science" or alchemy, before the steadiness and reason of science as a limited and "repeatable" experiment.

Essays can be thought of as discursive cabinets of wonder, collecting some of the compelling mysteries of life. To test this comparison, you may want to try the following:

1. Collect a group of objects or artifacts related to your essay or its contents. This relation may be quite direct: for instance, a project on

tigers may benefit from a careful consideration and description of the tiger's tooth you wear on a necklace. Other connections may be more suggestive. Perhaps the smooth metal ball bearing you found sitting next to some railroad tracks is the perfect industrial analogy for the Web server for your project on networks of communication.

2. Think too about objects you don't currently have but once had or wished for. Perhaps, for instance, a certain toy, talisman, or other belonging from your childhood opened the door to what you are writing about today. Your project on crystals may have begun with the amethyst geode you were given or the sand crystals you studied with a middle school microscope. Your interest in nutrition and hunger may have started painfully, when you lacked enough to eat, so perhaps you remember how good a can of fruit cocktail looked on the shelf of the store.

3. Keep in mind, too, things that aren't yours but may belong to you as they have come to belong to us all. Think, for instance, of how a painting you like by Claude Monet, Georgia O'Keefe, Vincent Van Gogh, or another great artist speaks to you. Is there a work of art that connects to your project or a scene from a film that speaks to it?

4. When you have found a few items for your essay's cabinet, consider how these may be described in words. Maybe you should open your essay with a tangible description of an object of importance and wonder. Or perhaps these objects and images will be used to form metaphors helping your readers grasp abstract ideas.

5. You may want to go a step beyond this prompt and consider forming your project as a cabinet of wonder. What would go into the cabinet? What texts, objects, or artifacts? What would the cabinet housing the project be like? How can you make or find it? Remember that the cabinet does not have to be rectangular: even the early "cabinets" of wonder took many forms, as artifacts often were displayed on shelves, housed in boxes of many kinds and shapes, or hung from walls or suspended from ceilings.

6. Consider how to match contents and form: what is the perfect container, collection, installation, presentation, or performance for your particular project?

7. As you continue to work on your project, keep an eye out for additional or better objects, artifacts, cabinets, and containers—just as you continue to draft and revise in search of the best narrations, descriptions, persuasions, and questions.

Readings: "Multihistories" and Elemental Cabinets on Almost Everything

The tradition of natural history dates back to Pliny's *Historia Naturalis*, written in 77 A.D. Using the original meaning of "historia" or "'istorin" as finding out for oneself, Pliny inquired into the whole of nature and claimed to have included twenty thousand facts in his book. Today's essayistic "historias" are more tightly focused but still shaggy and diverse, often showing how natural, cultural, and personal histories are needed to explain and explore the elements of the world. Even the physical elements of the periodic table are the subjects of a multihistory (see Phillip Ball's *The Ingredients: A Guided Tour of the Elements*).

In *A Natural History of the Senses*, a seminal text giving writers tools for such syncretic work, Diane Ackerman describes her method:

> What I wish to explore in this book is the origin and evolution of the senses, how they vary from culture to culture, their range and reputation, their folklore and science, the sensory idioms we use to speak of the world, and some special topics that I hope will exhilarate other sensuists as they do me, and cause less-extravagant minds at least to pause a moment and marvel. (xix)

A similar dynamic, replete with border crossings and topical asides, may be found in the research essays on diverse subjects gathered in the list below. Finding a few favorites among such titles is an enjoyable task for teachers and students interested in developing a multihistory as a research writing project.

SUBJECT	AUTHOR
The Alphabet	David Sacks
Aurora Borealis	George Bryson
Being Buried Alive	Jan Bondeson
Cod	Mark Kurlansky
Color in Painting	Phillip Ball and Victoria Finlay
Crying	Tom Lutz
Deafness	Oliver Sacks
Dueling	Barbara Holland
Endangered Languages	Mark Abley
The English Language	Bill Bryson
Extreme Behaviors	Jon Krakauer
Firearms	Kenneth Chase
Food	Felipe Fernández-Armesto
The Giant Squid	Richard Ellis
Glass, Paper, and Coffee Beans	Leah Hager Cohen
Grassland	Richard Manning
Hoaxes	Alex Boese
Human Cadavers	Mary Roach
Inanimate Simulations of Life	Gaby Wood

Invertebrate Animals	Sue Hubbell
Laughter	Robert Provine
Lawns and Turfgrass	Warren Schultz
Love	Diane Ackerman and Morton Hunt
Luck	Joshua Piven
Madness	Michelle Foucault
Mosquitoes	Andrew Spielman and Michael D'Antonio
New Forestry Practices	Jon Luoma
Olives	Mort Rosenblum
Oranges	John McPhee
Orchids	Susan Orlean
The Pencil	Henry Petroski
The Penis	David M. Friedman
Perfume	Cathy Newman
Phi	Mario Livio
Pilgrimage	Alain Be Bottom, Mick Brown, and Phil Cousineau
The Physical Elements	Phillip Ball
Private Body Parts	Terry Hamilton
Rainbows	Raymond L. Lee Jr. and Alister B. Fraser
Salmon	David R. Montgomery
Salt	Mark Kurlansky
The Screw and Screwdriver	Witold Rybczynski
The Senses	Diane Ackerman and David Abram
Tea	Roy Moxham
Tobacco	Ian Gately
Transsexuality	Joanne Meyerowitz
Tulips	Mike Dash
Truth	Felipe Fernández-Arnesto
Wolves	Barry Lopez
Writing	Georges Jean
Zero	Robert Kaplan and Charles Seife

Such works often trace the development of their specific subjects in broad cultural and historical contexts. For instance, Joseph Amato's *Dust: A History of the Small and the Invisible* ranges through medicine, sanitation, history, physics, philosophy, religion, business, social welfare, and mechanics to show how Western culture has obsessively attempted to rid itself of dust, only to encounter other small and invisible things, such as atoms, microbes, viruses, and prions, from which there is no escape.

Charles Seife's *Zero: The Biography of a Dangerous Idea* similarly retells the story of Western history, from the ancient Greeks onward, as a long denial of zero and the void it represents. As he shows how the Greek worldview came to be dominated by symmetry and geometry, Seife plainly states, "The whole Greek universe rested upon this pillar: there is no void." Zero remains an enigma in arithmetic: remember how strange it seemed when you learned that multiplying or dividing a number by zero yields zero? Zero quietly threatens to swallow all quantities. Other cultures were not so wary of the void, and Seife's history becomes a study of world cultures seen as ways of relating to zero. In cultures of the East, zero became one with infinity, as absence and presence danced in synchronicity and meshed in figures such as the Hindu god Shiva:

> As with the yin and yang of the Far East and Zoroaster's dualism of good and evil in the Near East, creation and destruction were intermingled in Hinduism. The god Shiva was both creator and destroyer of the world and was depicted with the drum of creation in one hand and a flame of destruction in another. However, Shiva also represented nothingness. One aspect of the deity, Nishkala Shiva, was literally the Shiva "without parts." He was the ultimate void, the supreme nothing—lifelessness incarnate. But of the void, the universe was born, as was the infinite. Unlike the Western universe, the Hindu cosmos was infinite beyond extent; beyond our own universe were innumerable other universes. (65)

Contact with the East led Westerners to incorporate zero. Arabic numbers, including zero, enabled the computations and transactions needed for commerce. In art, the vanishing point led to the illusion of three-dimensionality in realistic portrayals of people and scenes. Advances in mathematics—including the development of the Cartesian coordinates, algebra, probability theory, and calculus—came as zero was included in number schemes. Zero now figures everywhere in mathematics, chemistry, and physics. Seife describes the Cassimir effect, the tiny seductive force exhibited by vacuums and black holes. Do other universes wait on the far side of the black hole? Does zero become infinity again? Has Western science also joined absolute absence with presence?

Writers can use such histories to generate searches that wash their research subjects into larger fields of inquiry or dimensions. In this way, essay writing leads to more learning, and the world widens before us;

through the magic of metonymy and identification, our interests become cultural nomads, leading us on.

Film: Housing Our Discoveries

Perhaps there is no more interesting, contemporary creator of Cabinets of Wonder than the late sculptor Louise Nevelson. Like the famous short film of abstract expressionist Jackson Pollack doing action painting by dripping paint on glass, *Portrait of an Artist—Louise Nevelson, In Process* reveals how the artist draws, cuts, and assembles her ingenious patterns of wood scraps and metal into amazing, evolving patterns.

Perhaps the most important way any of us assay our needs into a functional Cabinet of Wonder is to build a house. *Falling Water* is a documentary that shows the legendary architect Frank Lloyd Wright creating his most famous and spectacular house—with a stream running through it—in Pennsylvania. While Wright's interaction with the family that is also his patron is sometimes contentious, building a house can be an act of love, as it is in *Life Is a House*. In that movie, Kevin Cline knows he is dying of cancer and ropes his children into living with him as he remodels an amazing home overlooking the ocean that will be their inheritance and remembrance. And then there is Jerry Andrus, one of America's most amazing magicians, whose magic stymied famous magicians in New York and Los Angeles because it was unique enough to be indecipherable. Archipelago, a group of three young filmmakers in Portland, Oregon, made a documentary of his life, *A Thing of Wonder*. Besides his tricks, he is an eccentric organist and gardener, and his house is certainly a Cabinet of Wonder for all his props and collectibles.

5 MULTIWRITING BLUES

We come again to the crossroad via a journey of the *ordo vagorum*, the dispersed race of struggling medieval monks searched for by Helen Waddell in *The Wandering Scholars*. These blues travelers moved from place to place to gather learning, experiences, songs, and lyrics while escaping from whatever threatened to pin them down, hold them too close, or set a final limit through violence, comfort, or long term employment.[1] Purveyors of the Latin lyric, they present a crossing of history, as the chop-logic of the scholastics and the hegemony of the church began to give way to a secular stance that becomes modern by first liberating an inquisitive and sensual past. Waddell notes that the rebirth of classical learning in the lives of these traveling clerks came from a rich tradition that could no longer be held dormant: "The scholar's lyric of the twelfth century seems as new a miracle as the first crocus; but its earth is the leafdrift of centuries of forgotten scholarship." For moderns, Waddell writes, the high classical Age of Augustans is "a thing set in amber, a civilization distinct and remote like the Chinese," but for the medieval scholar, it was "the upper reaches of a river that still flows past his door" (xii).

From the current postmodern convergence, where history becomes more eclectically available, the river can rush by like the "Texas Flood" in one of our favorite blues songs. But as Stevie Ray Vaughn plays and sings it, we are not swept up in the wall of water; instead we record and lament it. The singer reports on a tragedy he may be witnessing from a distance and gives the rushing water another kind of form, made of chords and moans. Similarly, we suggest working across genres, media, disciplines, and cultures not to scatter our efforts but to concentrate them, allowing the world to be balanced in a single project that finds the perfect form to evoke the story it wants to tell. While this text has probed more singular traditions of inquiry and communication, we now hope to rejoin them as manifestations of an ethic and way of being that unite questioning and composing in the service of staying intellectually alive.

We have made a wanderer's way through various traditions of discourse, turning each toward a freedom that syncretically gathers elements that had been forgotten, suppressed, or banned. Now, when so much is available to us and at hand, we need a basis for choosing what to use and the animating spirit that will hold meanings together across an apparent diversity of contents and styles. The consciousness of the questioning composer is now the subject, but this mystery can be studied only by analogy. Even the body of knowledge in biochemistry does not explain the experience of consciousness or the fact that we may have several qualitative shadings of it that determine our choices. Rather than speak, then, of the mind of the scientific inquirer, as Richard Feynmann does in essays such as "The Pleasure of Finding Things Out," or study cases of discovery throughout Western History, as Daniel Boorstin does in *The Seekers*, we turn to the blues as a way re-explaining composition at the crossroads.

This chapter concludes the book by sketching an analogy of composition and blues music as related forms of examined and perseverant experience. The lines of comparison or routes of transit between composition and the blues that we follow include the blues as:

- a survival strategy and way of talking back to the world; a habit and existential mode; a life that cuts an intellectual and emotional path through the morass of the problems and questions that confront us, or which we more freely choose;
- a flexible form of statement and counterstatement; a living tradition that gives us a set of discourses ready-made for our use, which we add to, recombine, morph, or distill;
- a philosophy John Edgar Wideman, inspired by reading the poetry of Sterling Plumpp, evokes with the blues: ". . . consolation and rumination, a long quarrel and tentative reconciliation with godhead or god-long-gone. . . . [b]lues (through paraphrase, analysis, contradiction, dialogue) as a path for coming to terms with existence" (81).

While earlier chapters have cast research writing as a mode of intellectual travel, persuasion as the loose talk of transformational collaboration, and the essay as a primordial way of ordering a world with too much in it to be fully explained or contained, we now hope to deepen these ideas by describing the blues as a running commentary on living that keeps people going through the continuing difficulties and surprising joys of life. In this blue light, each of the discursive traditions we have reviewed may be considered a manifestation of discursive and inquisitive living, where we follow our questions and write their traces, often in a multiplicity of available forms, for different purposes, audiences, and occasions. So, while Chapter 4 brings us to a juke joint, where the performance includes many layers, here we circle through the blues as another story of loose talk and travel for survival back toward the classroom, where we can relearn to practice some of the lessons of the music and its ethic.

This book may suggest to some a layered or sequenced curriculum for discourse studies, although not as directly as earlier works such as James Moffett's *Teaching the Universe of Discourse*. For instance, students who have completed a course that shifts research writing away from the captured facts of the term paper toward the nomadic journey of the Airstream tourist as intellectual seeker may be ready to next reconceive argument as mode of inquisitive action in the world designed to head all it touches toward an open space where conversation and conversion may occur. This same student may then be ready to accomplish the writing of a truly discursive essay that comes from assaying the subject and the world and having the confidence to realize that this is all one can do. Consider this chapter, then, less a course of its own—although composition as blues or blues as composition could be interesting as courses—and more the baseline for courses or projects at the crossroads, where composition becomes a way of life.

Think of the moving scene from Donald Murray's "The Listening Eye: Reflections on the Writing Conference," as Murray the master teacher waits in his office just before dawn on a winter morning to begin the work he has practiced so many times before. Students come to their conferences and talk about their papers while the teacher's counsel begins by being there, an experienced presence and guide who is willing to listen and strive to understand. His work is a commitment to the crossroads of subjects, interests, experiences, and background that his students bring into the office. At the end of the day, he is once again in the dark as the afternoon light fades. He writes:

> I am tired, but it is a good tired, for my students have generated energy as well as absorbed it. I've learned something of what it is to be a childhood diabetic, to raise oxen, to work across from your father at 115 degrees in a steel-drum factory, to be a welfare mother with three children, to build a bluebird trail, to cruise the disco scene, to be a teenage alcoholic, to salvage World War II wreckage under the Atlantic, to teach invented spelling to first graders, to bring your father home to die of cancer. I have been instructed in other lives, heard the voices of my students they had not heard before, shared their satisfaction in solving the problems of writing with clarity and grace. I sit quietly in the late afternoon waiting to hear what Andrea, my next student, will say about what she accomplished on her last draft and what she intends on the next draft. (96)

For most in our audience, considering teaching as blues may evoke a similar narrative, self-image, or sign of commitment that shows who you are in this regard and may help you make it through a trying day. However, there are other blues to find as well and other manners for composing an intellectual life that may be brought to bear. Some find the ethic of disciplined research in science, which holds failures as well as discoveries, to be its own kind of living blues. Others see painting, counseling, politics, ethnography, or urban studies as both parallel to the open traditions discussed in this book and animated by a philosophy and living energy reminiscent of this reflective and restless music. In this way, blues is not a master narrative but a way of redescribing and finding the rhythm, chords, solos, and voices of the important stories of your life.

The multiwriting blues is a way of reorganizing this work of inquiry and composition through which many traditions including bodies of knowledge, ways of perceiving, and manners of writing are opened for use in the fermentation of the unfolding question and the alchemy of rhetorical situations. This compositional method is an "either/and" practice that allows its practitioners to compose academic discourses, such as formal arguments or classic ethnographies, and texts once marginalized in academia, including personal confessions; experiential argumentation; wandering essays; performance art; and incidental genres, such as memos or lists. The manner of relating these texts may include juxtaposition or mixing, but often an overarching form is found that sublimates all to its end. For instance, a project as museum exhibit may include historical and personal narratives; lists of facts; "found" texts, including letters and journals; and a variety of images, dioramas, or simulations. But both viewers and exhibitors quickly see that now each piece must be part of an orchestrated display. Similarly, the "neo-post" analogy of the Cabinet of Wonder suggests how essays may hold objects or media while reordering a suggestively unfamiliar world. The juke joint similarly concentrates experience in a single form but widens to include multifaceted performances, on stage and in the audience, that order the world only for a moment or at most an evening. However, the ramifications of the night may continue in memory, romance, or regret.

While not all of us want to play at the juke or build museum displays, we suggest that teaching move toward helping students become directors of variegated discourses who experiment with content and form as they experience the world. Like other composition teachers, we are intrigued by the chimera of "transferable skills" and would like to believe that the method for finding the unity of an argument or opening an essay that students discover in particular projects can help them in others. Beyond such knowledge and skills, however, we are interested in imparting, modeling, and studying—and providing invitations toward and ample practice in—a manner of being or a "blues life" of writing, reflecting, questioning, and finding out more that is the restless pleasure of existence in an uncertain world.

Hip-hop, punk, rock, and country are more familiar to our students and classical and jazz are more often thought worthy of intellectual study or included in high culture. But blues is perhaps more centrally a study of the experiential learning, intellectual survival, and pleasure in the midst of pain that we find at the heart of reflective life. Blues is an emancipatory music that seeks to free people from their chains, whether spiritual or physical, by discovering and acknowledging the many ways in which we are not free. Born of slave chants and work songs, blues also includes the gospel message of good news, even while noting how life is often out of sync with it. But even stating this sad or painful fact can be a starting point toward perseverance as the music circles certain key questions: Why is life hard? Why has misfortune befallen me? Where and how can things be made better? What is it that makes this life worth it? What power propels me? One of the lessons of blues music is that tragedy, trauma, and trouble can be transformed into poetry, rhythm, and part of the base of experience we need to handle new situations as they arise. However, the blues also teaches that life must include risk, adventure, and a willingness to try out new worlds. It is an art of change that reflects upon conditions, reinvigorates spirits, and helps us to survive in a complicated world that finally does not honor the retrenchment of old viewpoints or versions of self.

In *Stomping the Blues*, a classic guide to the culture around the blues, Albert Murray delineates the difference between the music and its source. The blues is an emotional condition that blues music confesses, expresses, and treats through a cathartic discourse of experience in its multitude of forms. Murray's phenomenological chapter "The Blues as Such" begins with the stealthy often daily reappearance of the blues, signifying its unsettling effect:

> Sometimes you forget all about them in spite of yourself, but all too often the very first thing you realize when you wake up is that they are there again, settling in like bad weather, hovering like plague-bearing insects, swarming precisely as if they were indeed blue demons dispatched on their mission of harassment by none other than the Chief Red Devil of all devils himself; and yet perhaps as often as not it is also as if they squat obscene and vulturelike, waiting and watching you and preening themselves at the same time, their long rubbery necks writhing as if floating. (3)

The blues are the weight and sorrow of mortal life, inhabiting our daily problems or our projections of problems to come. They often come quietly, invisibly, and without shock or awe; at times they bring trouble or foreshadow the trouble to come. Other times, they are the same old blues, coming for the familiar reasons, announcing once again the homecoming of troubles we thought had moved on. The blues come as heartbreak or the frustrations of knowing we have no power, or they take the form of lonely homelessness that keeps us on the move, or as mistakes, coming back at us in ways we'd rather not see. In any case, the problem at hand reveals a deep well of blues that connects and absorbs these sufferings and merges them with the misery that human life can be.

As the songs suggest, the blues are like weather—a rain that seems like it will never stop. Murray continues:

> No wonder Hamlet came to debate with himself whether to be or not to be. Nor was it, or is it, a question of judging whether life is or is not worth living. Not in the academic sense of Albert Camus' concern with the intrinsic absurdity of existence per se. Hamlet's was whether things are worth all the trouble and struggle. Which is also what the question is when you wake up with the blues there again, not only all around your bed but also inside your head as well, as if trying to make you wish that you were dead or had never been born. (6)

When we have the blues, the need is to dispel them or, if we are hearty or wise, make creative use of them. Murray outlines a series of methods:

1. Acknowledge their presence: often, they just want our attention, and denying them makes them stronger;
2. Reveal their identity or name them: "to know a name is also to be onto a game" (9). Angela Y. Davis connects naming within blues music to the West African practice of *nommo*, in which the speaker/singer conjures the power of an entity by saying its name (128);
3. Imitate and mock them: give into them, only to use them against themselves;
4. Use counteragents:
   a. Voodoo: used to lift what may be a curse;
   b. Alcohol or narcotics: but these can help the blues to thrive as well.

(Murray 9–16)

The most effective "counteragent," however, is to make the blues into art. Blues music counteracts miserable emotions first by languishing in them and allowing them to have their say. But in blues music, lamentation becomes part of a richer fabric, mixing with other emotion in a hybrid discourse through which musicians and their audience commune in the continuing complexity of existence. The blues lament, in the next tune, becomes a "stomping blues" (such as those that give Murray's book its name), or a walking blues, expressing the need to travel, for pleasure or necessity. Or it may be a love song about someone new or the abiding, unfolding joy of knowing the same person more deeply. All of these are also central forms within the music. The paradigmatic blues of life gone bad is contextualized, remixed, and renovated in performances that are always about survival, even when at moments the music may wonder how this is possible.

For Murray, the music is rivaled only by religion as a creative counterforce. For the Sunday churchgoer, he notes, the blues may seem the devil's work, but the actual relationship between the music and religion is complex. They are salves of different kinds. Religion is concerned with the eternal soul; its path out of the blues involves waiting for a better world. Attendees at the Sunday morning service are motivated by the guilt of sin and leave charged with determination to resist the temptations of Baal. Blues music makes everyday earthly life bearable and provides the means for continuance. Saturday night revelers defiantly and joyously stomp the blues through song and dance, savoring life's pleasures, especially the sensual ones that even poverty cannot steal. Yet both the Saturday night juke joint parties and Sunday morning church services are rituals of affirmation and purification:

> Not all ceremonial occasions are solemn. Nor are defiance and contestation less fundamental to human well-being than are worship and propitiation. Indeed they seem to be precisely what such indispensably human attributes as courage, dignity, honor, nobility, and heroism are about. (42)

Thinking of blues music as defiant defies easier formulations of the blues as a discourse of acquiescence and resignation. The characteristic story told by the blues singer involves being the victim of misfortune and mistakes in a cold world full of mean, untrustworthy others. Acceptance of life's travails is a starting point for the music, and tune titles reflect this: "Born under a Bad Sign," "The Thrill Is Gone," "Black and Blue," or "Trouble." In the gospel that is performed communally, this acceptance becomes a belief that there is a better life beyond this world, that the heavenly chariot will "swing low" and take them to a better world. Similar accounts in African-American narratives of slaves flying off into the air parallel this transcendental response to the tragedy and displacement of slavery.[2]

However, it is this willingness in the blues—often performed individually or in small groups but reflecting a communal consciousness—to admit all parts of experience and to continue living and experiencing *anyway* that is the repeated outcome of this music. This is seen easily in the convention of other blues compositions that suggest that other responses to tragedy include not only a transcendental historical consciousness represented by the ability to leave or travel ("Wander This World" or "Walking Blues") but also an immersive historical consciousness that "goes with the flow" ("Stormy Monday" or "Everyday I Have the Blues") and a revolutionary one that offers resistance and hopes to change the world, one life at a time ("Gotta Be Some Changes Made," "I Can't Be Satisfied," or "Blues Power"). Many locations, conditions, experiences, and deprivations can be re-christened, commemorated, bemoaned, and endured as blues.

In *Listening to the Blues*, Bruce Cook suggests that the *oeuvre* of blues musicians or composers reflects the totality of their experiences. He interviews Robert Pete Williams, former convict and Louisiana bluesman, who built his first guitar in the vernacular manner of using what you have—in this case a board and baling wire. Williams says that his music comes from "the air" and speaks of life as it is, has been, and may be. Any content is possible, but the blues is also a disciplined practice. He tells Cook:

> The blues is something gonna tame your mind. You got a girl friend. She's in New York. Say you left her, and she wants to see you. She may start moanin' and whistlin'. She got you on her mind. You is the blues. I is the blues. Hattie [his wife] is the blues. Say Hattie is gone. I take a few drinks and start to sing. Got Hattie on my mind. Don't help me to talk to other people. I just start to pick the blues. You got your wife on your mind. No woman you can pick can satisfy your mind. Ain't gonna be satisfied until you get back to her. (40)

After a long afternoon of listening to Williams talk, play, and sing and of sharing food and drink with him, Cook concludes,

> And if Robert Pete Williams has created his blues out of the whole of his life, so has every other bluesman worthy of the name. Disappointment in love is cited by him and so many others as the purest sort of blues experience, yet Bukka White put it to me with that special sort of wry eloquence of his that "the blues was born behind a mule." Don't forget, in other words, that life isn't all how-I-miss-you-baby and mean-mistreatin'-mama; most of it is spent behind a mule, or washing dishes, or working on the line in some factory—if you're lucky enough to have a job at all. This is what I mean about the blues coming from the totality of man's experience. In Robert

Pete Williams' case, his imprisonment and subsequent parole were the shaping experiences of his life. That is why so much of his music seems to express a kind of nameless and absolute loneliness, a sense of isolation that is distinctive in the music created by American bluesmen. (44)

That loneliness is partly the outcome of a discourse that involves thinking. Anyone engaging in reflection about her world is likely to feel, over and over, temporarily outside it as she evolves. Studying the experience, music, and lyrics of Gertrude "Ma" Rainey, Bessie Smith, and Billie Holiday, in *Blues Legacies and Black Feminism*, Angela Y. Davis recounts blues music as an ongoing reflection through open commentary on all manners and problems of life. She writes:

> The blues realm is all-encompassing. In contrast to the condemnatory and censuring character of Christianity, it knows few taboos. As a cultural form that has long been a target of racist-inspired marginalization, the blues categorically refrains from relegating to the margins any person or behavior. Because the blues realm is open to discourse on every possible subject affecting the people who created it, it need not banish religion. Rather, what it rejects is religion's manner of defining the blues as an expression of an inferior people. The openness of the blues realm—its repudiation of taboos of all sorts—is rendered possible by virtue of the fact that the blues always decline to pass judgment. Their nonjudgmental character permits ideas that would be rejected by the larger society to enter into blues discourse. (133–34)

The women Davis studies are notable for opening the music to the new possibilities presented by women seeking emancipation from many types of oppression. But they also highlighted new or seldom expressed ways of living for women that could be stated in the open, nonjudgmental discourse of the blues.

She recounts how changing social conditions in the early twentieth century presented new possibilities for African-American existence:

> While the material conditions for the freedom about which slaves had sung in their spirituals seemed no closer after slavery than they had seemed before, there were nevertheless distinct differences between the slaves' personal status under slavery and during the post-Civil War period. In three major respects, emancipation radically transformed their personal lives:
> 1. There was no longer a proscription on free individual travel;

2. Education was now a realizable goal for individual men and women;
3. Sexuality could be explored freely by individuals who now could enter into autonomously chosen personal relationships. (xv)

While the field chants of the slaves captured a common identity, arranging individual variations in a pattern, the blues as practiced by Rainey and Smith and recast in jazz by Holiday valorized the travails and joys of personal life. The blues is able to tell things as they are, without the sentimentality of most popular music. Sexuality, especially, was the province of Rainey and Smith, who did not shy away from narrating themselves as partners, and women, to be desired, occasionally feared, and always reckoned with. Davis shows the complexities, ambiguities, and ironies of the singers' stances. While their freedom is not absolute, neither is their enslavement. "What gives the blues such fascinating possibilities of sustaining feminist consciousness," she writes, "is the way they often construct seemingly antagonistic relationships as noncontradictory oppositions. A female narrator in a women's blues song who represents herself as entirely subservient to male desire might simultaneously express autonomous desire and a refusal to allow her mistreating lover to drive her to psychic despair" (xv).

She marshals substantial evidence, including Rainey's version of "Oh Daddy Blues." For much of the song, the narrator seems despondent:

> Just like a rainbow I am faded away
> My daddy leaves me 'most every day
> But he don't mean me no good, why?
> Because I only wish he would
> I've gone insane
> I'm forever tryin' to call his name

Later, she begins to envision a different future charged with her sexual power:

> Oh, papa, think when you away from home
> You just don't want me now, wait and see
> You'll find some other man makin' love to me, now
> Papa, papa you ain't got no mama now.
>
> (xv)

Davis suggests that even lyrics that surrender to violence, degradation, and despair—as blues songs sometimes do—are rife with ambiguity when performed. When sung with spirit, detachment, irony, or a sense of satire, the lyrics about being a victim, finding appeasement, or experiencing self-immolation can show hope and joy or at least suggest that the picture is more complicated than it seems. Such performances articulate various realities at once within a richly ambiguous way of being blue. The lyrics of Rainey and Smith inscribe some of the worst features of cross-gender relationships—betrayal, pain, violence, even murder—and often cast women in the submissive role of loving their men as the men beat them or desiring to do just as their "daddy" desires. However, the nuances of the performances—whether oddly spirited, showing life continuing through despair, or subtly revealing an ironic reluctance, as if the singer doesn't believe the message society has given her—suggest a more ambiguous meaning that evokes the blues as a music of transit and multiplicity of experience, rather than fixed or singular messages. Davis's argument builds towards Holiday's "Strange Fruit," where a traditional and culturally popular musical form, the jazz ballad, becomes a music of social protest breaking taboos of expression to describe the worst violence of whites against blacks—lynching. David Margolick and Hilton Als's *Strange Fruit: The Biography of a Song* shows the complexity of this piece, from its creation by a Jewish songwriter through Billie Holiday's performance of it on very different occasions.

The "Saturday Night Function" at the juke joint or dance hall of which Murray speaks increases the ambiguity, as the band's slow blues backing the singer's lamentation of being left for dead by a lover become a lead-in to a railroad stomp about anticipation of the uncertain pleasures of Chicago, St. Louis, Memphis, or Kansas City. But the joy of the backbeat is conditioned by the dark narrative of flight from wrongdoing, wrongful accusations, or a past with contents that cannot be stated, while the night in the city promises more violence, another fleecing or repeated heartbreak. The blues juxtaposes or blends freedom and loneliness, love and loss, sin and being sinned against. It mixes the realization of mortality with the knowledge that one is not dead yet. At the far side of its oppositions is the enlightened understanding that all the troubles, hardships, pleasures, and dreams are parts of the same hard-lived life.

Blues music is an art of traditional forms, which are open to innovation, recombination, statement and counterstatement. It is a living tradition and a form ever in the making. In this it is connected to other discourses and traditions. As Anne Berthoff has said, "Forming is the mind in action. It is what we do when we learn; when we discover or recognize; when we interpret; when we come to know. Forming is how we make meaning." Such forming is done through a variety of mental strategies: "abstraction, symbolization, selection, 'purposing'; it requires or enables us to coordinate and subordinate, to amalgamate, discard, and expand: it is our means of giving shape to content" (4–5).

In the torrent of notes coming from Stevie Ray Vaughn's guitar, the wilting melancholy of Billie Holiday's voice, the call and complexly related response of Robert Johnson's playing and haunting whine, the blues are formed and rearranged as nuances so that shaded meanings rise. Further, the singular innovation of the bent "blue" note nomadically enters multiple traditions. It emanates from Miles Davis's cool trumpet and the growl of Chuck D.'s protest rap, just as a wide musical vocabulary can help us to see how the blues is itself an expression of African flexibility and bending of pitch meeting the Western scale. The blues is the messenger, bringing the fluctuations of yodeling from the Bambenzele and Biaka "pygmies" in the rainforests of the Congo and Cameroon across the Diaspora and into not only Leon Thomas's singing on Pharaoh Saunders's famous jazz album *The Creator Has a Master Plan* but also Jimmie Rodgers's country wailing and yodeling and the wavering glissando of a hundred popular artists, from Christine Aguilera and Mariah Carey to Jonny Lang and Kelly Clarkson. Similarly, African dancing grows not only through the teaching of African drummers outside that continent but Afro-Caribbean percussionists and the Drum Circle movement of Arthur Little and others (where many students are white). Afro-American dancers have persisted in incorporating African dance, as in the troupe of Alvin Ailey. In *Island Possessed*, Katherine Dunham describes her experiences expanding her dancing career through training in Haiti, which involved joining the Damballah clan of Voudoun.[3]

In *Jazz Dance: The Story of American Vernacular Dance*, Marshall and Jean Stearns look at the long history of dance that includes sexually explicit African dance. It continues not only in hip-hop dancing but in the way the modernist rediscovery of emotion in art was dependent upon what science was learning—that we act out of the shape of our nerve endings. That is, a scientific map of the human body—emphasizing the greater nerve endings in the head, hands and genitals—is obvious in African art and dance; it is basic and venerable, not "primitive." The restless migrations of Africans and Americans is still finding its way to the dance floor, whether it's the nearly forgotten Lindy Hop that Malcolm X danced, the break dancing that continues, or the latest steps being invented, even now, in a club in Los Angeles or South Beach in Miami.

The pleasures of inquiry and writing seem more abstract and likely to come in the library cubicle rather than the juke joint, railroad car, concert hall, dance floor, or sidewalk, yet its similarities to the blues as a habit of making meaning are worth considering. Beyond the immediate satisfactions of good grades, the praise of their teachers, or pride in a job well done, students write because they are curious, because the discourse carries questions that beckon them, and because life has thrust its problems and mysteries upon them. There is always the stray student, like a cat who meows too much, who does not know what to write about, who is not interested in anything we've studied so far or anything at all, it seems, and whose life, the student tells us, is without incident or occasion. But more common is the student already saturated with interests, questions, and a passion to know. Such students become academic learners by realizing that personal issues are partly public and are related to works by researchers, writers, and artists in all sorts of communicative forms. Jerred Hermann's interest in alternative fuels and resource sustainability led him to a study of architecture through which he designed and wrote about the "green" house of his dreams, which was comfortable and beautiful, as well as efficient, wise, and useful as a model for others. Eve Turek's project on American pilots missing in Vietnam grew out of local knowledge of a single case, but grew as she entered a worldwide community of people working together, and sometimes with or against governments, to try to find the answer to this series of mysteries.

Students with "boring" lives, of course, have only to start talking about horses, silicon chips, Quakerism, or life with deaf parents to show others the rare qualities of their experience, even if they find it odd that anyone finds *that* interesting. The encouragement of classmates and their many questions can help such students see that they have something unique to share. At times, some students become too used to writing repeatedly about a certain interest or area of expertise. Part of the challenge of teaching is to ask students to put aside perennial subjects and research something they are only curious about, with little preconceived knowledge. Such students can later track back to see how their earlier and new interests may be synthesized, as our student Randy Kromwall did when combining his long interest in magic with a new knowledge of writing theory to see each as both practiced illusion and seductive brush with one's mortality and whatever may lay beyond. Another student combined long experience as an athlete and sports fan with the academic study of criminology to research a feature story on an intramural program at a prison and the life histories of its participants. Such synthesis in writing is in the blues and Voudoun tradition of syncretism, where new gods (ideas) are added to the pantheon as they arise. This is what the Haitian proverb means when it says that Haitians are 99 percent Catholic and 100 percent Voudoun. All religions and traditions are built upon others and must be flexible enough to travel and adapt if they are to survive.

As is the case for a blues musician, the writer must also match content and message to form, asking in effect what kind of blues this is and how to express it in words, chords, rhythms, tempos, and the occasional solo. Our teaching has been an attempt to make this question of forms more open and interesting for students. As Derek Owens has said in *Resisting Writings (and the Boundaries of Composition)*, helping student build a "polyfocal vocabulary of discourse" should be one of our pedagogic goals and a way to practice through discourse the political inclusion we preach (10). Multiwriting is a utopian stance that assumes a free discursive world, with infinite choices of content and form, as if the whole polyfocal (or polyvocal) world was open for use. When connected to traditions of discourse—essaying, persuasive writing, research writing—such an assumption of limitless possibility yields an emancipatory reading, through which traditions themselves become methods of invention, that help us to make choices while generating forms. While an emerging understanding of the essay may yield a cabinet of wonder or museum installation, a story of rhetoric and persuasion can inform a student's work on a public demonstration or an email campaign. As students' repertoires and knowledge grow, they can better work on larger project of mixed forms.

In 2005, a group of our students worked with many others on campus to organize an Earth Day Mini-Conference that included presentations of many kinds. These ranged from PowerPoint presentations by environmental groups in town to a Global Café where students worked in teams to create a more eco-conscious campus culture. There were hands-on activities, including planting a community garden and "ground truthing" a United States Forest Service lumber sale to be sure the right trees were marked for sale. This mixing of forms and purposes touches the intelligences and interests of a mixed audience, creating an effect of transformation through invitation rather than force.

We see this dynamic of multiple choices leading to mixed forms at work in individual projects. As well as the usual worries about finding the right words or writing correctly, our students struggle creatively with other issues. One had come into possession of a uniform from Saddam Hussein's Republican Guard. Was it right to include this with his project or better to keep it private or give it to the authorities? Another student wondered: what is the right beginning for a project that will include narratives, arguments, facts, and multiple viewpoints; an interesting story; a series of questions; and a list of unexpected truths gathered from research? He settled on an ornate door leading into a small world that the project permeated. Electronic forms bear similar study. Should the project be distilled into bulleted PowerPoint or dispersed via hypertext?

Is a complex site design with multiple frames too cluttered? How can it be simplified? Should it be?

Such a writer is like a blues narrator or composer—free but not entirely so, or chained but discreetly testing the limits of one's oppression and stretching them. Their position may also be compared to that of a builder in the vernacular tradition who make use of materials at hand but also are mindful of cultural forms and traditional patterns. In *Dwellings: The Vernacular House Worldwide,* Paul Oliver notes that learning to build is part of becoming a participatory member of many societies. Rather than assigning such tasks to specialists or professionals, the culture sees the making of shelter as fundamental to being human. It is also an act of connection to cultural traditions and places:

> For countless millions of people the bond between themselves and the place where they live transcends the physical frame of their habitation. It is this double significance of dwelling—dwelling as the activity of living and residing, and dwelling as the place or built form which is the focus of residence—which encompasses its manifold cultural and material aspects" (15).

Such building becomes an act of using what one has to construct a habitat through which one comes into being. The houses made by the homeless of New York City recorded by Margaret Morton's photographs, collected in her *Fragile Dwellings,* are cosmological statements, cultural artifacts made largely of debris, and shelters of choice made by those who live in them. Mr. Lee's house in The Hill settlement, held together by ropes, string, and a multitude of elaborate knots, suggests fierce inter-relationships that tie the world together while also keeping some people out. The inside of Lee's house was known mainly only to him, and even would-be robbers were discouraged by knots that looked simple but could be undone only by Lee, their creator.

Student composers can enact similar "homes" within the project, as they construct with the materials they collect and fashion their project to convey its meanings to an audience. Beginning within traditions, such as those we have surveyed here, students often push into an open space where previous knowledge of content or conceptions of form falls away and the seductive mystery of a new space opens. So a project that begins as a reflection on a service learning experience at a residence for senior citizens finds its center in a comic essay of misadventure called "Beaten by a Walker." Similarly, an off-hand remark about changing hairstyles opens the way for a project that tells the story of race relations in America through considering the author's changing hair. What began as a prescribed project on how to raise pigs becomes an ethnography of pig farmers who are the first to admit that they are a breed apart. Similarly, a student who starts off to persuade others not to eat McDonald's food changes her approach to describe how the exact replication of the burger tastes and appearance occurs. The project takes us to industrial New Jersey, where the tastes of America are coerced and manufactured by a flavor industry intent on giving us the same old Big Mac, distinct from the Whopper, which it also has produced.

The project may then deepen its persuasion by moving us into a state of awareness and uncertainty where we question all we eat. It is also internally persuasive for the author, who has been "moved" to a new place where she can entertain the question of form in a new way: how can she best give readers the experience of simulated food? What began as a theme potentially controlled by a thesis now becomes a textual carnival that includes a mini-history of the flavor development industry; an interview with the university's food toxicologist on how we experience tastes and why we crave certain flavors and food textures; a chemical study of high fructose corn syrup, the master ingredient of American food; a virtual tour of a produce section, showing how even nonpackaged food may constitute an "improved" reality; and a model of the perfect unblemished burger, presented on a pedestal and sprayed bronze.

This vernacular construction allows people to work together using available materials while remaining open to new possibilities of form. As the course unfolds, participants should feel as if they are on a journey together, where the destination is not prescribed but may well be interesting. We have approached this sense of common commitment in part by allowing students to comment upon syllabi and assignments, when they often ask for greater clarity on how much work is expected, leading to discussions of how much is enough. We then set a minimum threshold that may include, for instance, a certain number of pages of writing or genres and additional media or forms. But the idea, as our experienced students help us tell beginners, is always to go far beyond these standards and to make a project that grows as the project itself unfolds and calls for more. We are the vessel we have called into existence.

As the term goes on, we continue to pair students with classmates and with others outside the group. These may include writing tutors, who our Writing Center director trains to tutor multiwriting; other faculty, who often have something to contribute to particular projects, depending on interest and expertise; and community members, who can be key to expanding students' thinking. For instance, a project by a student on air pollution took off when she met local citizens engaged in monitoring and working to better air quality in our town; they shared with her years of experience and their different viewpoints on what should be done. We often help to stoke this potential for expanded thought through asking students to include interviews as either distinct pieces within projects or among the sources of longer essays. As well as working with individual projects, we suggest common themes of threads for the class, through readings or class visits by artists, travelers, or scholars whose work or lives may parallel those of students. For instance, presentations by a painter or filmmaker allow for imaginative use of these media as students consider how their projects could be painted or filmed.

Finding a rough unity remains an open problem for composing at the crossroads as students expand their thinking and composing over genres, media, disciplines, or cultures. We offer various exercises for unity, focusing upon common metaphors or the organizing effects of particular forms. We also repeatedly ask students to write and recast the central questions of their project and to try to eventually get these down to a very short list. While we do not ask students to "narrow the topic" in the way that many instructors do, we find that a well-phrased question makes all the difference, as a project that begins by asking "Can the salmon of the Northwest be saved?" find its center in a study of habitat that asks, "What kind of restoration projects work? And how do we know?" We find that such projects become more specific as the students become more knowledgeable and deeply engaged. Even a project that weighs a question as large as the existence of God or the nature of rational thought becomes more concrete and intriguing as the writers' autobiography relates to additional sources and the question becomes lived rather than abstractly presented.

Getting students to work beyond the limits of higher education's infrastructure of credits and grades is a mystery we continue to examine. Perhaps the key is in trying to erase the word *student*. The pedagogy we advocate works to the extent that it finds the human being within the student. It asks people to learn beyond the grade and past the barest of expectations. Its invitation remains open. At times, people refuse it by making projects that are only good enough to get by. However, we have seen many cases in which such students taking a different course go at their projects with a vengeance, as if to make up for past refusals. For instructors at a larger school, where the opportunity to teach students more than once may not exist, we suggest consideration of how to plant the seed in reluctant students. Perhaps the best way to begin is by asking them how a seed can be planted. How can I get you to open up? What really excites you? Is there something you want to tell the world? What makes it hard for you to write?

On due days, the projects roll in housed in a wide range of containers, with a multitude of contents and styles. This display of forms may include materials such as chicken wire, rubber, cloth, wood, plastic, paper, silicon, and slate, to name a few. Some projects come as books; others on CD or mini-DV. Boxes and trunks abound, with museum displays and shadow boxes mixed in. Texts are presented along with photographs, drawings, songs, sculpture, artifacts, scrolls, plant specimens, microscope slides, dolls, or computer simulations. Students have also worked collaboratively to make the whole class's work into a series of exhibits or curiosa, or installations in the campus art gallery or student union. Here students connect back to the roots of the museum as a place of the muses, where the projects surprise us like gifts reinvented from earlier, more mundane versions.

Project performances offer a chance for another invention. The blind taste test reveals how well we know certain food items. No mistaking the Reese's cup or a Pringle's chip. Instead of recapping what has been done, the performance (rather than a "presentation") is a way to keep going and to bring the project to life for a live audience who want to be entertained and enlightened. Projects find further nuances of meaning in performances that dialogically enact, heighten, or switch the stance or style of the "hardcopy" project. Student Bryan Suereth's project on jazz musician Sun Ra attempted a "harmonic convergence" between the artist (Sun Ra), the performer (Suereth), and the chorus (his classmates, who chanted in unison and in the round). Sue Ruth's the *eMpTV Guide*, a mock magazine showing the emptiness of television culture made valid points, but her presentation showed that turning off the TV was both hard to do and essential. Her presentation featured a video, with alternating images of silly TV shows—games shows, *Entertainment Tonight*, *The Real World*—with scenes of warfare, violence, destruction, and environmental waste. Ruth provided the sound track, live, through her own talk performance, speaking of cultural apathy and the hypnotizing effect of trivial images in a world that matters. The screen went to a test pattern just as Ruth went silent.

We are often asked about assessment. It is hard to know how to judge projects such as these. Again, we suggest thinking through the implications of both vernacular architecture and the blues. In each tradition, the premium is on working together and seeing how we can both validate the current state of things and continue into a future that may be better or worse but will come. So, we ask students to collaborate with us on criteria and expectations, which includes lists of qualities we would like to see in the deadline project but also suggests that we want the projects to fire the imaginations of its viewers or include a vision for how the project may be expanded by its author in times to come. Our goal in reading any project is to witness what the project is now on the way to asking about what it might become. Even failed projects thus become invitations toward further research and invention, and the writing life.

We often end courses with a reflection exercise where students also follow various prompts to "refract" their work and sometimes the work of classmates, bending the light to view latent possibilities of the current project and the new inquiries that appear on the edges of the old. We have also used an "idea journal" prompt in which students record different ideas for research projects that arise as they work toward completion of current ones. Such *overplanned improvisation*, where many routes are seen and practiced, leaves us poised and expectant—in a state similar to the "beginner's mind" espoused by Buddhist master Shunryu Suzuki—to see and use the new forms that arise as the occasions, purposes, and audiences of discourse shift and morph. Invention is a manner of participating in a world that needs to be changed if humans are to survive or thrive. The ideal of continual invention through inquiry also may reanimate the college experience to include knowledge and skill-building and practice in critique while binding these elements through the acts of questioning, finding out, relating, and debating.

John Edgar Wideman evokes blues composition in music and the poetry of Sterling Plumpp as an art of change. "Blues announces the end of the world," Wideman writes. "[T]he old world you've known or thought you knew till the blues jumps up and grunts, Huh-huh, no-no-no, boy, it ain't like that at all." The blues bring with them new experience to mull, "something more for you to learn, to cry over or grin about or celebrate or mourn." This hesitation and reintegration is built into the music: "Don't you forget there's always the break, the hesitation, hitch between one beat, one word, one note, one line, one breath and the next. Slide and glide as best you can, my friend, there's still the unexpected you got to deal with" (81). Inquisitive writing is the cool, academic complement to blues music's ambiguously mournful or celebratory stance. But inquiry can be passionate, as well; like blues music, it is sometimes a binding experience, through which we pursue and occasionally feel we find reintegration with the world. In each, the transitory nature of life is an opportunity to experience more while one is able.

We end by looping back to the *lukasa* of the Luba. Mary and Allen Roberts remind us again that this memory board is not only a layered combination of overlapping forms as media but part of the slipstream of the world, constantly trans-"formed" through human choice. They write:

> The mnemonics presented in this chapter, ranging from pictorial to sculptural, contemplative to kinetic, constitute the theater of Luba royal experience. Luba mnemonics are microcosmic and macrocos-

mic at the same time. These expressive forms are "keys to a code designed to present to the understanding a whole kind of doctrine in a single flash." Indeed "artworks . . . become vehicles for reaching some kind of fundamental truth" (Napier 1992:134), or at least for giving the *impression* of having reached such truth. "Truth," of course is always in the eye of the beholder, in the words of the lukasa narrator, in the poetry of the numbi singer, in the fingers of the kasanzi plucker, and in the feet of the dancer. His or her ability to persuade others through a rendition of the past will determine how history is made. For as Richard Scheechner rightly states, "to 'make history' is not to do something but to do something with what has been done. History is not what happened but what is encoded and transmitted. Performance is not merely a selection from data arranged and interpreted; it is behavior itself and carries in itself kernels of originality, making it the subject for further interpretation, the source of further study" (1985:51). The initiations, recitations, and spectacles of Mbudye lie somewhere between history and performance on the border between convention and creation, where past, present, and future conflate "to re-present a past for the future performance-to-be" (ibid.). (147)

Like the Cabinet of Wonder, the *lukasa* combines the imagined reality and really imagined history of people bound together by the remnants of what they and their ancestors have chosen to recall. The *lukasa*, like the blues its lore will help to spawn on its migration through the slave trade to a "new" world, is a map whose only "key" to the highway of the future is the open road of discovering and revising questions that refuse to leave our consciousness. Blues is the school of life built firmly upon the shoulders of the learner. In *Thinking in Jazz: The Infinite Art of Improvisation*, Paul Berliner reminds us that blues and jazz musicians literally must take action to be taught what they crave to learn. In a section entitled "Paying Dues as Learners," he says:

Although the jazz community's largely supportive atmosphere is a prominent theme in personal narratives by improvisers, this is not the complete story. Students face enormous challenges in mastering both their respective instruments and the complex musical language for which, until recently, there have been few written aids. Moreover, the driving passion of the experts, even those who assume the role of teacher is, of course, their own music. None assumes exclusive control over the training of their students, nor do they typically provide a program of instruction comprehensive enough to form the complete basis for the education of students. Even the young musician in a lengthy apprenticeship with a master artist-teacher supplements this training with various other learning opportunities. The jazz community's traditional educational system places its emphasis on learning rather than on teaching, shifting to students the responsibility for determining what they need to learn, how they will go about learning, and from whom. Consequently, aspiring jazz musicians whose educational background has fostered a fundamental dependence on teachers must adopt new approaches to learning. Veterans describe the trials and tribulations that accompany the learner's efforts to absorb and sort out musical knowledge as examples of "paying dues." (510)

The multiwriting blues ask students to face themselves over and over, realizing that all learning is necessarily autobiographical, whether they are expressing themselves or attempting to be "objective" or "analytical." Do they want to undergo the rite of passage during graduation as experts who "have all the answers" contained in a few endlessly practiced forms or as amateurs capable of discovering—in the pleasure of finding things out through talking, traveling, and essaying an ever-changing and dangerous world—the most important questions of their lives? As teachers of composition and rhetoric and more, we similarly must stare into the mirror of our practice and ask ourselves some difficult questions. Do we want to help students follow in our footsteps? Or do we want to use our experience to teach them to teach us what matters to them and how they might best learn, apply, and perform it with the freedom to travel through and across the boundaries of diverse and emerging genres, disciplines, media, and cultures? Will we "fix" these students or prepare them to sing out loud and clear, like the famous blues guitarist Luther Allison, "I'm a Soul-fixin' man [or woman]!"?

Musing: A Synesthesia for Inquiry in the Hands of Others

Intellectual work is a social practice. Even rare, genius-polymaths find guides and search for colleagues and interlocutors, even dreaming them up if need be. In our workaday world, we have found that much of the fun of writing comes from doing it together—with one another and even for each other. The call and response structure of blues music, accented during performance, is an analogy. In *Blues Legacies and Black Feminism*, Angela Y. Davis cites blueswoman Koko Taylor, who knows the blues as a universal condition that operates individually, selecting us one by one to have an experience that bonds us to others who have gone through some of the same:

Now when I write a song, I'm thinking about people in general, everyday living. Just look around, you know. Say, for instance, like when I wrote this tune "Baby Please Don't Dog Me." You know what I'm saying. I'm thinking about, O.K., here is some woman begging and she's pleading. Baby please don't dog me, when you know that you're doing wrong yourself. . . . Now that shoe might not fit my feet. That shoe might not fit your feet. But that shoe do fit somebody's feet. It's some woman out there is really thinking, she really feels the way that I'm singing about, what I'm talking about in this song. It's some woman somewhere really feels this way. There are the words she would like to say. (56, quoted in the film *Wild Women Don't Have the Blues*)

Once this collaborative process is set in motion, little must be done to prompt it. We have been surprised by our students' desire and ability to complexly integrate their works with the ideas and projects of others. Students will explain how some portions of their projects came from classmates or form bridges between their projects and others. Students also craft their projects to stand out, check to see what others are doing, and then craft their projects to add a new element or sensation to the work of the class.

The research and writing others do enters our lives in a variety of ways. We may read it in a book or report, but we are also likely to hear it from friends who tell us about things they have learned in ways that pique our interest. Or perhaps we stumble across compelling information on a curious subject as we search the Web for something else. The research we do can similarly reach others in ways that are surprising and stoke their curiosity. Here are prompts for reflecting upon the form(s) your work may take. The two exercises may guide you toward the use of multisensory and interactive forms for presenting your research, including exhibits and learning kits. The writing project will help you to continue thinking about the forms your research may take, by considering the effects of forms on your audience and the relationship of forms to your contents.

We are drawing closer to a crossroads that we are still learning to envision, where people engaged in questions relax in the company of other searchers and share the charged air. The structures and distinctions we have long dwelled inside will begin to crumble there—where there is no need for courses, credits, or lists of expected outcomes, and no students or teachers; instead there is conversation, commitment, mystery, and surprise, among humans on Earth, in this universe. Certainly we are far from such a utopia, but we are also already there and always have been. The blues fell like rain this morning, reminding us that we are here together and have to decide how we will relate.

Exercise 5.1: "Staring Up" the List—Meditating on Forms

Form is a usefully vague word that can mean many things. The *Oxford English Dictionary*, for instance, lists twenty-two definitions, many with several parts, grouped into three broad categories. This is only for "form" the noun; it may also be a verb, "to form." We are most interested in the definitions grouped into the first category for "form" as noun: "the shape or arrangement of parts." For writers, definition nine in this category I. is close to the point: "Style of expressing the thoughts and ideas in literary or musical composition, including the arrangement and order of the different parts of the whole." But as we begin to find form by discovering it inside content, another definition, I.4, must be considered. This is taken from the old philosophic method known as Scholasticism: "The essential determinant principle of a thing; that which makes anything (matter) a determinate species or kind of being; the essential creative quality." This definition suggests that each project has only one essential form, which writers must find.

However, it is also possible for a project to have many forms and to take on different qualities as you organize it into a Web site or blog, draft it as an essay, write about it in your journal, or narrate it to your friends. And the OED also has a definition to fit this variety of forms, I.5.b: "One of the different modes in which a thing exists or manifests itself; a species, kind, or variety." Such forms vary not only with the content of the project but also as the writer finds ways to reach different audiences and accomplish various purposes in regard to the project. In this way, one more definition may also be relevant. "Form" once referred specifically to a part of a window, the "tracery," or inner frame of gothic style windows, which held the glass in place. This form made possible a visible connection between outside and inside. As you consider forms, you may want to meditate on their window-like qualities. What kind of view into the project does each form grant? How does it relate the rest of your work and thinking to the larger world around it and to an expectant audience who wants to see?

To begin thinking more practically about forms, consider the list below, gathered from observation and conversation during a twenty-four-hour period:

seed pod	spider hole
orange construction cone	contract
sand dune	needle
pyramid	Empire State Building
national anthem	open house
lighted sign	gold fish

Persian rug	unusual necklace
Persian garden	voice mail
camera	Monet's Water Lilies
pipe	jazz piano
moebius strip	funk bass
manikin	sushi
snowflake	blue bottle
ceremonial robe	newspaper
tea cup	airport security screening
rehearsal	belt buckle
high heel	railing
safe	assault

1. Review the list, stopping to picture and think about each item. Which are forms you particularly enjoy? Do you find any of them disconcerting or alien? Which familiar items seem suddenly strange to you?

2. Do you see any connections among items on the list? Perhaps, for instance, you see how several items, ranging from the ceremonial rite of the airport security screen to the paradoxical form of the "safe," used to house items we feel the least secure about, have to do with protection, surveillance, and the desire to prevent harm. Some items may also lead you to picture several things at once: a pipe for smoking, the plumbing under your sink, a long pipeline carrying oil, or a perfect wave with "pipeline" for surfing.

3. Some items may also lead you to reflect upon how human-made forms either emulate or dispel those in nature. Persian rugs and gardens, for instance, reflect a complicated, intricate view of the cosmos and the role of humans as order-makers within it. The Big Mac, on the other hand, is a strangely unnatural form, with a "secret sauce" and "beef." This masks, of course, its role in turning rainforests into cattle ranches.

4. Next, make your own list of interesting forms that you encounter, hear mention of, think about, or picture during the next twenty-four hours. Remember that the word *form* is open to natural forms, human-made objects, performances or ceremonies, and kinds of writing or art, among other possibilities.

5. After making your list, study it and meditate upon it for at least twenty minutes. Rather than "staring down" the list, looking so hard that meaning dissolves, "stare up" gently, allowing meanings to arise and dance. Allow your mind to wander to the images, stories, analyses, and connections that the items inspire.

6. At this point, you are ready to consider how these forms or others may play a part in your research project. Are items on this list related

to your project? Note those that seem immediately connected, but also consider items that seem to have no connection. Find one form that is intriguing or odd but is apparently unrelated to anything else on your list or to any of the academic or personal work you are currently doing. Circle this.

7. See if this form arises in new ways during the next few days. Sometimes the items that seem incongruous are about to become central in our work or lives. This is also a good tip for revising writing: find the parts of the piece that do not seem to fit. Instead of editing them out, continue to reflect upon them. It may be that they hold the key to a deeper revision of the piece that allows you to think new thoughts and arrive at different viewpoints.

8. As you work on your project, continue to think about how forms relate to it. You may find that one form becomes a way of organizing your work or its container. Forms may also become interesting ways to write projects. See Dahlia Lithwick and Brandt Goldstein's *Me V. Everybody: Absurd Contracts for an Absurd World* to see how one form of writing, the contract, becomes a vehicle for pointing out the maddening and amusing oddities of social life and relations in America.

9. Forms may also lead to interesting performances. A project on surveillance, for instance, may take the written form of an FBI dossier on an American "suspect," which may be presented live by including a video tape from a hidden camera that has been watching the room as the class files in and settles in for the day's session.

As you work toward a completed project, using one or several forms, look back at the beginning of this exercise and consider how your forms fit or change the definitions. Have you found one essential form or a number of different but related ones? How do your forms frame a window-like view of the project? Check the OED in your college library to see which additional definitions seem most useful.

Exercise 5.2: Insects in the Stream

For many students, Community Service Learning (CSL) experiences are among the most meaningful parts of college, and community service work has become increasingly important to colleges and universities that want to overcome the stereotype of the detached "ivory tower" of the academy and reconnect higher education to society.

As part of their CSL work, students at many universities have created "learning kits" for use by K–12 and home-schooled students, and their teachers and parents, on a variety of subjects across the disciplines. These college students incorporate their own research into areas of interest in forms that allow others to interact with the materials in enjoyable and multifaceted ways. For instance, Martin Hartmannsgruber's learning kit for elementary age students on the insect life of streams in the region included materials to use while examining a stream such as a guide to identifying common insects; a matching game to help kids continue to identify insects, with a playing board crafted from wood to resemble a stream; and a field guide to the ecosystem of the stream, especially showing how predation and oxygen levels affect insect life. How can your research be made into such a kit? Consider some of the following questions:

- What aspects of your research are most interesting? What parts of it are most likely to get someone excited or intrigued? How can your kit begin to incorporate these features of your subject?
- What other outcomes did you imagine for your kit? What should your audience learn from it? What thoughts, feelings, or actions would you like it to inspire?
- What field trip could accompany your subject?
- What stories from your life or the lives of others illustrate the intriguing qualities, fertile mysteries, urgency, or significance of your project?
- What games did you enjoy playing as a child? Can any of these be incorporated into your project?
- What games do you see children playing today? Can any of these be used?
- What did you read as a child? What do children read today? Is there a way, for instance, to incorporate magic or fantasy into your work? Perhaps a "cross-section" book, like those that show the workings of castles, skyscrapers, or the human body could be useful?
- Would an experiment or demonstration help your audience engage your subject?
- Would activities involving library research, research on the Web, or interviews be useful for your audience to try?
- What sort of writing or other creative activities can be incorporated into the kit? Can the kit inspire other additional mini-kits or other projects?
- Should the kit include opportunities for involvement with appropriate organizations or agencies?

If you find this way of reimagining your project works for you, you may want to take the next steps and create the project as a learning kit.

Project: Exhibiting the Senses

1. First, build your awareness of the contents and forms of exhibits by viewing one or several. You will find exhibits at museums or historical centers but try classroom buildings and your college library as well to see what exhibits they include.

2. Pay careful attention and jot notes, looking especially for some of these features:

- Does the exhibit have a title?
- How is the display constructed: does it use display cases, free-standing displays (like dinosaur skeletons), video screens, dioramas (for example, a simulated woodland habitats behind glass), simulations of scenes or characters, controlled environments (like the rain forest room at botanical gardens), or activity stations for interactive learning?
- What do you read when studying the exhibit? How would you describe the texts used in the exhibit? What genres of writing do you see?
- What do you see at the exhibit? Check for paintings, drawings, photographs, sculpture, models or simulations, and objects and artifacts.
- What do you hear at the exhibit? How is sound used?
- Are the other senses activated by the exhibit? If so, how?
- Are plays or historical reenactments used? If so, describe these.
- Check for interactive elements, such as games, puzzles, or quizzes, or chances for the audience to choose to take in additional information. (For instance, at the Experience Music Center in Seattle viewers/listeners use special headsets to hear additional tunes, by Jimi Hendrix, early punk rock and the blues, and other choices.)

3. Next, review the exhibit as a whole. This may require going back through it. Consider some of the following:

- How would you describe the order or organization of the exhibit? Why do you think this order is used? Why does it start as it does? What is in the middle? How is an ending made?
- What key questions does the exhibit explore or attempt to answer? This may be stated or implied.
- What effects did the exhibit have on you? What effects do you think it is meant to have? What are we to think or do after viewing it? What does it mean to teach us?
- What parts or elements of the exhibit worked best for you? Why?

4. Discuss the exhibit you saw with classmates, including those who examined other exhibits. What approaches or elements among those you have experienced or heard about interest you the most?

5. Now, turn your attention back to your research project. Imagine that you are to make an exhibit from it. This time, begin by considering purpose and desired effects. What would you like your research project as exhibit to show or teach the audience? What thoughts, feelings, or actions do you wish it to inspire?

6. How can these purposes and effects be enacted? What methods or forms should you use? Why? How would the exhibit you imagine making be like the ones you have seen? What cues have helped you to improvise toward your own creation?

7. Create a catalog of your projected project, which may include descriptions of the following:
- manner of display
- texts
- images
- artifacts
- films
- plays/enactments
- sounds
- textures/tastes/smells
- interactive elements

Be sure to take into account restraints concerning space, time, and available technology. You may want to start by dreaming of a utopian exhibit that spares no expense in time or money and then decide upon the most essential, appropriate, and feasible elements for the exhibit you actually make this term.

8. Consider the order of your exhibit. What organizational pattern or logic would you use? What would come first in the exhibit? What would come next? What would be at the end of the exhibit? Why? Instead of an outline of the project, you may want to try an architectural sketch, blueprint, or floor plan of the project as an exhibit.

9. Now it is time to begin creating your exhibit. Be open to possible changes you see as you work. Even your purpose and desired effects may shift or radically change as the exhibit begins to take form. You may want to keep a journal to track these interesting shifts in your thinking and in the emerging forms of your project.

Readings: Books of Unusual Forms

We experience forms all around us: cruising through cities with a post-modern feel or through the strip malls; walking through a cityscape of skyscrapers and sidewalks; or enjoying a rest in the shade of a live oak tree, replete with Spanish moss. Our bodies are forms to contemplate and care for, and the Earth itself is a form carved by natural processes from continental drift to glaciations and altered by humans in ways that have become destructive more than creative. Teachers can help students experience this world of forms through a variety of activities, including tours of art museums and galleries, or natural history museums, where the brontosaurus bones become a memorable, awesome form. An architectural tour of campus or the town or city can be especially intriguing, especially if an expert is along to help build our lexicon for seeing and naming forms. Music provides another avenue for thinking about form as structure, function, and connection or analogy: jazz as overplanned improvisation, the symphony as drama, and the piano solo as essay, to name a few analogies between music and writing.

For writers and many others, however, the book is a form that continues to fascinate. You may experience this fascination as you read, hold, and smell you favorite books or experience the collection of a favorite library. The book arose as many forms do, from a history of concerns with function and aesthetics or convenience and magic. Books are now made routinely to resemble one another by following the rectangular pattern of the golden section. They are linear progressions set within boxes. However, the variety within this structure begins to show how books match form to purpose.

Books are seldom so helplessly bookish as in the reference section. One of our favorite research and library orientation strategies has been to show students the reference room and get them started discovering not only the reference books that might fit their immediate interests but also the unexpected references that may awaken their fancy. For instance, the music reference section at our university library includes works such as *The Encyclopedia of Jazz,* by the controversial jazz writer Leonard G. Feather; Sybil Marcuse's *Musical Instruments, A Comprehensive Dictionary;* and the six-volume *Guinness Encyclopedia of Popular Music,* edited by Colin Larkin. Also on the shelf are *The Bibliography of Black Music,* by Dominique-Rene De Lerma; *A Thousand and One Nights at the Opera,* by Frederick Herman Martens, and William E. Studwell's *Christmas Carols: A Reference Guide.* The odd find is The *Encyclopedia of Automatic Musical Instruments,* by Q. David Bowers, which describes in text as well as grainy black and white photographs a miscellany of music boxes, player pianos, "guitarophones," and other devices.

This would fit perfectly on our own Curiosa reference section of books we've collected over the years, such as *A Dictionary of Superstitions,* where we learn that rare and creepy double nuts are NEVER to be eaten by one person, and Jay Robert Nash's *Darkest Hours: A Narrative Encyclopedia of Worldwide Disasters from Ancient Times to the Present.* Section headings of this morbid gray tome include "Major

Air Crashes," "Major Avalanches and Landslides," "Major Plagues," "Epidemics," "Famines and Droughts," and "Major Mine Disasters." Perhaps even more intriguing is *Things: The Objects Devised by Man's Genius Which are the Measure of his Civilization*, edited by Geoffrey Grigson and Charles Harvard Gibbs-Smith and written by a team of twenty-six writers. Topics in this treasury of historical narratives, with an intricate cover image like an *I Spy* puzzle, include bagpipes, buttons, false teeth, silk, tapestries, and vacuum cleaners. The entry on "calculating machines" foreshadows computers, speaking of "electronic brains" that humans may set to work but that will run computations on their own.

In "The Garden of the Forking Paths," Jorge Luis Borges imagines a book that contains the world and is also a labyrinth. This idea changes our experience of the *ficcíon* in which the book is described; is this short narrative, a part of the larger, encompassing fiction of the labyrinth? Which text contains which? Similarly, *Tilt: A Skewed History of the Tower of Pisa*, by Nicholas Shrady, suggests the tower's form with its clever tilt. Fans of geometry may peruse A. W. F. Edwards's *Pascal's Arithmetical Triangle: The Story of a Mathematical Idea*, which embodies its form with a triangular structure showing how Pascal's work relates both to the earlier work of Greek, Hindu, and Arabic mathematicians and to the later discoveries of Newton and Leibniz, leading to calculus. Those who prefer the smooth form of circles may want to try Iain Sinclair's *London Orbital: A Walk around the M25*, with illustrations by Dave McKean, or the essays that end up where they started in James Burke's *Circles: Fifty Round Trips through History, Technology, Science, Culture*.

The world's largest book may be *Bhutan: A Visual Odyssey across the Last Himalayan Kingdom*, by writer Michael Hawley and a team of photographers and editors. This book is five feet tall and more than three wide, its size picked to match the grandeur of the landscape. *GOAT: The Greatest of All Time*, edited by Benedict Taschen, offers a heavyweight tribute to Mohammed Ali—it weighs seventy-five pounds. Books have been collectors' items through much of history. Several on-line resources give a quick look at such collections. For example, The Miniature Book Society (www.mbs.org) shows miniature books from around the world.

The prehistory of the book can be glimpsed through codices, now often published in book form. The *Codex Borgia: A Full-Color Restoration of the Ancient Mexican Manuscript*, edited by Gisele Díaz and Alan Rodgers, orders the world through iconography, while the *Codex Wallerstein: A Medieval Fighting Book from the Fifteenth Century on the Longsword, Falchion, Dagger, and Wrestling*, edited by Grzegorz Zabinski and Batlomeij Walczak, provides instruction on these Western martial arts.

The book art movement makes use of methods from painting to papermaking and often includes written texts matched with images. We suggest several Web sites showing some of the diversity of book art today:

- www.mkimberlypress.com, The M Kimberly Press site, featuring the work of master book artist Mare Blocker
- www.centerforbookarts.org, The Center for Book Arts in New York City
- www.wellesley.ed/Library/wombks/homepage/page1.html, exhibit of women in book arts, Wellesley University

What unusual books can you find, imagine, or make?

Film: Appearing Nightly—A Film of Blues

Sometimes we remind ourselves that we shouldn't "judge a book by its cover," in part to recall that no writing will fully capture the writer. Similarly, no music can fully render the musician, who is constantly evolving. But even if films are freeze-frames of art- or artists-in-progress, some remind us of the flexibility, adaptation, and discovery of musicians. We can see them playing, hear them thinking sub/super-consciously. Just as the variety of books in the readings above demonstrate that reading must be stylized to attract its audience, the films about the blues we mention here remind us that this music shape-changes according to its audience.

Many baby boomers came to blues through the rock 'n' roll that paid it tribute or ripped it off, depending upon your point of view. The Ann Arbor Blues Festival in 1969 was the Woodstock of Blues and featured aging blues musicians like the ancient Sun House, who had to be escorted on stage by his already elderly son. The Maysle Brothers looked at the dangerous side of rock music in *Gimme Shelter*—which built upon the Altamont Concert that ended in death—where the Rolling Stones moved rock away from the safety of the Beatles. The Stones turned Muddy Waters's "I Can't Be Satisfied" into "Satisfaction" and inscribed the power of Voudoun as potential historical revolution in tunes like "Satanic Majesty."

In the sea of booze, drugs, money, and glory, many a rocker—like Brian Jones of the Rolling Stones, Janis Joplin, Jim Morrison, and (more than any other) Jimi Hendrix—died young. This music was both an explosion and implosion of form, and all who courted it reverberated with its mysterious push. In *The Blues Brothers*, John Belushi (who would join the throng who died young) and Dan Ackroyd play characters who enter the world of blues as alumni of an orphanage that includes the famous jazz musician Cab Calloway. To help the orphanage they break lots of taboos to assemble the band. They have to buy instruments from the savvy Ray Charles, who plays a blind music storeowner, and they get a big push from Aretha Franklin, whose character breaks into song in the diner where she works. Assembling the band from cheesy places like the Ramada Inn is a parody of westerns like *The Magnificent Seven* (the name of an actual East Coast band), but the musicians, including Steve Cropper, are a seasoned pleasure. All the car chases aside, this movie gets at the elevation of the blues from nameless juke joint into the kind of arena that blues greats would eventually play. Mark saw the Rolling Stones booed when they came on stage in Boulder, Colorado, in 1970, after they made the mistake of letting the great B. B. King with Sonny Freeman and the Unusuals open for them and bring down the house.

This idea that blues rides its musicians the way Voudoun gods ride the "horse" of the faithful who are "possessed" leads to films that are very different forms. Robert Palmer's *Deep Blues* (borrowed from the book of the same title) takes the author back into the South where he grew up. Much of his life had been an attempt to follow the history of the blues until it disappeared into the mythology of Africa (for example, in his book *Savannah Syncopators*). *Can't You Hear the Wind Howl* is a film that looks at the much-mythologized but still-haunted life of the great Robert Johnson, and John Hooker stars as a real person behind the hypnotic voice in *John Lee Hooker—Come See About Me.*

For viewers less familiar with the blues, a perfectly tame way to begin is with *Adventures in Babysitting*. Elizabeth Shue plays the babysitter who has an unanticipated wild night on the town with the children she is looking after. In an attempt to save her charges from the Mob, she enters the back door of a blues club, where every person through the door must sing the blues to leave. This scene has the late, great Albert Collins on guitar, and when the babysitter begins in the tamest way imaginable, by saying her name, the band shifts into high gear behind her. It's an effortless introduction to the blues, which is always at home stating the ordinary in amazing ways.

If you haven't heard young white blues guitarslingers like Jonny Lang, Kenny Wayne Shepherd, or Sean Costello, you may want to view the cult film *Crossroads*, which guitarist Ry Cooder wrote the score for. Ralph Macchio plays the young white classical guitar protégé at Julliard who also wants to find and record Robert Johnson's last, alleged missing, blues song. As his character, Eugen, he breaks Robert's friend Willie Brown out of his old folks' home in New York, and they travel to the Delta to get Willie's soul back from Legba, African god of the crossroads. Eugene must face and defeat (using Mozart and blues) the Devil's guitarist, played by infamous studio musician and heavy metal rocker Stevie Vie.

Yet there are even stranger venues for entering this music. In *Genghis Blues*, blind African-American blues musician Paul Pena loses his wife and retreats to his basement, where he hears some amazing music on HAMM radio that he has no name for. This documentary follows Pena's seven-year search for the source of what turns out to be Tuvan throat-singing, which he somehow teaches himself by listening and practicing. Joining forces with the Feynmann Society—supporters and successors to the infamous astrophysicist and eccentric Richard Feynmann—Pena journeys to Tuva, in the most remote part of Asia, to participate in the national throat-singing contest. He not only serenades them in this amazing musical tradition but mixes it with the blues, which they applaud.

Another odd way into the evolving blues in film is *Schultz Gets the Blues*. A German buried alive in routine takes a life-changing journey to hear the Cajun music he has loved from afar. While this kind of Indie film finally has an audience, Jamie Fox makes rhythm and blues mainstream by winning an Oscar for *Ray*, the film that chronicles the riveting and difficult life of Ray Charles. While this musician overcame blindness, drug addiction, and the pressures of both the road and recording companies to prosper, the key moment in the film is when Ray faces the record producer who is telling him what to do and says—in the tradition of all these films—"the music gonna do what it gonna *do*." Blues is a force beyond any individual's goals or schemes.

NOTES
WORKS CITED
INDEX

NOTES

Introduction

1. *Educate* comes from the Latin root *educere*, to lead forth. Stephen Weber, president of San Diego State University, has linked this term to what he sees as the need for higher education to progressively discover new knowledge, develop new public structures for inquiry and dialogue, and work with others to enact a global network of human intellect, similar to the "noosphere" envisioned by the paleontologist/religious philosopher Pere Pierre Teilhard de Chardin (Weber, 2005). See Teilhard's *The Phenomenon of Man* and *The Divine Milieu* for a rendering of this thought.

2. Fonseca's work can be seen in the Native American Permanent Collection of the Portland, Oregon, Art Museum. The quotation appears on a placard in the display.

3. See especially the Massachusetts Institute of Technology Open Courseware Project at http://ocw.mit.edu.

I. A Crossroads in Space and Time

1. This draining of the Happening spirit in composition is paralleled in the wider culture of the United States, where social protest is routinely regarded as potential terrorism while the country tunes into the spectacle of reality television, where the culture of competition, materialism, and narcissism circulate, as if in a feedback loop, telling us who we are or should be. Guy Debord's *La Société du Spectacle* (*The Society of the Spectacle*) suggests that the spectacle itself, broadening to swallow the public world, has created the society it needs to thrive, which looks only to it for its codes, commodities, laws, and limits.

2. This metaphor of discursive islands finds interesting parallels in works about islands and the people who live up on them. For instance, Gunnar Hansen's *Plundering Paradise: The Hand of Man on the Galapagos Islands* shows how Darwin's laboratory of natural selection has become a contact zone populated by expatriots from around the world, poachers, and scientists competing over its heritage and future. At times, the isolation of islands can give us a window to the past, as the Gullah people of the Sea Islands of South Carolina and Georgia have shown the Creole and African heritage of their residents, through language, song, visual art, stories, and other cultural forms. William S. Pollitzer's *The Gullah People and Their African Heritage* remains a classic guide, and the groundbreaking earlier work of linguist of Lorenzo Dow Turner is recounted in

Africanisms in the Gullah Dialect. The film *The Language You Cry In: The Story of a Mende Song* recounts the work of Turner, as well as that of the anthropologist Joseph Opala and others in connecting Gullah culture of the island to the British slave holding caste on Bunch Island. *Daughters of the Dust*, another good film mentioned in the chapter's film section, shows one Gullah family preparing to leave their home for the promise of a different life in the north, mindful that their lives and culture may be irretrievably altered.

3. Weathers's usage of grammar suggests earlier definitions of the term. For the Greeks, grammar was a study of literature in all its elements, including its renderings of and role within history and culture. As the term *grammar* began to take on its current limits as a way of studying the structure of language, it simultaneously splintered, as if in rebellion against constraints, to also mean a study of the occult. A broader, inventive conception of the term remains in infrequent usage as the set of principles or basic elements that constitute a particular discipline, media, or culture. A core grammar of multiwriting, which might offer an evolving set of questions or terms for use in any field or situation, has yet to be written.

4. See recent works on multigenre pedagogy, including Cheryl Johnson and Jayne Moneysmith's *Multiple Genres, Multiple Voices: Teaching Argument in Composition and Literature.*

5. Emergence theory tracks the "collaborative intelligence," to use essayist Susan Griffin's term, of systems that run with a sense of purpose without an overarching master mind. This has been a useful model as we've worked toward a pedagogic structure in which students take cues from each other, from published examples of discourses and from earlier student work. See Steven Johnson's *Emergence: The Connected Lives of Brains, Cities, and Software* for an introduction. "Public work" articulates and expands the social dimension of life and work and seeks an expanded field of meaning. See the work of Harry C. Boyte, especially *Everyday Politics: Reconnecting Citizens and Public Life*, or check the Web site of the Center for Democracy and Citizenship at the University of Minnesota: www.publicwork.org.

6. Bira Almeida's *Capoeira: A Brazilian Art Form: History, Philosophy and Practice* remains a multidimensional guide to the intellectual, spiritual, and cultural dimensions of the art and was instrumental in making it known outside Brazil.

7. Eldon was a brilliant young Reuters photographer who was stoned to death in Somalia. *The Journey Is the Destination* is a one-volume compendium of his personal journals of multimedia collages. It is also discussed in Chapter 2 of this book.

2. Research Writing as a Key to the Highway

1. For instance, *The Legacy of Conquest* shows how the "conquest" of the West, despite the Romantic myth of manifest destiny, was a case of economic expansion that entailed, as it often does, the displacement and death of those standing in the way. Further, the story of the West cannot be understood except as many stories, which should be considered in its complexity. Using an Eastern

metaphor, Limerick compares this multiple history to a subway system of many stations. While every station is distinct and could be a center for viewing the entire system, most of us do not view the system in this partial way. "On the contrary, the idea of the system as a whole makes it possible to think of all the stations at once—to pay attention to their differences while still recognizing their relatedness, and to imagine how the system looks from its different points of view" (292).

2. Studies of the rise of conventions are now myriad in discourse studies. While this chapter summarizes work on the history of research writing and the term paper, it is paralleled by studies of the history of science writing, including the poignant story of the rise of the experimental article structured by the APA style, told in Charles Bazerman's *Shaping Written Knowledge: The Genre and Activity of the Experimental Article in Science.* Another interesting source for addressing the notions of conventionality and fashion in literature and theory is Robert Grudin's bizarre novel *Book*, where a band of theorists may be involved in the disappearance of a writer in their English department who quietly rebels by heeding a muse. The footnotes in this rather bookish book foment their own rebellion, calling attention to their marginal status by occupying the main text like a student radical would the President's office. This book is an unconventional choice for introductory courses in literary theory, in which instructors would like students to think both with and beyond particular critical viewpoints while considering the purposes of literature to the world.

3. See Robert Davis and Mark Shadle, "Building a Mystery: Alternative Research Writing and the Academic Act of Seeking," *College Composition and Communication* 51. 3 (Feb. 2000): 417–46.

4. While Johnson considers examples ranging from new conceptions of the World Wide Web to the complex organizations of neighborhoods, the most telling examples may be ants, who go about their business without direction from the queen but also know what to do under most circumstances, and slime mold, a supposedly simple organism with the amazing intelligence needed to disassociate itself into tiny components, then come together into large forms, depending on its environment and needs.

5. See again the *CCC* article "Building a Mystery," where we review these alternative strategies at more length.

3. The Loose Talk of Persuasion

1. For the full text of this skit, see http://www.mindspring.com/mfpatton/sketch.htm at the interactive Socrates Argument Clinic; http://www.mindspring.com/mfpatton/sclinic.htm, a subset of Patton's Argument Clinic; and http://www.mindspring.com/mfpatton/, made by Michael and Cheryl Patton at the University of Montevallo.

2. See www.orgnet.com/divided.html.

3. See especially M. M. Bakhtin's *Rabelais and His World.*

4. In "The African American Female Ontology," Beverly Johns writes of the difficult interface between that African-American women's ways of being and those prescribed by a Western academy codified by white males. She calls for

a movement at once formative and deconstructive through which people may be both conversant with dogma and able to think and live beyond it through another knowledge of a different history and a past that predates the rise of Western modernity. Cynthia A. Tyson's essay "From the Classroom to the Field: Teacher, Researcher, Activist" shows how many parts of her work are bound by the work of activism, where the work of the academic becomes engaged in processes of social change.

5. While Dobrin is no friend to the concept of "alternative" or "hybrid" discourses, his critique is based on a more democratic sense of language, in which "academic discourse" is not codified as a norm distinct from its "alternatives." Dobrin suggests that all discourses are hybrid, mixed, and resistant to codification; this is the nature of discourse, which is never fixed in form. He further suggests that the danger of introducing "hybrid" or "alternative" discourses to academic culture is that the powerful mechanisms of academic literacy will simply assimilate these discourses, rendering them powerless to truly change anything.

In this book, we have attempted to broaden the discursive field so that academic literacies are placed in a broader set of forms and discourses for intellectual work. Yet, this remains an academic work, perhaps illustrating Dobrin's claims, even as we hope to resist or recast them.

6. We saw Rich's troupe perform, powerfully, at the Western Campus Compact Continuums of Service Conference in Bellevue, Washington, April 2003.

7. For statewide statistics for 2001–3 compiled by the U.S. Department of Agriculture, see the Oregon Center for Public Policy Web site, http://www.ocpp.org/cgi-bin/display.cgi?page=issue041119.

4. The Essay as Cabinet of Wonder

1. See Frances Yates's *The Art of Memory* for more on this memory theatre. Mary Nooter Roberts also compares the memory theatre to the memory palace conceived by Camillo's contemporary, the Jesuit missionary Matteo Ricci, to hold a vast number of Chinese characters. Ricci used this imaginary palace to show young Confucian scholars how to use Western devices to learn Chinese oral traditions. See Jonathan Spences's *The Memory Palace of Matteo Ricci*.

2. Roberts shows how many of these forms find a central meaning through use in the initiation rites of the secret society the Mbudye, culminating in the power to use or make the *lukasa* (117–49).

3. Those considering a pilgrimage should look at Junior Juke Joint on the Web (http://www.deltablues.net) or Steve Cheseborough's *Blues Traveling: The Holy Sites of Delta Blues*.

4. Le Guin's evocation of the mother tongue came in her commencement address for Bryn Mawr College in 1986 and is published in the collection of essays and reviews *Dancing at the Edge of the World: Thoughts on Words, Women, Places*.

5. Multiwriting Blues

1. Such wandering clerks enjoyed an awful reputation, as Waddell recounts in her chapter on the Ordo Vagorum. The church did not approve of travel, holding

up the ideal of industry at home, but this cursed lot would not stay still. They did, however, enjoy the hospitalities of others. Waddell recounts anonymous comments from the eighth-century *Regula Magistri*:

> Their feet are weary with the hardness of the way, and they would like them bathed; but they would rather have their inwards drenched with infinite refilling of the cup than the fomentation of the feet, and when the table has been cleared by their starving host, and the crumbs swept away, they shamelessly insist on their mighty thirst, and if by any chance there is no goblet handy, they'll mix it up in the same plate, and when they are stuffed and sodden to the pitch of vomiting, they say it is a hard life. And before they go to bed, more exhausted after their labours at table than by their journey, they tell all the toils of the way, and beguile still more relishes and still more cups from their host, as for the reason of their wandering, a pilgrimage, we'll say? Or perhaps captivity. (Waddell 177 *Regula* 736)

The account of comic bad behaviors continues for another page and a half.

2. Slaves flying back home to Africa is a well-documented part of African-American folklore, as Pontheolla T. Williams explains this in her book *Robert Hayden: A Critical Analysis of His Poetry*. Looking at one of his poems, she explains:

> Closely related to his Afro-American history poems but actually an Afro-American folk theme poem is "O Daedalus, Fly Away Home. . ." The poem is a skillful blend of Afro-American folk and classical subject matter. An epigraph included in the first two versions of the poem indicates that it is based on the "Legend of the Flying African," which Hughes and Bontemps state is a part of the folklore of the Georgia Sea Island blacks. . . Enchanted by the night, the music, and the girl, the speaker reflects on his slave heritage and his African roots. He recalls that his "gran" was one of those slaves who escaped slavery by flying back to Africa: . . . The classical Daedalus image compliments the "flying gran" image. The images together symbolize the blend of Western civilization with that of Africa, which the Afro-American actually represents.

3. Citing both Dunham's book and Francis Huxley's interesting look at Haitian Voudoun in The Invisibles, Ishmael Reed takes great pains in his novels—especially Mumbo Jumbo and The Last Days of Louisiana Red—to show how most clans use three drums as a stand-in for multiplicity and the plurality of religion he traces back to a polytheistic Egypt. Only the Petro or Red Cult has two drums, which may represent confrontation and the limits of binary thinking.

WORKS CITED

Print Sources

Abley, Mark. *Spoken Here: Travels among the Threatened Languages.* Boston: Houghton, 2003.

Abram, David. *The Spell of the Sensuous: Perception and Language in a More-Than-Human World.* New York: Pantheon, 1996.

Ackerman, Diane. *A Natural History of Love.* New York: Random, 1994.

———. *A Natural History of the Senses.* New York: Random, 1990.

Aczel, Amir D. *The Riddle of the Compass: The Invention That Changed the World.* Rpt. ed. Harvest, 2002.

Addams, Jane. *Twenty Years at Hull House: With Autobiographical Notes.* New York: Signet, 1999.

Alexie, Sherman. *Reservation Blues.* Warner, 1996.

Almeida, Bira. *Capoeira: A Brazilian Art Form—History, Philosophy, and Practice.* 2nd ed. Berkeley, CA: North Atlantic, 1986.

Amato, Joseph. *Dust: A History of the Small and the Invisible.* Berkeley: U of California P, 2000.

Anderson, Chris. *Edge Effects: Notes from an Oregon Forest.* American Land and Life Series. Iowa City: U of Iowa P, 1993.

Andrews, Ted. *Animal-Speak: The Spiritual and Magical Powers of Creatures Great and Small.* St. Paul: Llewellyn, 1998.

Antin, David. *Tunings.* New York: New Directions, 1984.

Anzaldúa, Gloria. *Borderlands: La Frontera = the New Mestiza.* San Francisco: Aunt Lute, 1987.

Baer, Robert. *Sleeping with the Devil: How Washington Sold Our Soul for Saudi Crude.* New York: Crown, 2003.

Bakhtin, M. M. *Rabelais and His World.* Bloomington: Indiana UP, 1984.

Ball, Phillip. *Bright Earth: Art and the Invention of Color.* New York: Farrar, 2001.

———. *The Ingredients: A Guided Tour of the Elements.* Oxford: Oxford UP, 2002.

Ballenger, Bruce. *Beyond Note Cards: Rethinking the Freshman Research Paper.* Portsmouth: Boynton/Cook, 1999.

Bantock, Nick. *The Gryphon: In Which the Extraordinary Correspondence of Griffin and Sabine Is Rediscovered.* San Francisco: Chronicle, 2001.

Barth, John. "A Nightsea Journey." *Lost in the Funhouse: Fiction for Print, Tape, Live Voice*. New York: Doubleday, 1968. 3–13.

Bartholomae, David. "Inventing the University." *When a Writer Can't Write*. Ed. Mike Rose. New York: Guilford, 1985. 134–65.

Basso, Keith. *Wisdom Sits in Places: Landscape and Language Among the Western Apache*. Albuquerque: U of New Mexico P, 1996.

Bataille, Georges. *The Accursed Share: An Essay on the General Economy*. Vol. 1: Consumption. Trans. Robert Hurley. New York: Zone, 1988.

Bateson, Gregory. *A Sacred Unity: Further Steps to an Ecology of Mind*. Ed. Rodney E. Donaldson. New York: Bessie/Harper, 1991.

Baudrillard, Jean. *America*. Trans. Chris Turner. London: Verso, 1988.

Bazerman, Charles. *Shaping Written Knowledge: The Genre and Activity of the Experimental Article in Science (Rhetoric of the Human Services)*. Madison: U of Wisconsin P, 1988.

Bégout, Bruce. *Zeropolis: The Experience of Las Vegas*. Photos. Julie Cook. London: Reaktion, 2003.

Belenky, Mary Field, Blythe McVicker Clinchy, Nancy Rule Goldberger, and Jill Mattuch Tarule. *Women's Ways of Knowing: The Development of Self, Voice and Mind*. Tenth Anniversary Edition. New York: Basic, 1997.

Bellow, Saul. *Seize the Day*. New York: Viking, 1961. Originally published in the *Partisan Review*, 1956.

Benjamin, Lois, ed. *Black Women in the Academy: Promise and Perils*. Gainesville: UP of Florida, 1997.

Benjamin, Walter. "Paris, Capital of the Nineteenth Century." *Reflections*. Ed. Peter Demetz. Trans. Edmund Jephcott. New York: Wolff/ HBJ, 1978.

———. "Theses on the Philosophy of History." *Illuminations*. Ed. with introd. Hannah Arendt. Trans. Harry Zohn. New York: Schocken, 1969. 253–64. http://mason.gmu.edu/~cforchem/oldsite/benjamin.html.

Berliner, Paul. *Thinking in Jazz: The Infinite Art of Improvisation*. Chicago: U of Chicago P, 1994.

Berry, Wendell. *Traveling at Home*. With wood engravings by John De-Pol. San Francisco: North Point, 1989.

———. *The Unsettling of America: Culture and Agriculture*. San Francisco: Sierra Club, 1977.

Berthoff, Ann E. *The Making of Meaning: Metaphors, Models and Maxims for Writing Teachers*. Montclair, NJ: Boynton Cook, 1981.

Billig, Michael. *Arguing and Thinking: A Rhetorical Approach to Social Psychology*. Cambridge: Cambridge UP, 1987.

Bizzell, Patricia. "The Intellectual Work of 'Mixed' Forms of Academic Discourses." Schroeder, Fox, and Bizzell, *ALT Dis* 1–10.

Blitz, Michael, and C. Mark Hurlbert. *Letters for the Living: Teaching*

Writing in a Violent Age. Urbana, IL: National Council of Teachers of English, 1998.

Boese, Alex. *The Museum of Hoaxes*. New York: Dutton/Penguin, 2002.

Bondeson, Jan. *Buried Alive: The Terrifying History of Our Most Primal Fear*. New York: Norton, 2001.

Boorstin, Daniel. *The Seekers: The Story of Man's Continuing Quest to Understand His World*. New York: Random, 1998.

Borges, Jorge Luis. "The Garden of Forking Paths." *Labyrinths: Selected Stories and Other Writings*. Ed. Donald A. Yates and James E. Irby. Trans. Donald A. Yates, et al. Pref. André Maurois. New York: New Directions, 1962. 19–29.

Bowden, Charles, and Virgil Hancock. *Chihuahua: Pictures from the Edge*. Albuquerque: U of New Mexico P, 1996.

Bowers, Q. David. *Encyclopedia of Automatic Musical Instruments*. New York: Vestal, 1972.

Boyte, Harry. *Everyday Politics: Reconnecting Citizens and Public Life*. Philadelphia: Pennsylvania UP, 2004.

Bronowski, Jacob. *The Ascent of Man*. Boston: Little, Brown, 1976.

Brown, Edward. *A Brief Account of Some Travels in Hungaria, Serbia, Bulgaria, Macedonia, Thessaly, Austria, Syria, Carinthia, Carniola and Friuli. As also some observations on the silver, copper, quicksilver mines, baths and mineral waters in those parts: With the figures of some Habits and Remarkable places*. London: Printed by T. R. for Benjamin Tooke, 1673.

Bryson, Bill. *Mother Tongue: English and How It Got That Way*. New York: Morrow, 1990.

———. *A Short History of Nearly Everything*. New York: Broadway, 2003.

Bryson, George. *Northern Lights: The Science, Myth and Wonder of Aurora Borealis*. Photos. Calvin Hall and Daryl Pederson. Seattle: Sasquatch, 2001.

Burke, James. *Circles: Fifty Trips through History, Technology, Science, Culture*. New York: Simon, 2000.

Burkhart, Bryan, and David Hunt. *Airstream: The History of the Land Yacht*. San Francisco: Chronicle, 2000.

Butler, Smedly D. *War Is a Racket*. Rpt. ed. Los Angeles: Feral, 2003.

Butrym, Alexander J. *Essays on the Essay: Redefining the Genre*. Athens: U of Georgia P, 1989.

Campbell, Joseph. *The Hero with a Thousand Faces*. Rpt. ed. Princeton: Princeton UP, 1972.

Cavallaro, Dani. *The Body for Beginners*. New York: Writers and Readers, 1999.

Chase, Kenneth Warren. *Firearms: A Global History to 1700*. Cambridge, UK: Cambridge UP, 2003.

Cheseborough, Steve. *Blues Traveling: The Holy Sites of Delta Blues.* 2nd ed. UP of Mississippi, 2004.

Cobb, Edith. *The Ecology of Imagination in Childhood.* New York: Columbia UP, 1977.

Cohen, Leah Hager. *Glass, Paper, Beans: Revelations on the Nature and Value of Ordinary Things.* New York: Doubleday/Currency, 1997.

Cole, David. *Enemy Aliens: Double Standards and Constitutional Freedoms in the War on Terrorism.* New York: New Press, 2005.

Connell, Evan S. *A Long Desire.* Rev. ed. Farrar, 1988.

Connors, Robert J. *Composition-Rhetoric: Backgrounds, Theory and Pedagogy.* Pittsburgh, PA: U of Pittsburgh P, 1997.

Cook, Bruce. *Listen to the Blues.* New York: Scribner, 1973.

Cousineau, Phil. *The Art of Pilgrimage: The Seeker's Guide to Making Travel Sacred.* Berkeley, CA: Conari, 1998.

Covino, William. *The Art of Wondering: A Revisionist Return to the History of Rhetoric.* Portsmouth: Heinemann, 1988.

———. *Magic, Rhetoric, and Literacy: An Eccentric History of the Composing Imagination.* Albany: SUNY P, 1994.

Cowan, James. *A Mapmaker's Dream: The Meditations of Fra Mauro, Cartographer to the Court of Venice.* Boston: Shambhala/Random, 1996.

Crowley, Sharon, and Debra Hawhee. *Ancient Rhetorics for Contemporary Students.* 2nd ed. Boston: Allyn and Bacon, 1999.

Dash, Mike. *Tulipomania: The Story of the World's Most Coveted Flower and the Extraordinary Passions It Aroused.* New York: Three Rivers, 1999.

Davis, Angela. *Are Prisons Obsolete?* New York: Open Media/Seven Stories, 2003.

———. *Blues Legacies and Black Feminism: Gertrude "Ma" Rainey, Bessie Smith and Billie Holiday.* New York: Vintage, 1999.

Davis, Miles, with Quincy Troupe. *Miles: The Autobiography.* New York: Touchstone/Simon, 1989.

Davis, Robert, and Mark Shadle. "'Building a Mystery': Alternative Research Writing and the Academic Act of Seeking." *College Composition and Communication* 51.3 (2000).

———. "A Piñata of Theory and Autobiography: Research Writing Breaks Open Academe." *Research Writing: A Sourcebook for Teachers* 79–90. Ed. Pavel Zemliansky and Wendy Bishop. New York: Heinemann, 2004.

Debord, Guy. *La Societe du Spectacle.* Paris: Gallimard, 1996.

———. *The Society of the Spectacle.* Trans. Donald-Nicholson Smith. New York: Zone, 1995.

De Botton, Alain. *The Art of Travel.* New York: Pantheon, 2002.

———. *The Consolations of Philosophy.* New York: Vintage, 2001.

De Chardin, Pier Teilhard. *The Divine Milieu.* Harper, 2001.

Delcourt, Marie. *Pericles*. N.p.: Gallemard, 1939.

De Lerma, Dominique-René. *The Bibliography of Black Music*. Fwd. Jessie Carney Smith. Westport: Greenwood, 1981–84.

Deleuze, Gilles, and Felix Guattari. *A Thousand Plateaus: Capitalism and Schizophrenia*. Trans. Brian Massumi. Minneapolis: U of Minnesota P, 1987.

Devita, Phillip R., ed. *The Naked Anthropologist: Tales from around the World*. New York: Wadsworth Modern Anthropology Library, 1991.

Dewey, Ken. "X-ings." Sanford, *Happenings and Other Acts* 206–10.

Díaz, Gisele, and Alan Rodgers. *The Codex Borgia: A Full-Color Restoration of the Ancient Mexican Manuscript*. Intro. Bruce E. Byland. New York: Dover, 1993.

Dobrin, Sidney I. "A Problem with Writing (about) 'Alternative' Discourse." Schroeder, Fox, and Bizzell, *ALT Dis* 45–56.

Douglas, William O. *Of Men and Mountains*. New York: Harper, 1950.

Dunham, Katherine. *Island Possessed*. Chicago: U of Chicago P, 1994.

Edwards, A. W. F. *Pascal's Arithmetical Triangle: The Story of a Mathematical Idea*. Baltimore: Johns Hopkins UP, 2002.

Eldon, Dan. *The Journey Is the Destination: The Journals of Dan Eldon*. Ed. Kathy Eldon. San Francisco: Chronicle, 1997.

Elkins, James. *The Object Stares Back: On the Nature of Seeing*. New York: Simon, 1996.

Ellis, Richard. *The Search for the Giant Squid*. New York: Lyons, 1998.

Fakundiny, Lydia. "On Approaching the Essay." *The Art of the Essay*. Ed. Lydia Fakundiny. Boston: Houghton, 1991. 1–19.

Feather, Leonard. *The Encyclopedia of Jazz*. New York: Horizon, 1960.

Fernández-Armesto, Felipe. *Food: A History*. London: Macmillan, 2001.

———. *Truth: A History*. New York: Bantam, 1997.

Feynman, Richard. "The Pleasure of Finding Things Out." *The Pleasure of Finding Things Out: The Best Short Works of Richard Feynman*. Ed. Jeffrey Robbins. Fwd. Freeman Dyson. Cambridge: Helix/Perseus, 1999. 1–26.

Finlay, Victoria. *Color: A Natural History of the Palette*. New York: Ballantine, 2002.

Foucault, Michel. *Madness and Civilization: A History of Insanity in the Age of Reason*. Trans. Richard Howard. New York: New American Library, 1965.

Freidman, David M. *A Mind of Its Own: A Cultural History of the Penis*. New York: Penguin, 2001.

Fuentes, Carlos. *A New Time for Mexico*. Berkeley: U of California P, 1997.

Gandhi, M. K. *An Autobiography: The Story of My Experiments with Truth*. Trans. Mahadev Desai. Fwd. Sissela Bok. Rpt. ed. Boston: Beacon, 1993.

Gately, Iain. *Tobacco: The Story of How Tobacco Seduced the World.* New York: Grove, 2001.

Gibson, William. "My Obsession." *Wired* Jan. 1999: 102.

Ginsberg, Allen. "When the Mode of Music Changes and the Walls of the City Shake." *Poetics of the New American Poetry.* Ed. Donald M. Allen and Warren Tallman. New York: Grove, 1974.

Gladwell, Malcolm. *The Tipping Point: How Little Things Can Make a Big Difference.* Boston: Little, Brown, 2000.

Gleick, James. *Chaos: Making a New Science.* New York: Viking, 1987.

Glenn, Cheryl. *Rhetoric Retold: Regendering the Tradition from Antiquity through the Renaissance.* Carbondale: Southern Illinois UP, 1997.

———. "Sex, Lies, and Manuscript: Refiguring Aspasia in the History of Rhetoric." *CCC* 45.2 (1994): 180–99.

Gómez-Peña, Guillermo, and Coco Fusco. *Dangerous Border Crossers: The Artist Talks Back.* London: Routledge, 2000.

Good, Graham. *The Observing Self: Rediscovering the Essay.* New York: Routledge, 1988.

Goodall, H. L. "Bud" Jr. *Writing the New Ethnography.* Walnut Creek: AltaMira, 2000.

Gordon, Deborah. *Ants at Work: How an Insect Society Is Organized.* Illustrated by Michelle Schwengel. Norton, 2000.

Gray, J. Glenn. *The Warriors: Reflections on Men in Battle.* 2nd ed. Lincoln: U of Nebraska P, 1998.

Greene, Brian. *The Elegant Universe: Superstrings, Hidden Dimensions, and the Quest for the Ultimate Theory.* New York: Norton, 1999.

Greenfield, Lauren. *Girl Culture.* Intro. Jean Jacobs Brumberg. San Francisco: Chronicle, 2002.

Griaule, Marcel. *The Pale Fox.* Trans. Stephen G. Infantino. Chino Valley: Continuum Foundation, 1986.

Griffin, Susan. "The Red Shoes." *The Eros of Everyday Life: Essays on Ecology, Gender and Society.* New York: Anchor, 1996. 161–76.

Grigson, Geoffrey, and Charles Harvard Gibbs-Smith, eds. *Things: A Volume of Objects Devised by Man's Genius Which Are the Measure of His Civilization.* New York: Hawthorn, n.d.

Grudin, Robert. *Book: A Novel.* Rpt. ed. New York: Penguin, 1993.

Hall, Michael L. "The Emergence of the Essay and the Idea of Discovery." Butrym, *Essays on the Essay* 73–91.

Hamilton, Terri. *Skin Flutes and Velvet Gloves: A Collection of Facts, Fancies, Legends and Oddities about the Body's Private Parts.* New York: St. Martin's, 2003.

Hansen, Gunnar. *Islands at the Edge of Time: A Journey to America's Barrier Islands.* Washington, DC: Island Press, 1996.

Hawley, Michael. *Bhutan: A Visual Odyssey across the Last Himalayan Kingdom.* Cambridge: Friendly Planet, 2004.

Heat-Moon, William Least. *Blue Highways: A Journey into America.* Boston: Little, Brown, 1982.

Hedges, Chris. *War Is a Force That Gives Us Meaning.* New York: Anchor, 2003.

Heilker, Paul. *The Essay: Theory and Pedagogy for an Active Form.* Urbana, IL: NCTE, 1996.

Hodgson, Barbara. *The Tattooed Map: A Novel.* San Francisco: Chronicle, 1995.

Holland, Barbara. *Gentlemen's Blood: A History of Dueling.* New York: Bloomsbury, 2003.

Hubbell, Sue. *Waiting for Aphrodite: Journeys into the Time before Bones.* Illustrated by Liddy Hubbell. Boston: Houghton, 1999.

Hunt, Morton M. *The Natural History of Love.* Rev. ed. New York : Anchor, 1994.

Huxley, Francis. *The Invisibles: Voodoo Gods in Haiti.* New York: McGraw, 1969.

James, C. L. R. *Beyond a Boundary.* New York: Pantheon, 1984.

Jean, Georges. *Writing: The Story of Alphabets and Scripts.* Trans. Jenny Oates. New York: Abrams, 1992.

Johns, Beverly. "The African American Female Ontology." Benjamin, *Black Women in the Academy* 53–64.

Johnson, Cheryl, and Jayne Moneysmith. *Multiple Genres, Multiple Voices: Teaching Argument in Composition and Literature.* Boynton-Cook, 2005.

Johnson, Steven. *Emergence: The Connected Lives of Brains, Cities and Software.* Rpt. ed. New York: Scribner, 2002.

Kane, Joe. *Savages.* Rpt. ed. New York: Vintage, 1996.

Kaplan, Robert. *The Nothing That Is: A Natural History of Zero.* Illustrated by Ellen Kaplan. Oxford: Oxford UP, 2000.

Kauffman, Robert Lane. "The Skewed Path: Essaying as Unmethodical Method." Butrym, *Essays on the Essay*, 253–71.

King, Martin Luther, Jr. *The Autobiography of Martin Luther King*, Jr. Ed. Clayborne Carson. New York: Intellectual Property Management/Warner, 2001.

Kingston, Maxine Hong. *The Woman Warrior: Memoirs of a Girlhood among Ghosts.* New York: Vintage, 1977.

Kirby, Michael, and Richard Schechner. "An Interview with John Cage." Sanford, *Happenings and Other Acts* 51–71.

Kolodny, Annette. *The Lay of the Land: Metaphor as Experience and History in American Life and Letters.* Chapel Hill: U of North Carolina P, 1975.

Kolpen, Jana. *The Secrets of Pistoulet: An Enchanted Fable of Food, Magic and Love.* New York: Stewart, 1996.

Krakauer, Jon. *Into the Wild.* New York: Villard, 1996.

Kroker, Arthur, and David Cook. *The Postmodern Scene: Excremental Culture and Hyper-aesthetics.* New York: St. Martin's, 1986.

Kurlansky, Mark. *Cod: A Biography of the Fish that Changed the World.* New York: Walker, 1997.

Lagemann, Ellen Condliffe. "The Challenge of Liberal Education." National Meeting of the American Association of Colleges and Universities, Washington, DC, 1 Feb. 2003.

Lan, Haixia. "Contrastive Rhetoric: A Must in Cross-Cultural Inquiries." Schroeder, Fox, and Bizzell, *ALT Dis* 269–80.

Langewiesche, William. *American Ground: Unbuilding the World Trade Center.* New York: North Point, 2002.

Lanham, Richard. *The Electronic Word: Democracy, Technology, and the Arts.* Chicago: U of Chicago P, 1993.

Larkin, Colin, ed. *The Guinness Encyclopedia of Popular Music.* Middlesex: Guinness, 1992.

Larson, Richard L. "The 'Research Paper' in the Writing Course: A Non-Form of Writing." *College English* 44 (1982): 811–16.

Latour, Bruno, and Steve Woolgar. *Laboratory Life: The Construction of Scientific Facts.* Intro. Jonas Salk. 2nd ed. Princeton: Princeton UP, 1986; Sage, 1979.

Lee, Raymond L., Jr., and Alister B. Fraser. *The Rainbow Bridge: Rainbows in Art, Myth, and Science.* University Park: U of Pennsylvania P and Bellingham: SPIE Press, 2001.

Le Guin, Ursula K. *Dancing at the Edge of the World: Thoughts on Words, Women, Places.* New York: Grove, 1989.

Lessig, Lawrence. *The Future of Ideas: The Fate of the Commons in a Connected World.* New York: Random, 2001.

Leyner, Mark. *Et Tu, Babe.* New York: Harmony, 1992.

Limerick, Patricia. *The Legacy of Conquest: The Unbroken Past of the American West.* New York: Norton, 1987.

Lithwick, Dahlia, and Brandt Goldstein. *Me v. Everybody: Absurd Contracts for An Absurd World.* New York: Workman, 2003.

Livio, Mario. *The Golden Ratio: The Story of Phi, the World's Most Astonishing Number.* New York: Broadway, 2002.

Long, Laura Lai. "Full (dis)Course Meal: Some Words on Hybrid/Alternative Discourses." Schroeder, Fox, and Bizzell, *ALT Dis* 139–54.

Lopez, Barry Holstun. *Of Wolves and Men.* New York: Scribner, 1978.

LuMing Mao. "Re-clustering Traditional Academic Discourse: Alternating with Confucian Tradition." Schroeder, Fox, and Bizzell, *ALT Dis* 112–25.

Lunsford, Andrea, and John J. Ruszkiewicz. *Everything's an Argument.* Boston: Bedford/St. Martin's, 1999.

Luoma, Jon R. *The Hidden Forest: Biography of an Ecosystem.* New York: Owl/Holt, 1999.

Lutz, Tom. *Crying: A Natural and Cultural History of Tears.* New York: Norton, 1999.

Lutz, William D. "Making Freshman English a Happening." *CCC* 22 (Feb. 1971): 35–38.

Lyotard, Jean François. *The Postmodern Condition: A Report on Knowl-*

edge. Trans. Geoff Bennington and Brian Massumi. Minneapolis: U of Minnesota P, 1984.

Mabokela, Reitumetse Obakeng, and Anna L. Green, eds. *Sisters of the Academy: Emergent Black Women Scholars in Higher Education.* Sterling: Stylus, 2001.

Macrorie, Ken. *The I-Search Paper*. Rev. and rpt. of *Searching Writing*. Portsmouth: Boynton/Cook, 1988.

———. *Uptaught*. Portsmouth. Boynton/Cook, 1970.

Manguel, Alberto. *A History of Reading*. London: Harper, 1996.

Manji, Irshad. *The Trouble with Islam: A Muslim's Call for Reform in Her Faith*. New York: St. Martin's, 2004.

Manning, Richard. *Grassland: The History, Biology, Politics, and Promise of the American Prairie*. New York: Penguin, 1995.

Marcuse, Sibyl. *Musical Instruments: A Comprehensive Dictionary*. New York: Doubleday, 1964.

Margolick, David, and Hilton Als. *Strange Fruit: The Biography of a Song*. Fwd. Hilton Als. New York: Ecco, 2001.

Martens, Frederick Herman. *A Thousand and One Nights of Opera*. New York: Appleton, 1926.

Marx, Leo. *The Machine in the Garden: Technology and the Pastoral Ideal in America*. New York: Oxford UP, 1964.

Mauriès, Patrick. *Cabinets of Curiosities*. New York: Thames and Hudson, 2002.

McDonald, Bernadette, and Douglas Jehl, eds. *Whose Water Is It?: The Unquenchable Thirst of a Water-Hungry World*. Washington, DC: National Geographic, 2003.

McKeon, Richard. *Rhetoric: Essays in Invention and Discovery*. Ed. Mark Backman. Woodbridge: Ox Bow, 1987.

McPhee, John. *The Control of Nature*. New York: Farrar, 1989.

———. *Encounters with the Archdruid*. New York: Farrar, 1971.

———. *Oranges*. New York: Farrar, 1967.

McRae, Michael: *The Siege of Shangri-La: The Quest for Tibet's Sacred Hidden Paradise*. New York: Broadway, 2002.

Meyerowitz, Joanne. *How Sex Changed: A History of Transsexuality in the United States*. Cambridge: Harvard UP, 2002.

Mills, Nicolaus, and Kira Bruner, eds. *The New Killing Fields: Massacre and the Politics of Intervention*. New York: Basic, 2002.

Milosz, Czeslaw. *Milosz's ABC's*. Trans. Madeline G. Levine. New York: Farrar, 2001.

Moffett, James. *Teaching the Universe of Discourse*. Portsmouth: Boynton/Cook, 1968, 1983.

Montaigne, Michel de. "On the Cannibals." *The Essays: A Selection*. Trans and ed. M. A. Screech. London: Penguin, 1993. 79–92.

———. "On Educating Children." *Essays* 37–73.

———. "On Three Kinds of Social Intercourse." *Essays* 247–59.

Morson, Gary Saul, and Caryl Emerson. *Mikhail Bakhtin: Creation of a Prosaics*. Stanford, CA: Stanford UP, 1990.

Morton, Margaret. *Fragile Dwelling*. Intro. Alan Trachtenberg. New York: Aperture, 2000.

Moxham, Roy. *Tea: Addiction, Exploitation and Empire*. London: Constable, 2003.

Muensterberger, Werner. *Collecting: An Unruly Passion*. San Diego: Harvest, 1994.

Murray, Albert. *Stomping the Blues*. Twenty-Fifth Anniversary Edition. Cambridge: Da Capo, 2000.

Murray, Donald. "The Listening Eye: Reflections on the Writing Conference." *College English* 41 (Sept. 1979): 13–18.

Nafisi, Azar. *Reading* Lolita *in Tehren: A Memoir in Books*. New York: Random, 2003.

———. "The Republic of the Imagination." *Washington Post Book World* 5 Dec. 2004.

Nash, Robert Jay. *Darkest Hours: A Narrative Encyclopedia of World-wide Disasters from Ancient Times to the Present*. Chicago: Nelson-Hall, 1976.

Nash, Walter. *Rhetoric: The Wit of Persuasion*. Oxford, UK: B. Blackwell, 1989.

Newman, Cathy. *Perfume: The Art and Science of Scent*. Washington, DC: National Geographic, 1998.

Okakura, Kakuzo. *Book of Tea*. Mineola, NY: Dover, 1966.

O'Hanlon, Redmond. *No Mercy: A Journey to the Heart of the Congo*. New York: Knopf, 1997.

O'Keeffe, Linda. *Shoes: A Celebration of Pumps, Sandals, Slippers and More*. Photos. Andreas Bleckmann. New York: Workman, 1996.

Oliver, Paul. *Dwellings: The Vernacular House Worldwide*. New York: Phaidon, 2003.

Olson, Charles. "Apollonius of Tyana." *Selected Writings*. Ed. and intro. Robert Creeley. New York: New Directions, 1966. 133–58.

———. *The Special View of History*. Ed. Ann Charters. Berkeley: Oyez, 1970.

Ondaatje, Michael. *The Collected Works of Billy the Kid*. New York: Norton, 1974.

———. *The English Patient*. New York: Knopf, 1999.

Opie, Iona, and Moira Tatem, eds. *A Dictionary of Superstitions*. New York: Oxford UP, 1989.

Orlean, Susan. *The Bullfighter Checks Her Makeup: My Encounters with Extraordinary People*. New York: Random, 2002.

———. *The Orchid Thief*. New York: Random, 1998.

Owens, Derek. "Composition as the Voicing of Multiple Fictions." *Into the Field: Sites of Composition Studies*. Ed. Anne Ruggles Gere. New York: MLA, 1993. 159–75.

————. *Resisting Writings (and the Boundaries of Composition)*. Dallas: Southern Methodist UP, 1994.

The Oxford English Dictionary. Oxford: Clarendon, 1933.

Parenti, Christian. *The Soft Cage: Surveillance in American From Slavery to the War on Terror*. New York: Basic, 2003.

Pax, Salam. *The Clandestine Diary of an Ordinary Iraqi*. New York: Grove, 2003.

Persig, Robert. *Zen and the Art of Motorcycle Maintenance: An Inquiry into Values*. Reissue ed. New York: Bantam, 1984.

Petrosky, Henry. *The Pencil: A History of Design and Circumstance*. New York: Knopf, 1989.

Piven, Joshua. *As Luck Would Have It: Incredible Stories from Lottery Wins to Lightning Strikes*. New York: Villard, 2003.

Plato. *The Complete Works of Plato*. Ed. John M. Cooper and D. S. Hutchinson. Indianapolis: Hackett: 1997.

Pliny, the Elder. *Natural History*. http://www.perseus.tufts.edu/cgi-bin/ptext?doc=Perseus:text:1999.02.0138:toc.

Pollitzer, William S. *The Gullah People and Their African Heritage*. Rpt. ed. Athens: U of Georgia P, 2005.

Powell, Malea. "Listening to ghosts: An alternative (non)argument." Schroeder, Fox, and Bizzell, *ALT Dis* 211–22.

Power, Samantha. *A Problem from Hell: America and the Age of Genocide*. New York: Perennial, 2003.

Pratt, Mary Louise. "Arts of the Contact Zone." *Profession 91*. New York: MLA, 1991. 33–40.

Provine, Robert R. *Laughter: A Scientific Investigation*. New York: Viking, 2000.

Putnam, Robert D. *Bowling Alone: The Collapse and Revival of the American Community*. New York: Simon, 2000.

Putnam, Robert D., and Lewis M. Feldstein, with Don Cohen. *Better Together: Restoring the American Community*. New York: Simon, 2003.

Pynchon, Thomas. *The Crying of Lot 49*. New York: Harper, 1999.

————. *Gravity's Rainbow*. New York: Viking, 1973.

Raymo, Chet. *The Path: A One-Mile Walk through the Universe*. New York: Walker, 2003.

Reed, Ishmael. *The Last Days of Louisiana Red*. Washington, DC: Dalkey, 2000.

————. *Mumbo Jumbo*. New York: Scribner, 1996.

Reisner, Marc. *Cadillac Desert: The American West and Its Disappearing Water*. New York: Viking, 1986.

Rheingold, Howard. *Smart Mobs: The Next Social Revolution*. Cambridge: Perseus, 2002.

Roach, Mary. *Stiff: The Curious Lives of Human Cadavers*. New York: Norton, 2003.

Roberts, Mary Nooter, and Allen F. Roberts, eds. *Memory: Luba Art and the Making of History*. New York: Museum of African Art, 1996.

Romano, Tom. *Blending Genre, Altering Style: Writing Multigenre Papers*. Portsmouth: Boynton/Cook, 2000.

———. *Writing with Passion: Life Stories, Multiple Genres*. Portsmouth: Heinemann, 1995.

Rosenblum, Mort. *Olives: The Life and Lore of a Noble Fruit*. New York: North Point, 1996.

Roy, Arundhati. *War Talk*. Cambridge: South End, 2003.

Royster, Jacqueline Jones. "Academic Discourses or Small Boats on a Big Sea." Schroeder, Fox, and Bizzell, *ALT Dis* 23–30.

———. "When the First Voice You Hear Is Not Your Own." Chair's Address. Conference on College Composition and Communication, Washington DC, Mar. 22, 1995.

Russell, David. *Writing in the Academic Disciplines: A Curricular History*. Carbondale: Southern Illinois UP, 1991.

Rybczynski, Witold. *Home: A Short History of an Idea*. Rpt. ed. Penguin, 1987.

———. *One Good Turn: A Natural History of the Screwdriver and the Screw*. New York: Scribner, 2000.

Ryden, Kent. C. *Mapping the Invisible Landscape: Folklore, Writing, and the Sense of Place*. Iowa City: U of Iowa P, 1993.

Sacks, David. *The Alphabet*. London: Hutchinson, 2003.

Sacks, Oliver. *Seeing Voices: A Journey into the Land of the Deaf*. Berkeley: U of California P, 1989.

Sanders, Scott Russell. *The Paradise of Bombs*. Athens: U of Georgia P, 1987.

———. "The Singular First Person." *Sewanee Review* 96 (1988): 658–72.

Sanford, Mariellen R., ed. *Happenings and Other Acts*. New York: St. Martin's, 1992.

Sassen, Saskia. *Globalization and Its Discontents: Essays on the New Mobility of People and Money*. New York: New Press, 1999.

Schroeder, Christopher, Helen Fox, and Patricia Bizzell, eds. *ALT Dis: Alternative Discourses in the Academy*. Portsmouth: Boynton/Cook, 2002.

Schultz, Warren. *A Man's Turf: The Perfect Lawn*. Photos. Roger Foley. New York : Potter, 1999.

Seife, Charles. *Zero: The Biography of a Dangerous Idea*. New York: Viking 2000.

Sendak, Maurice. *Where the Wild Things Are*. New York: Harper, 1963.

Shrady, Nicholas. *Tilt: A Skewed History of the Tower of Pisa*. New York: Simon, 2003.

Silko, Leslie. *Ceremony*. New York: Viking, 1977.

Sinclair, Iain. *London Orbital: A Walk around the M25*. London: Penguin, 2003.

Singer, Peter. *One World: The Ethics of Globalization*. New Haven: Yale UP, 2002.

Sirc, Geoffrey. *English Composition as a Happening*. Logan: Utah State UP, 2002.

Sís, Peter. *Tibet through the Red Box*. New York: Farrar, 1998.

Smith, Henry Nash. *Virgin Land: The American West as a Symbol and Myth*. Cambridge: Harvard UP, 1950.

Snell, Bruno. *The Discovery of Mind: The Greek Origins of European Thought*. Trans. T. G. Rosenmeyer. Cambridge: Harvard UP, 1953.

Slotkin, Richard. *Regeneration through Violence: The Mythology of the American Frontier, 1600–1860*. Middletown: Wesleyan UP, 1973.

Sobel, Dava. *Longitude: The True Story of a Lone Genius Who Solved the Greatest Scientific Problem of His Time*. Rpt. ed. New York: Penguin, 1996.

Spellmeyer, Kurt. *Common Ground: Dialogue, Understanding, and the Teaching of Composition*. Englewood Cliffs: Prentice Hall, 1993.

Spence, Gerry. *How to Argue and Win Every Time*. New York: St. Martin's Griffin, 1996.

Spence, Jonathan. *The Memory Palace of Matteo Ricci*. New York: Penguin, 1985.

Spielman, Andrew, and Michael D'Antonio. *Mosquito: A Natural History of Our Most Persistent and Deadly Foe*. New York: Hyperion, 2001.

Stafford, Barbara Maria, and Frances Terpak. *Devices of Wonder: From the World in a Box to Images on a Screen*. Object list by Isotta Poggi. Los Angeles: Getty Research Institute, 2001.

Stearns, Marshall, and Jean Stearns. *Jazz Dance: The Story of American Vernacular Dance*. New York: Schirmer, 1994.

Steinbeck, John. *The Grapes of Wrath*. New York: Viking, 1939.

———. *Travels with Charley: In Search of America*. New York: Viking, 1962.

Studwell, William E. *Christmas Carols: A Reference Guide*. New York: Garland, 1985.

Sunstein, Cass R. *Why Societies Need Dissent*. Oliver Wendell Holmes Lectures. Cambridge: Harvard UP, 2005.

Taschen, Benedikt, ed. *GOAT: Greatest of All Time: A Tribute to Mohammed Ali*. Cologne: Taschen, 2004.

Ternes, Alan, ed. *Ants, Indians, and Little Dinosaurs*. New York: Scribner, 1975.

Thomas, Lewis. *Late Night Reflections on Listening to Mahler's Ninth Symphony*. New York: Viking, 1983.

Tibetan Book of the Dead, The. Comp. Padma Sambhava. Ed. Graham Coleman and Thupten Jinpa. Trans. Gyurme Dorje. New York: Viking, 2006.

Toole, John Kennedy. *A Confederacy of Dunces.* Baton Rouge: Louisiana State UP, 1980.

Toulmin, Stephen. *Cosmopolis: The Hidden Agenda of Modernity.* New York: Free Press, 1990.

Tulku, Tarthang. *Openness Mind: Self-Knowledge and Inner Peace through Meditation.* Berkeley, CA: Dharma, 1978.

Turnbull, Colin. *The Forest People.* Reissue ed. Carmichael, CA: Touchstone, 1987.

Turner, Lorenzo, Katherine Wyly Mille, and Michael B. Montgomery. *Africanisms in the Gullah Dialect.* Southern Classics Series. Columbia: U of South Carolina P, 2002.

Turow, Scott. *Ultimate Punishment: A Lawyer's Reflections on Dealing with the Death Penalty.* New York: Farrar, 2003.

Tyson, Cynthia A. "From the Classroom to the Field: Teacher, Researcher, Activist." Benjamin, *Black Women in the Academy* 139–50.

Venn, George. *Marking the Magic Circle: Poetry, Fiction and Essays.* Photos. Jan Boles. Corvallis: Oregon State UP, 1987.

Vizenor, Gerald. *The Heirs of Columbus.* Middleton: Wesleyan UP, 1991.

Waddell, Helen. *The Wandering Scholars.* New York: Anchor; Doubleday, 1961.

Walker, Lester. *A Little House of My Own: 47 Grand Designs for 47 Tiny Houses.* London: Black Dog and Leventhal, 2000.

Weathers, Winston. *An Alternate Style: Options in Composition.* Portsmouth: Boynton/Cook 1980.

Weber, Stephen. *The Success of Open Source.* Cambridge: Harvard UP, 2004.

Weber, Stephen L. Inauguration Speech for President Khosrow Fatemi. Eastern Oregon University. La Grande, Oregon. 15 Jan. 2005.

Wells, Susan. "Rogue Cops and Health Care: What Do We Want from Public Writing?" *College Composition and Communication* 47.3 (October 1996): 325–41.

Weschler, Lawrence. *Mr. Wilson's Cabinet of Wonder.* New York: Vantage, 1995.

Wideman, John Edgar. *A Riff on Reading Sterling Plumpp's Poetry. Martin Scorsese Presents: The Blues a Musical Journey.* Ed. Peter Guralnick et al. Armistad/Harper, 2003. 81–83.

Williams, Pontheolla T. *Robert Hayden: A Critical Analysis of His Poetry.* Urbana: U of Illinois P, 1987.

Williams, Terry Tempest. *Refuge: An Unnatural History of Family and Place.* New York: Pantheon, 1991.

Willis, Meredith. *Deep Revision: A Guide for Teachers, Students and Other Writers.* New York: Teachers and Writers, 1993.

Wood, Gaby. *Edison's Eve: A Magical History of the Quest for Mechanical Life.* New York: Knopf, 2002.

Woodward, Bob. *Bush at War.* New York: Simon, 2002.

X, Malcolm, and Alex Haley. *The Autobiography of Malcolm X: As Told to Alex Haley.* New York: Ballantine, 1987.

Xing Lu. *Rhetoric in Ancient China, Fifth to Third Century b.c.e.: A Comparison with Classical Greek Rhetoric.* Columbia: U of South Carolina P, 1998.

Yates, Frances Ameila. *The Art of Memory.* Chicago: U of Chicago P, 1966.

Zabinski, Grzegorz, and Batlomeij Walczak. *Codex Wallerstein: A Medieval Fighting Book from the Fifteenth Century on the Longsword, Dagger, and Wrestling.* Paladin, 2002.

Zeldin, Theodore. *Conversation: How Talk Can Change Our Lives.* Mahwah, NJ: Hidden Spring, 1998.

———. *An Intimate History of Humanity.* London: Sinclair-Stevenson, 1994.

Zemliansky, Pavel, and Wendy Bishop: *Research Writing Revisited : A Sourcebook for Teachers.* Portsmouth: Boynton/Cook 2004.

Films

Adventures in Babysitting. Dir. Chris Columbus. Perf. Elisabeth Shue and Albert Collins. Walt Disney Video, 1987.

Battle of Algiers, The. Dir. Gillo Pontecorvo. Perf. Brahim Hadjadj and Jean Martin. Criterion Collection, 1967.

Blues Brothers, The. Dir. John Landis. Perf. Dan Aykroyd and John Belushi. MCA Home Video, 1980.

Bombhunters. Dir. Skye Fitzgerald. Spinfilm, 2005.

Buena Vista Social Club. Dir. Wim Wenders. Perf. Luis Barzaga and Joachim Cooder. Lions Gate, 2000.

Butch Cassidy and the Sundance Kid. Dir. George Roy Hill. Perf. Paul Newman and Robert Redford. Twentieth Century Fox, 1969.

Can't You Hear the Wind Howl. Dir. Peter Meyers. Perf. Kevin Moore. Winstar, 1998.

Clownin' Kabul. Dir. Enzo Balestrieri and Stefan Moser. Perf. Wildman Adams. Gesundheit! Institute, 2002.

Crossroads. Dir. Walter Hill. Perf. Ralph Macchio and Joe Seneca. Sony, 1986.

Daughters of the Dust. Dir. Julie Dash. Perf. Cora Lee Day and Alva Rogers. Kino International, 1991.

Dead Man Walking. Dir. Tim Robbins. Perf. Susan Sarandon and Sean Penn. MGM, 1996.

Deep Blues. Dir. Robert Mugge. Perf. Robert Mugge and Robert Palmer. Fox Lorber, 1999.

Dersu Uzala. Dir. Akira Kurosawa. Perf. Maksim Munzuk and Yuri Solomin. Kino Video, 2003.

Dying to Tell the Story. Dir. Kyra Thompson. Turner Home Entertainment, 1998.

El Norte. Dir. Gregory Nava. Force, n.d.

Emerald Forest, The. Dir. John Boorman. Perf. Powers Boothe and Meg Foster. MGM, 2001.

Erin Brockovich. Dir. Steven Soderbergh. Perf. Julia Roberts and Albert Finney. MCA Home Video, 2000.

Fahrenheit 9/11. Dir. Michael Moore. Sony, 2004.

Falling Water. Dir. Ken Burns and Lynn Novik. Direct Cinema Limited, 1995.

Fight Club. Dir. David Fincher. Perf. Edward Norton and Brad Pitt. Twentieth Century Fox, 1999.

Fog of War—Eleven Lessons from the Life of Robert S. McNamara. Dir. Errol Morris. Perf. Robert McNamara and Fidel Castro. Sony, 2004.

Genghis Blues. Dir. Roko Belic. Perf. Paul Pena, Kongar-ol, B. B. King, and Richard Feynman. New Video Group, 2000.

Giant Buddhas, The. Dir. Christian Frei. Switzerland, 2005. DVD in production: http://www.giant-buddhas.com/en/production/.

Glengarry Glen Ross. Dir. James Foley. Perf. Jack Lemmon and Al Pacino. Live/Artisan, 1992.

Hearts and Minds. Dir. Peter Davis. Perf. Georges Bidault and Clark Clifford. Criterion Collection, 1974.

Hotel Rwanda. Dir. Terry George. Perf. Xolani Mali and Don Cheadle. MGM, 2005.

Iron and Silk. Dir. Shirley Sun. Perf. To Funglin and Zhuang Genyuan. Lions Gate, 2005.

John Lee Hooker—Come See about Me. Dir. Joerg Bundschuh. Perf. John Lee Hooker. Eagle Vision, 2004.

Language You Cry In (Story of a Mende Song), The. Dir. Alvaro Toepke and Angel Serrano. San Francisco: California Newsreel, 1999.

Life as a House. Dir. Irwin Winkler. Perf. Kevin Kline and Kristen Scott-Thomas. New Line Video, 2001.

Listen to Me. Dir. Douglas Day Stewart. Perf. Jami Gertz and Kirk Cameron. Sony, 1989.

Magnificent Seven, The. Dir. John Sturges. Perf. Yul Brynner, Eli Wallach. MGM, 2001.

Milagro Beanfield War, The. Dir. Robert Redford. Perf. Reuben Blades and Richard Bradford. MCA Home Video, 1988.

Mystic River. Dir. Clint Eastwood. Perf. Tim Robbins and Sean Penn. Warner Home Video, 2003.

Olefas (The Pathfinder in U.S.). Dir. Nils Gaup. Veiviseren, 1987.

Picnic at Hanging Rock. Dir. Peter Weir. Perf. Rachel Roberts and Vivean Gray. Criterion, 1998.

Portrait of an Artist—Louise Nevelson in Process. Perf. Louise Nevelson. Homevision, 2000.

Postino, Il. Dir. Michael Radford. Perf. Philippe Noiret and Massimo Troisi. Miramax, 1995.

Pow Wow Highway. Dir. Jonathan Wacks. Perf. A. Martinez and Gary Farmer. Anchor Bay, 2004.

Ray. Dir. Taylor Hackford. Perf. Jamie Foxx and Kerry Washington. Universal Studios, 2005.

Rolling Stones, The—Gimme Shelter. Dir. Albert Mayles and David Mayles. Perf. Mick Jagger and Charlie Watts. Criterion Collection, 1970.

Schultz Gets the Blues. Dir. Michael Schorr. Perf. Horst Krause and Harald Warmbrunn. Paramount, 2003.

Seven Years in Tibet. Dir. Jean-Jacques Annaud. Perf. Brad Pitt and David Thewlis Annaud. Sony Pictures, 1998.

Sheltering Sky, The. Dir. Bernardo Bertolucci. Perf. Debra Winger and John Malkovich. Warner Home Video, 2002.

Smoke Signals. Dir. Chris Eyre. Perf. Adam Beach and Evan Adams. Miramax, 1998.

Thing of Wonder, A—The Mind and Matter of Jerry Andrus. Dir. Adrienne Leverette, Eric Schopmeyer, and Rob Tyler. Perf. Jerry Andrus. Archipelago, 2002.

Under the Tuscan Sun. Dir. Audrey Wells. Perf. Diane Lane and Sandra Oh. Walt Disney Video, 2004.

What about Bob. Dir. Frank Oz. Perf. Bill Murray and Richard Dreyfuss. Walt Disney Video, 2000.

Wild Women Don't Have the Blues. Dir. Christine Dall. Calliope Film Resources, 1989.

Music

Broonzy, Big Bill (William), and Charles Segar. "Key to the Highway." *Trouble in Mind.* Washington, DC: Smithsonian Folkways, 2000.

Davis, Miles. *Kind of Blue.* New York: Columbia, 1959.

Dylan, Bob. *Highway 61 Revisited.* Sony, 2003.

Guthrie, Woody. "This Land Is Your Land." *This Land Is Your Land: The Ashe Recordings.* Vol. 1. Washington, DC: Smithsonian Folkways, 1997.

Holiday, Billie. "Strange Fruit." Commodore, 1939. Reissued on Strange Fruit, Atlantic, 1972.

Johnson, Robert. "Crossroads Blues." *Complete Recordings.* New York: Sony, 1990.

Kent, Willie, and the Gents. *Live at B.L.U.E.S. in Chicago.* Vienna: Wolf Records, 1997.

King, Albert. "Blues Power." *Live Wire/Blues Power.* Memphis: Stax, 1991.

Public Enemy. *Fear of a Black Planet.* New York: Def Jam, 1990.

Rainey, Ma. "Oh Papa Blues (Oh Daddy Blues)." Paramount, 1927. Reissued on *Ma Rainey,* Milestone, 1974.

Saunders, Pharoah. *The Creator Has a Master Plan.* Tokuma, 2003.

Smith, Bessie. "Oh Daddy Blues." New York: Columbia, 1923. Reissued on *Bessie Smith: The World's Greatest Blues Singer.* New York: Columbia, 1972.

Vaughn, Stevie Ray. *Texas Flood.* New York: Epic, 1983.

INDEX

Robert L. Davis and Mark F. Shadle are professors of English–Writing at Eastern Oregon University in La Grande, Oregon, where Rob is currently the director of undergraduate studies. Both have experience in writing across the curriculum, are fellows in the Oregon Writing Project, and are cofounders of the Multiwriting Institute at www.mysteryhorn. org. They have regularly presented on multiwriting at the Conference on College Composition and Communication, the Young Rhetorician's Conference, the Rhetoric Society of America Conference, and the Oregon Rhetoric and Composition Conference. They have published on multiwriting in books such as *Research Writing Revisited,* edited by Wendy Bishop and Pavel Zemliansky, and in journals, including *College Composition and Communication.*